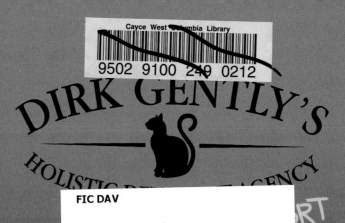

DIRK GENTLY'S
HOLISTIC DETECTIVE AGENCY

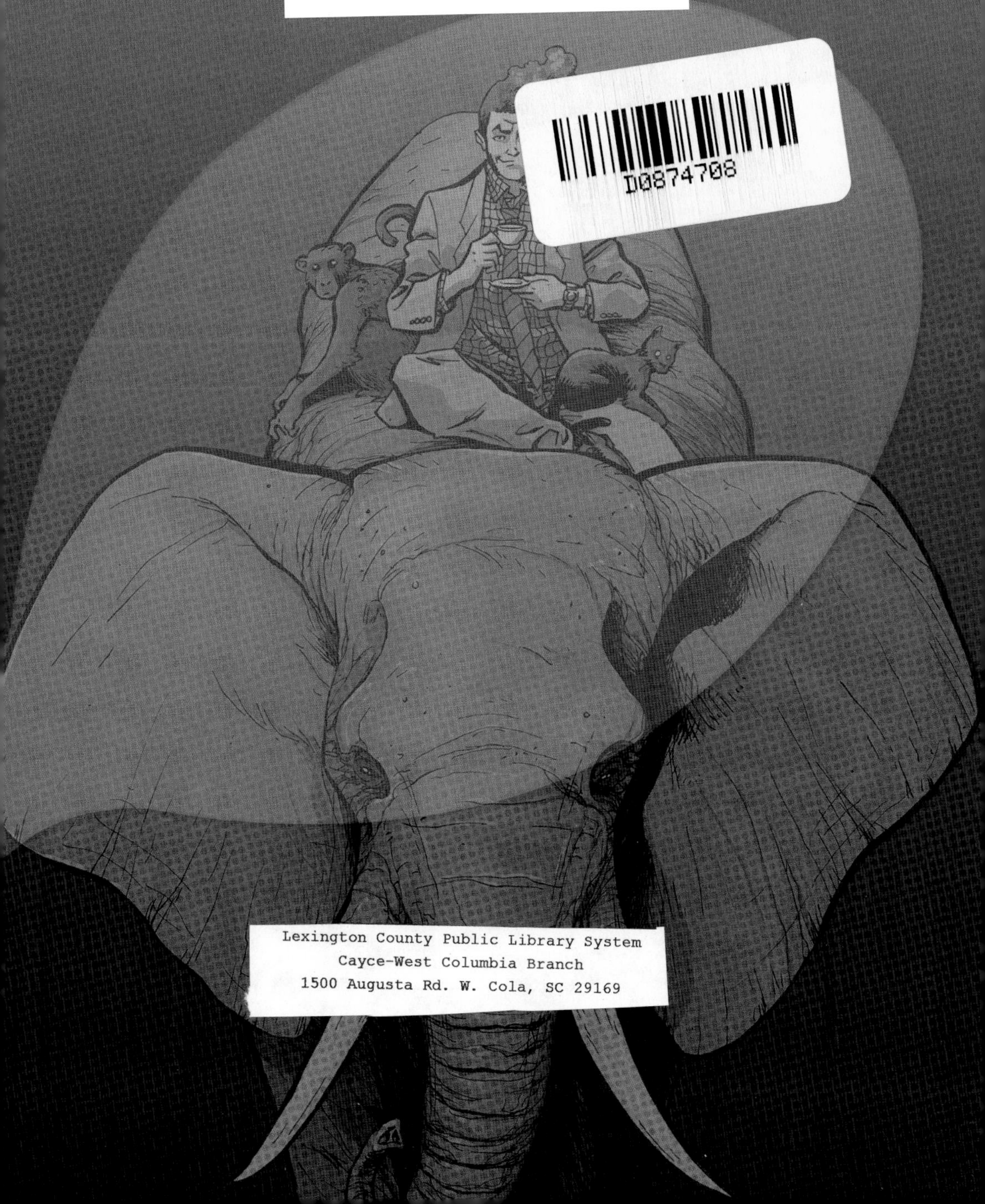

Become our fan on Facebook **facebook.com/idwpublishing**
Follow us on Twitter **@idwpublishing**
Subscribe to us on YouTube **youtube.com/idwpublishing**
See what's new on Tumblr **tumblr.idwpublishing.com**
Check us out on Instagram **instagram.com/idwpublishing**

www.IDWPUBLISHING.com

Published in association with Ideate Media.

Ted Adams, CEO & Publisher
Greg Goldstein, President & COO
Robbie Robbins, EVP/Sr. Graphic Artist
Chris Ryall, Chief Creative Officer/Editor-in-Chief
Matthew Ruzicka, CPA, Chief Financial Officer
Dirk Wood, VP of Marketing
Lorelei Bunjes, VP of Digital Services
Jeff Webber, VP of Licensing, Digital and Subsidiary Rights
Jerry Bennington, VP of New Product Development

ISBN: 978-1-63140-701-7   19 18 17 16   1 2 3 4

The Estate of Douglas Adams is donating a share of its royalties from the sale of this comic to the Save the Rhino Foundation.

Originally published as DIRK GENTLY'S HOLISTIC DETECTIVE AGENCY: A SPOON TOO SHORT issues #1–5.

For international rights, contact licensing@idwpublishing.com

Special thanks to Devon Byers, Jesus G. Romero, Andy Black, Ed Victor, Bruce Vinokour, and James Goss.

DIRK GENTLY'S HOLISTIC DETECTIVE AGENCY
A SPOON TOO SHORT

WRITTEN BY
Arvind Ethan David

ART BY
Ilias Kyriazis

COLORS BY
Charlie Kirchoff

LETTERS BY
Shawn Lee & **Robbie Robbins**

SERIES EDITS BY
Denton J. Tipton & **Chi-Ren Choong**

EXECUTIVE PRODUCER
Max Landis

Cover by **ROBERT HACK** • Cover Colors by **STEPHEN DOWNER**

Collection Edits by **JUSTIN EISINGER** & **ALONZO SIMON**

Collection Design by **CLAUDIA CHONG** • Publisher **TED ADAMS**

Dirk Gently's Holistic Detective Agency created by Douglas Adams.

CHAPTER ONE

Cover Art by **ILIAS KYRIAZIS**

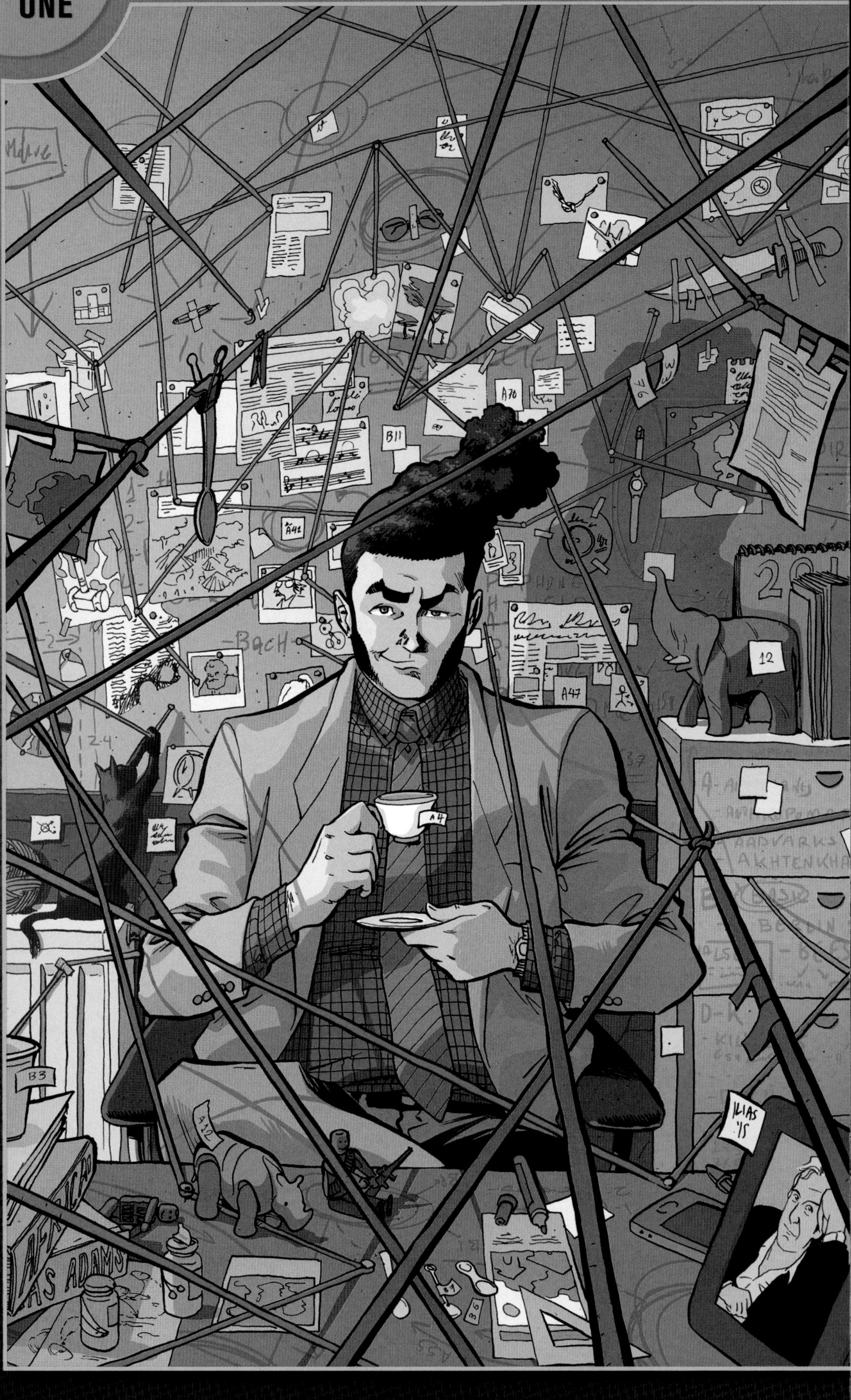

the great treehouse adventure
DRACULA
CHEESY
WHAT'LL IT BE, BOYS?
THUNK
THUNK
THUNK

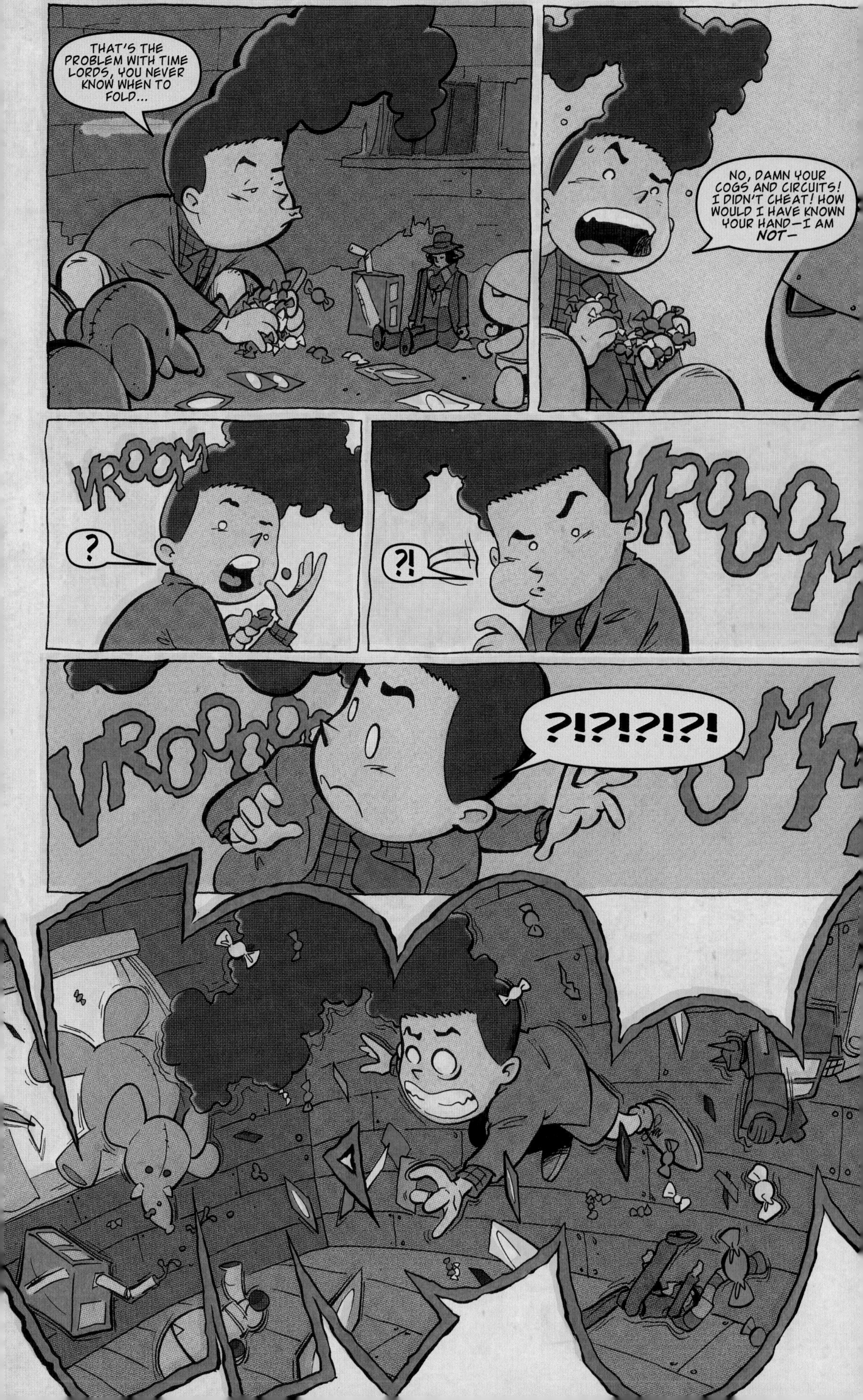
THAT'S THE PROBLEM WITH TIME LORDS, YOU NEVER KNOW WHEN TO FOLD...
NO, DAMN YOUR COGS AND CIRCUITS! I DIDN'T CHEAT! HOW WOULD I HAVE KNOWN YOUR HAND—I AM NOT—
VROOM
?
?!
VROOOOM
VROOOOOOOM
?!?!?!?!

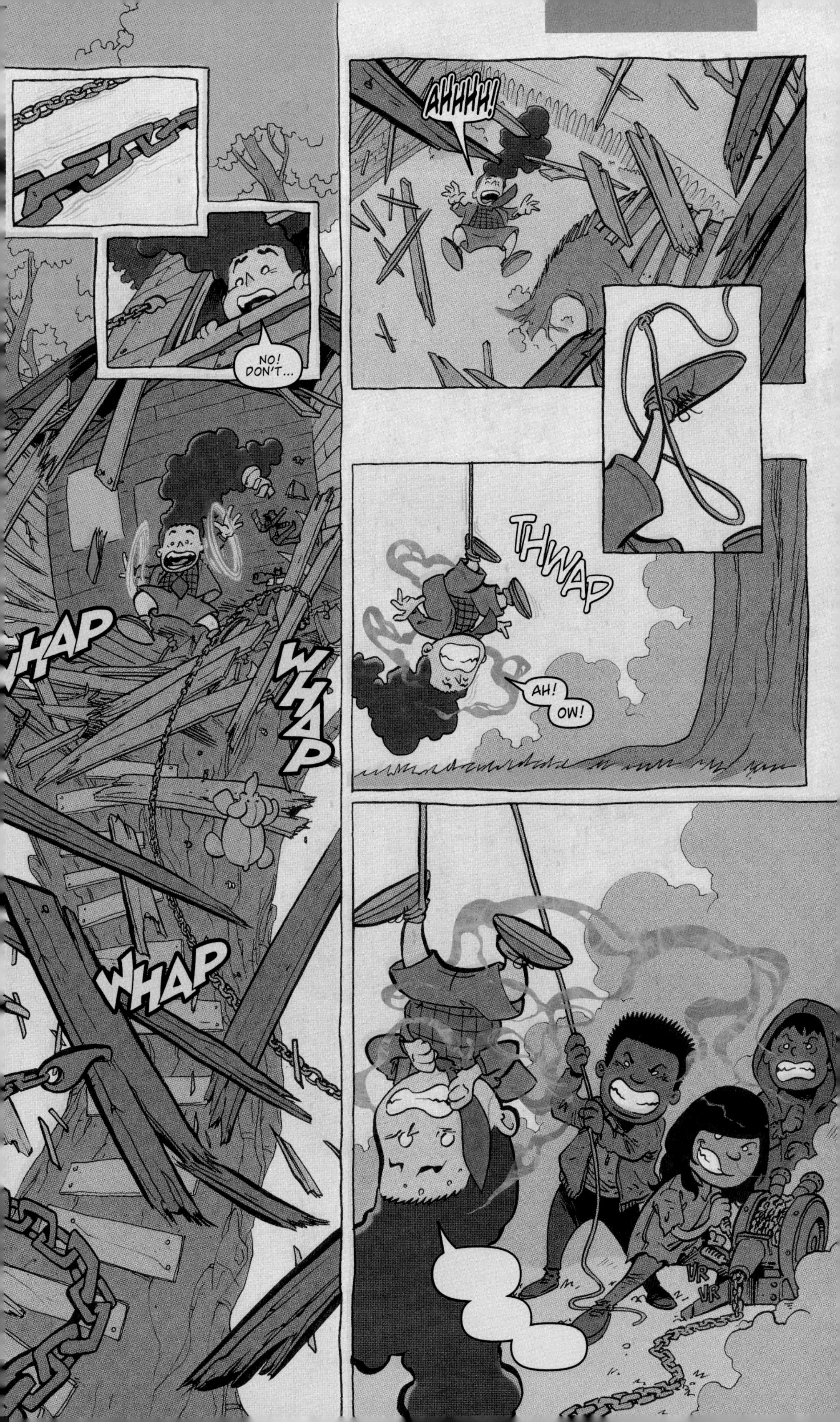
NO! DON'T...
WHAP
WHAP
WHAP
AHHHH!
THWAP
AH!
OW!
VR
VR

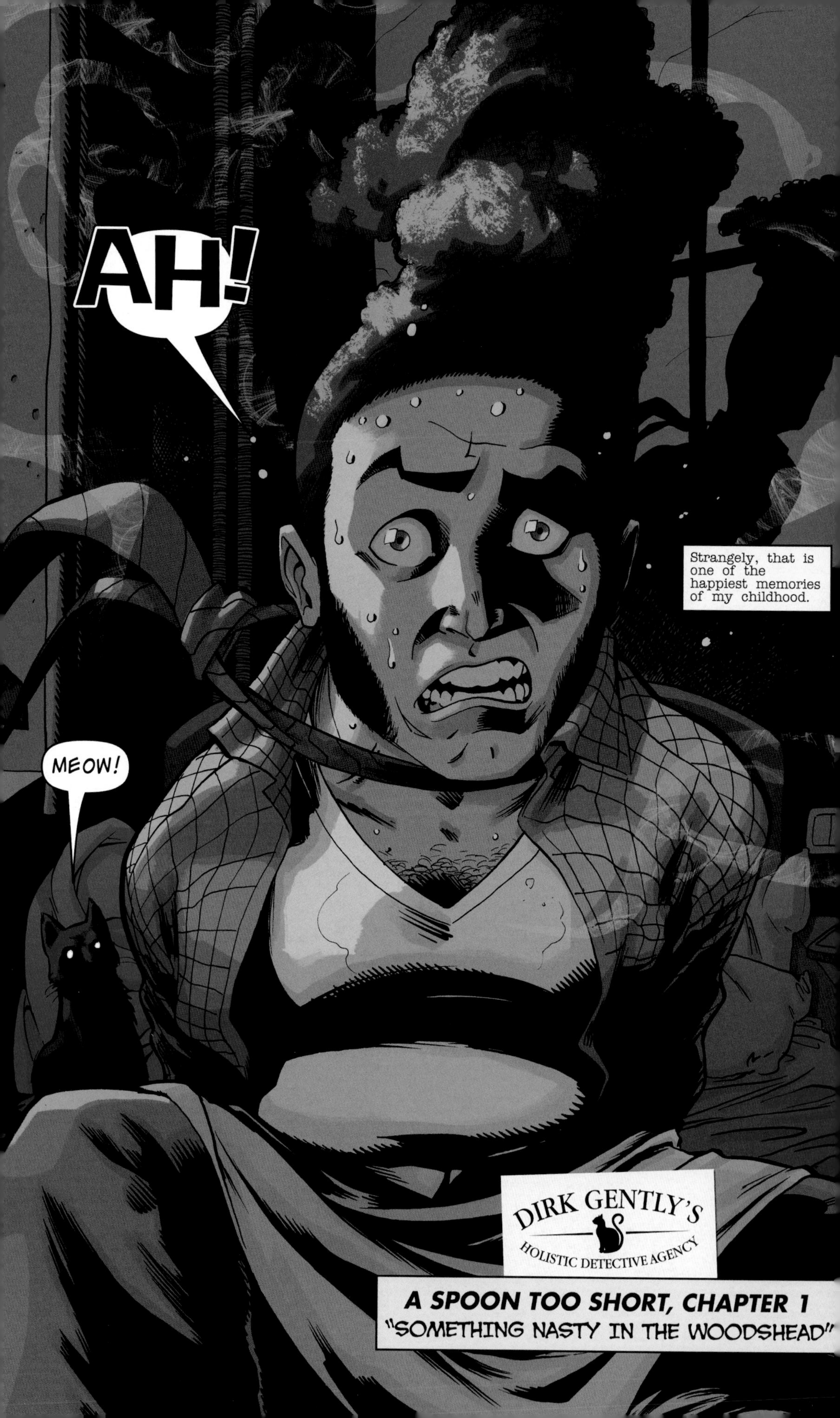
AH!
Strangely, that is one of the happiest memories of my childhood.
MEOW!
DIRK GENTLY'S HOLISTIC DETECTIVE AGENCY
A SPOON TOO SHORT, CHAPTER 1
"SOMETHING NASTY IN THE WOODSHEAD"

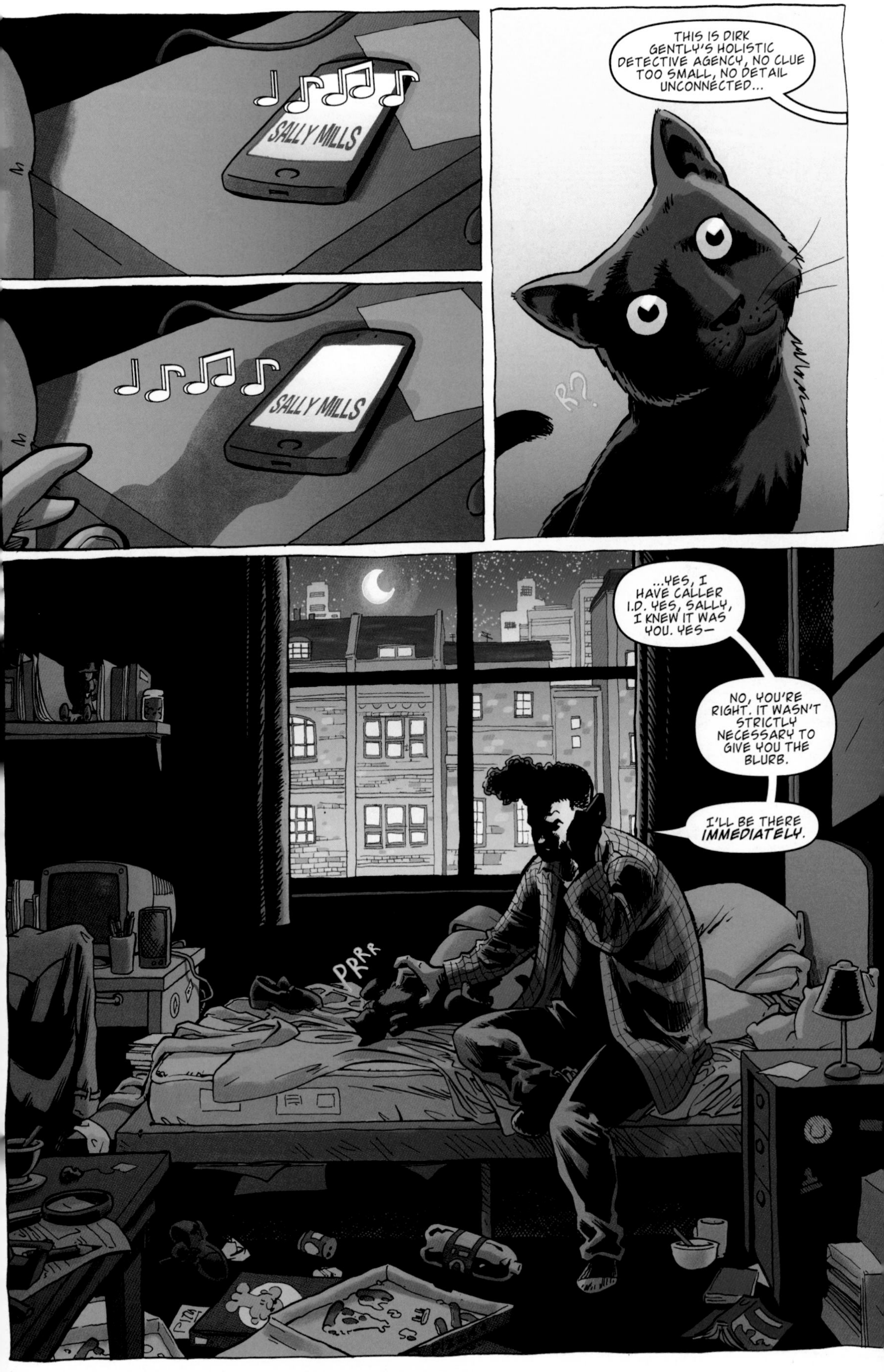
SALLY MILLS
SALLY MILLS
THIS IS DIRK GENTLY'S HOLISTIC DETECTIVE AGENCY, NO CLUE TOO SMALL, NO DETAIL UNCONNECTED...
R?
...YES, I HAVE CALLER I.D. YES, SALLY, I KNEW IT WAS YOU. YES—
NO, YOU'RE RIGHT. IT WASN'T STRICTLY NECESSARY TO GIVE YOU THE BLURB.
I'LL BE THERE *IMMEDIATELY*.
PRRR

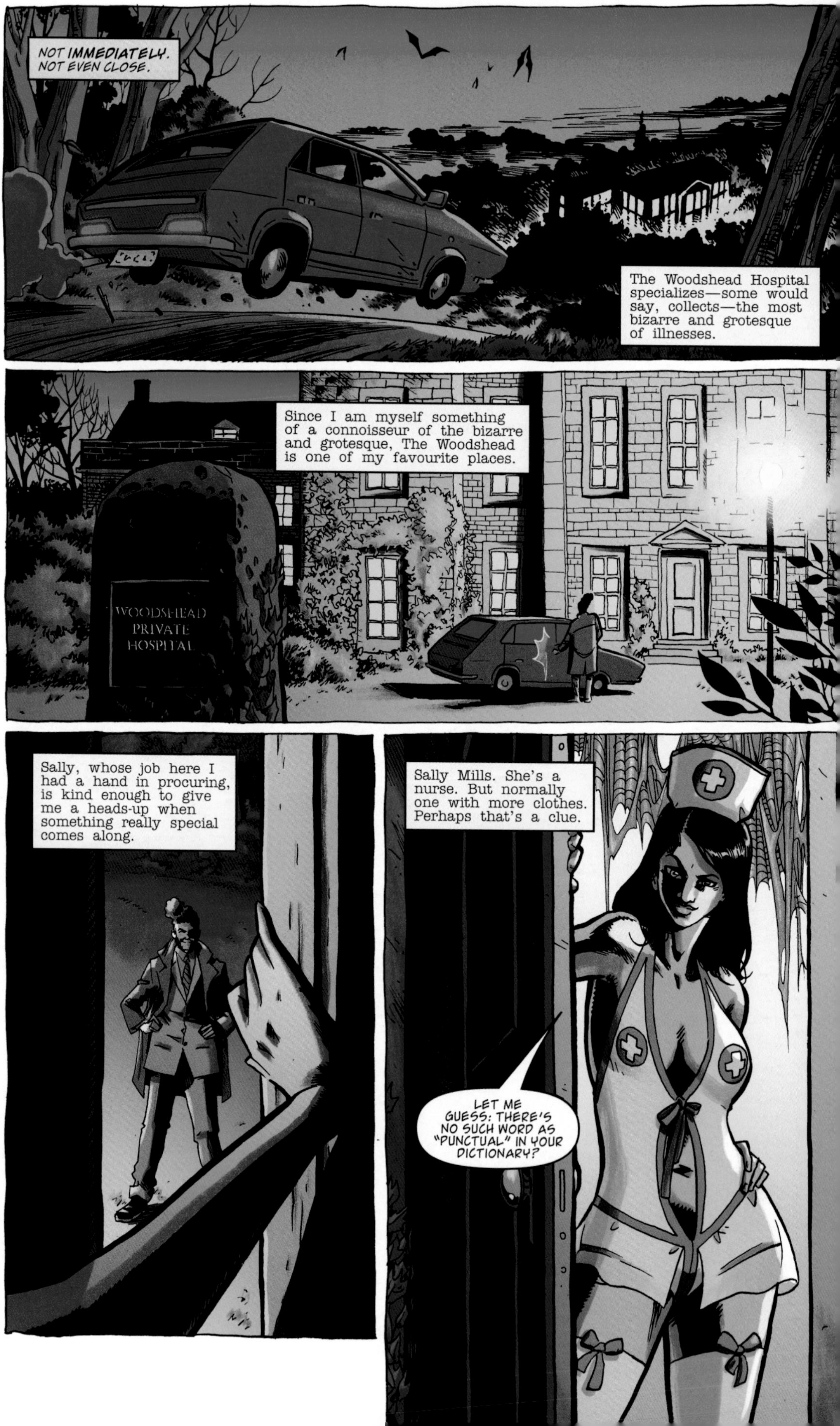
NOT IMMEDIATELY.
NOT EVEN CLOSE.
The Woodshead Hospital specializes—some would say, collects—the most bizarre and grotesque of illnesses.
Since I am myself something of a connoisseur of the bizarre and grotesque, The Woodshead is one of my favourite places.
WOODSHEAD PRIVATE HOSPITAL
Sally, whose job here I had a hand in procuring, is kind enough to give me a heads-up when something really special comes along.
Sally Mills. She's a nurse. But normally one with more clothes. Perhaps that's a clue.
LET ME GUESS: THERE'S NO SUCH WORD AS "PUNCTUAL" IN YOUR DICTIONARY?

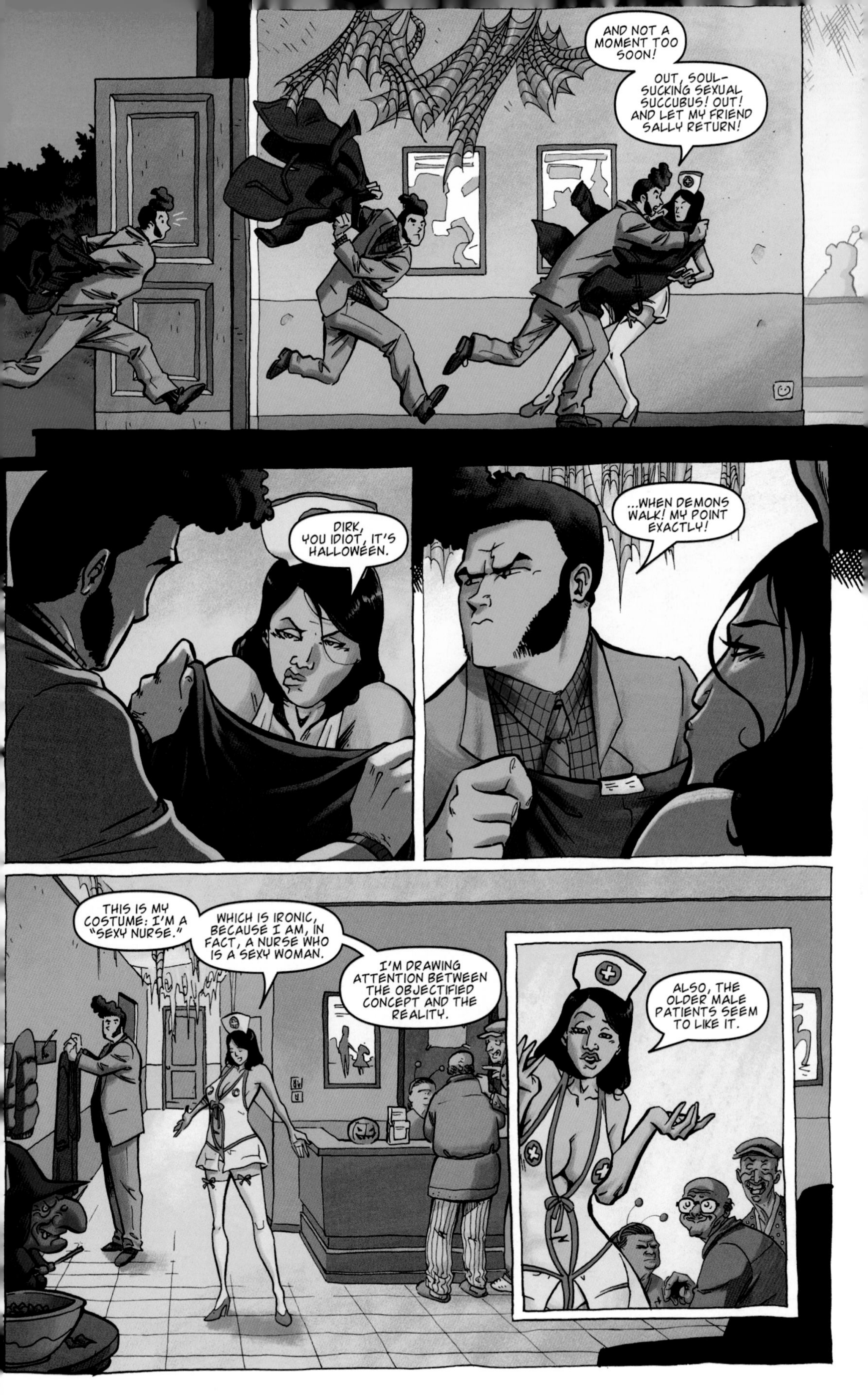
AND NOT A MOMENT TOO SOON!
OUT, SOUL-SUCKING SEXUAL SUCCUBUS! OUT! AND LET MY FRIEND SALLY RETURN!
DIRK, YOU IDIOT, IT'S HALLOWEEN.
...WHEN DEMONS WALK! MY POINT EXACTLY!
THIS IS MY COSTUME: I'M A "SEXY NURSE."
WHICH IS IRONIC, BECAUSE I AM, IN FACT, A NURSE WHO IS A SEXY WOMAN.
I'M DRAWING ATTENTION BETWEEN THE OBJECTIFIED CONCEPT AND THE REALITY.
ALSO, THE OLDER MALE PATIENTS SEEM TO LIKE IT.

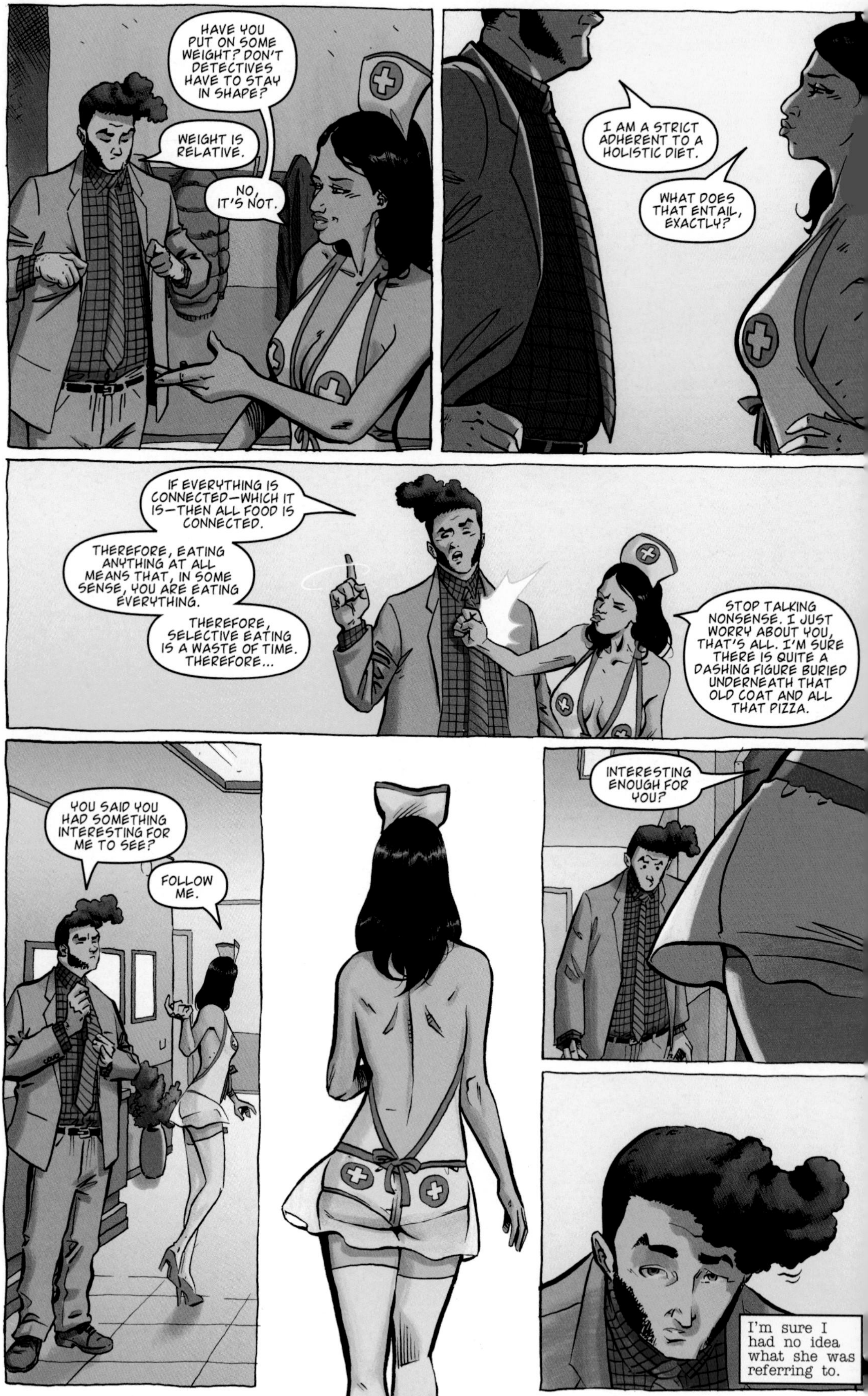
HAVE YOU PUT ON SOME WEIGHT? DON'T DETECTIVES HAVE TO STAY IN SHAPE?
WEIGHT IS RELATIVE.
NO, IT'S NOT.
I AM A STRICT ADHERENT TO A HOLISTIC DIET.
WHAT DOES THAT ENTAIL, EXACTLY?
IF EVERYTHING IS CONNECTED—WHICH IT IS—THEN ALL FOOD IS CONNECTED.
THEREFORE, EATING ANYTHING AT ALL MEANS THAT, IN SOME SENSE, YOU ARE EATING EVERYTHING.
THEREFORE, SELECTIVE EATING IS A WASTE OF TIME. THEREFORE...
STOP TALKING NONSENSE. I JUST WORRY ABOUT YOU, THAT'S ALL. I'M SURE THERE IS QUITE A DASHING FIGURE BURIED UNDERNEATH THAT OLD COAT AND ALL THAT PIZZA.
YOU SAID YOU HAD SOMETHING INTERESTING FOR ME TO SEE?
FOLLOW ME.
INTERESTING ENOUGH FOR YOU?
I'm sure I had no idea what she was referring to.

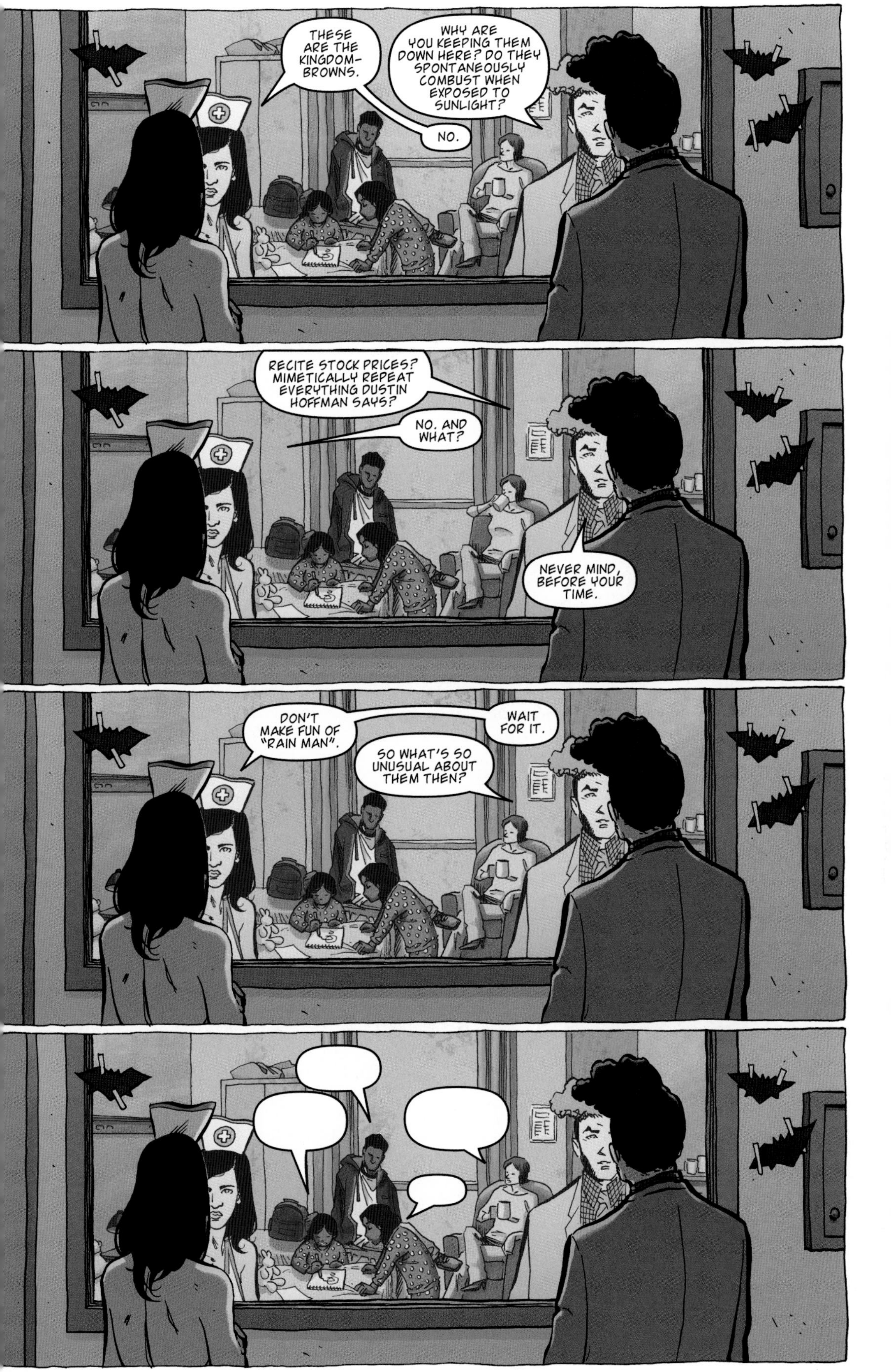
THESE ARE THE KINGDOM-BROWNS.
WHY ARE YOU KEEPING THEM DOWN HERE? DO THEY SPONTANEOUSLY COMBUST WHEN EXPOSED TO SUNLIGHT?
NO.
RECITE STOCK PRICES? MIMETICALLY REPEAT EVERYTHING DUSTIN HOFFMAN SAYS?
NO. AND WHAT?
NEVER MIND, BEFORE YOUR TIME.
DON'T MAKE FUN OF "RAIN MAN".
WAIT FOR IT.
SO WHAT'S SO UNUSUAL ABOUT THEM THEN?

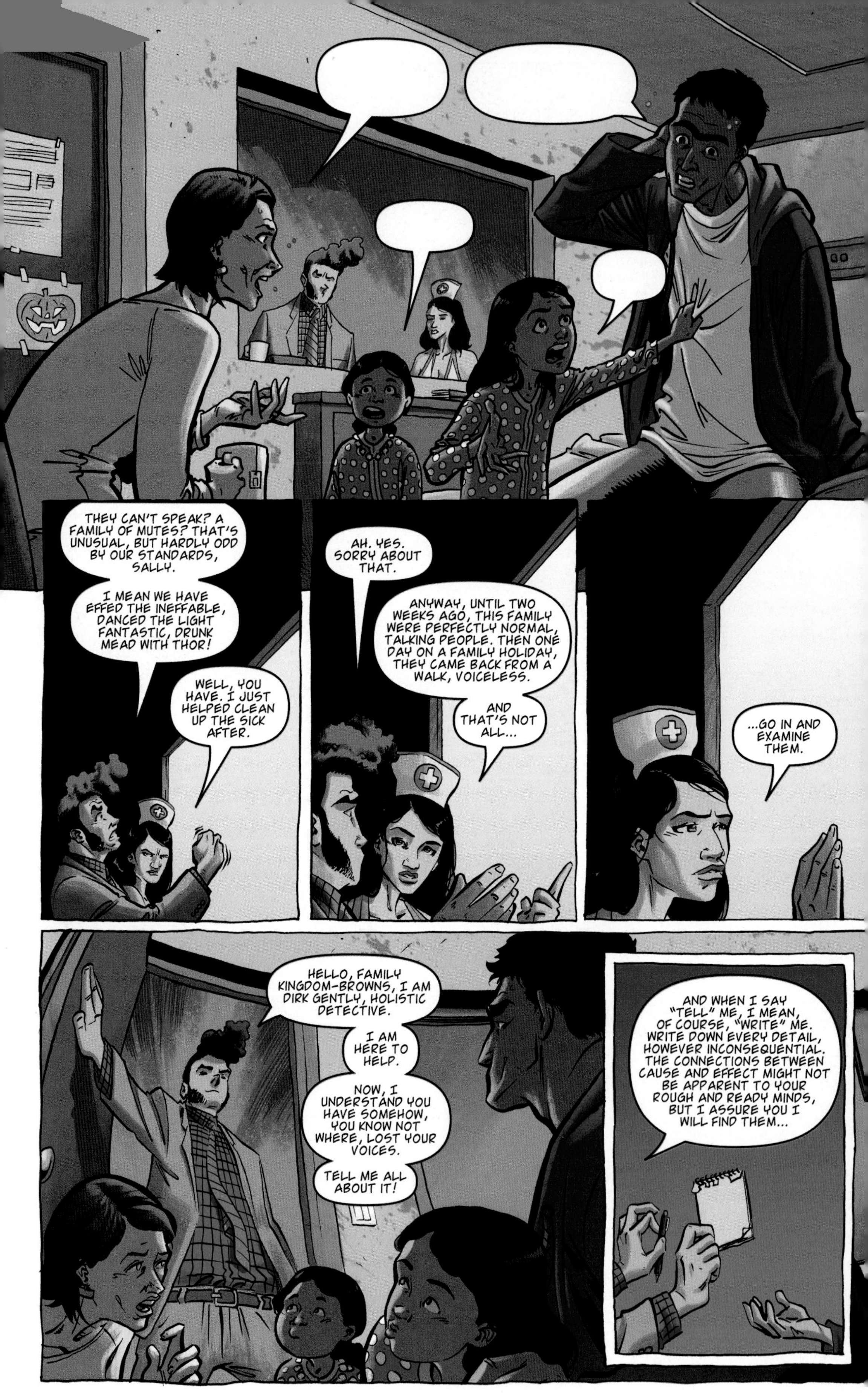
THEY CAN'T SPEAK? A FAMILY OF MUTES? THAT'S UNUSUAL, BUT HARDLY ODD BY OUR STANDARDS, SALLY.
I MEAN WE HAVE EFFED THE INEFFABLE, DANCED THE LIGHT FANTASTIC, DRUNK MEAD WITH THOR!
WELL, YOU HAVE. I JUST HELPED CLEAN UP THE SICK AFTER.
AH. YES. SORRY ABOUT THAT.
ANYWAY, UNTIL TWO WEEKS AGO, THIS FAMILY WERE PERFECTLY NORMAL, TALKING PEOPLE. THEN ONE DAY ON A FAMILY HOLIDAY, THEY CAME BACK FROM A WALK, VOICELESS.
AND THAT'S NOT ALL...
...GO IN AND EXAMINE THEM.
HELLO, FAMILY KINGDOM-BROWNS, I AM DIRK GENTLY, HOLISTIC DETECTIVE.
I AM HERE TO HELP.
NOW, I UNDERSTAND YOU HAVE SOMEHOW, YOU KNOW NOT WHERE, LOST YOUR VOICES.
TELL ME ALL ABOUT IT!
AND WHEN I SAY "TELL" ME, I MEAN, OF COURSE, "WRITE" ME. WRITE DOWN EVERY DETAIL, HOWEVER INCONSEQUENTIAL. THE CONNECTIONS BETWEEN CAUSE AND EFFECT MIGHT NOT BE APPARENT TO YOUR ROUGH AND READY MINDS, BUT I ASSURE YOU I WILL FIND THEM...

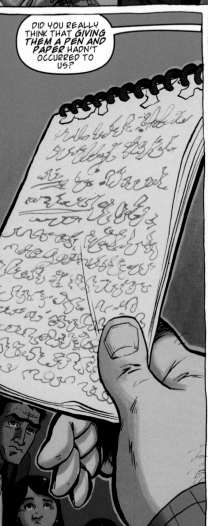

DID YOU REALLY THINK THAT *GIVING THEM A PEN AND PAPER* HADN'T OCCURRED TO US?

HMM. ARE THEY FOREIGN?

ONLY IF YOU COUNT HAMPSHIRE.

HYPOTHESIS: THEY ARE AN EMBEDDED SPY RING, CONCEALED UNDERCOVER IN DARKEST... HAMPSHIRE, CONDITIONED TO COMMUNICATE ONLY IN CYPHER.

ALTERNATIVE HYPOTHESIS: THEY ARE POSSESSED. THIS WRITING BEARS A STRONG RESEMBLANCE TO THE AUTOMATIC WRITING OF VICTORIAN MEDIUMS.

I hate it when Sally does eyebrows. I can't do eyebrows. Only Sally. And she's not even a Detective.

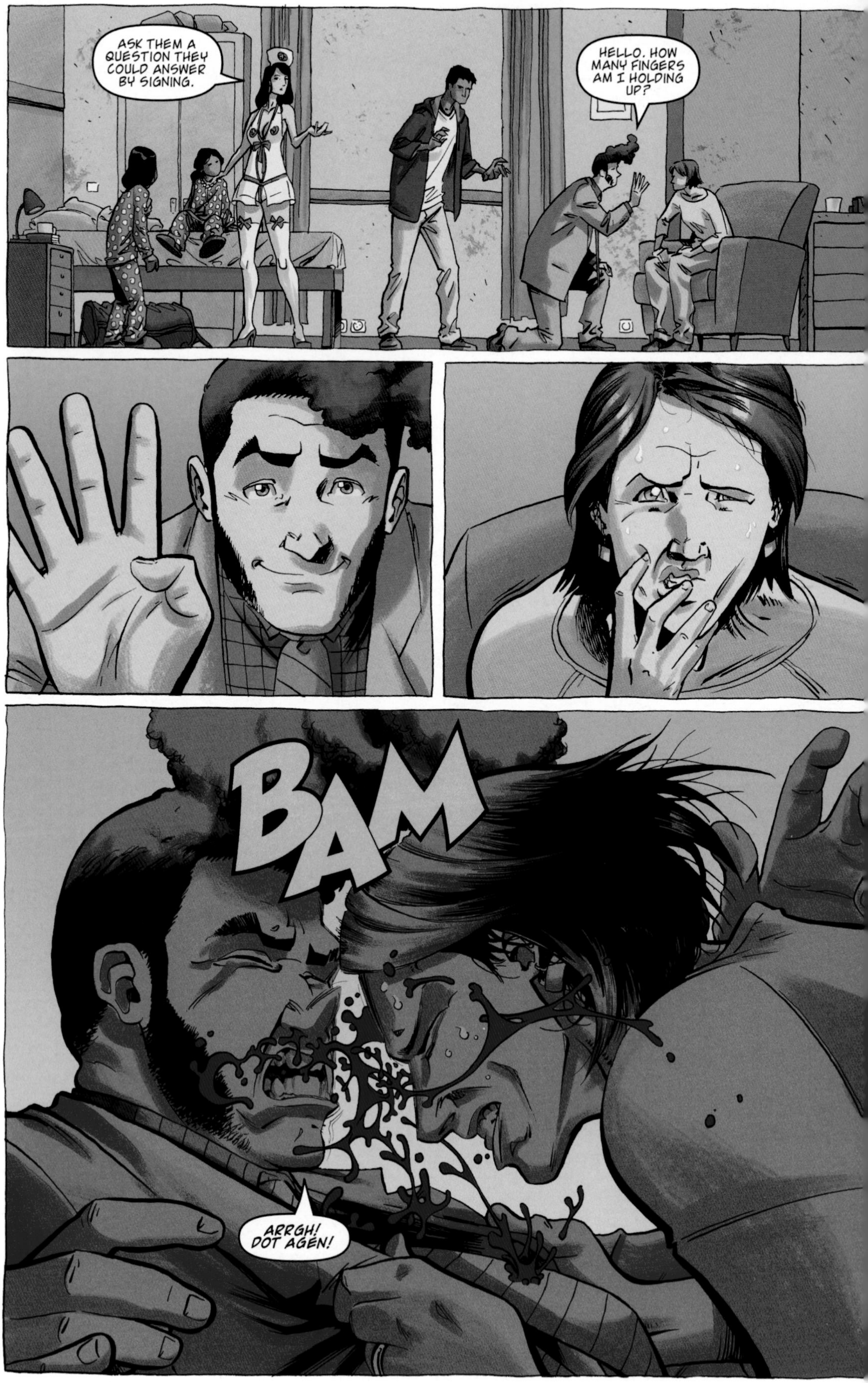
ASK THEM A QUESTION THEY COULD ANSWER BY SIGNING.
HELLO. HOW MANY FINGERS AM I HOLDING UP?
BAM
ARRGH! DOT AGEN!

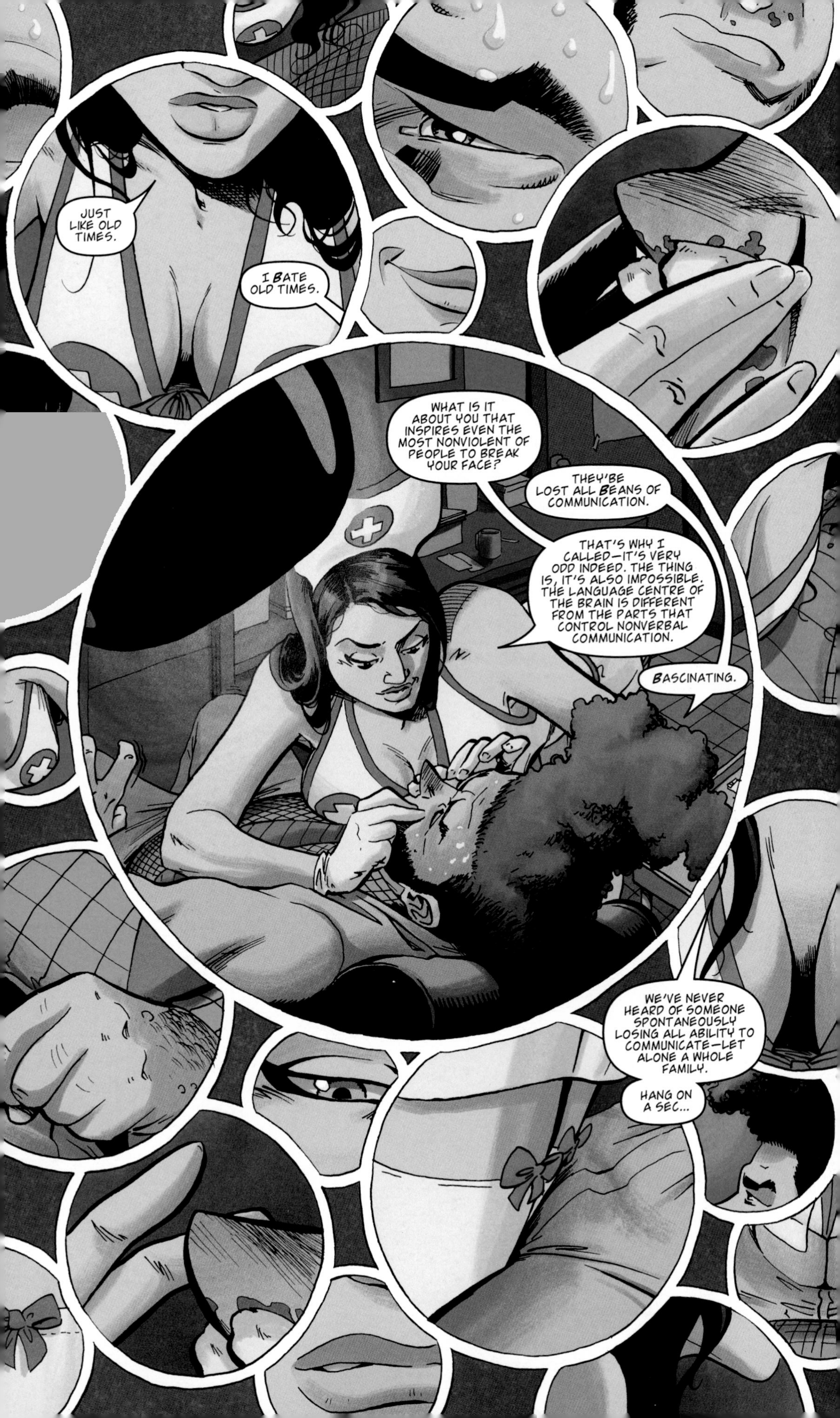
JUST LIKE OLD TIMES.
I BATE OLD TIMES.
WHAT IS IT ABOUT YOU THAT INSPIRES EVEN THE MOST NONVIOLENT OF PEOPLE TO BREAK YOUR FACE?
THEY'BE LOST ALL BEANS OF COMMUNICATION.
THAT'S WHY I CALLED—IT'S VERY ODD INDEED. THE THING IS, IT'S ALSO IMPOSSIBLE. THE LANGUAGE CENTRE OF THE BRAIN IS DIFFERENT FROM THE PARTS THAT CONTROL NONVERBAL COMMUNICATION.
BASCINATING.
WE'VE NEVER HEARD OF SOMEONE SPONTANEOUSLY LOSING ALL ABILITY TO COMMUNICATE—LET ALONE A WHOLE FAMILY.
HANG ON A SEC...

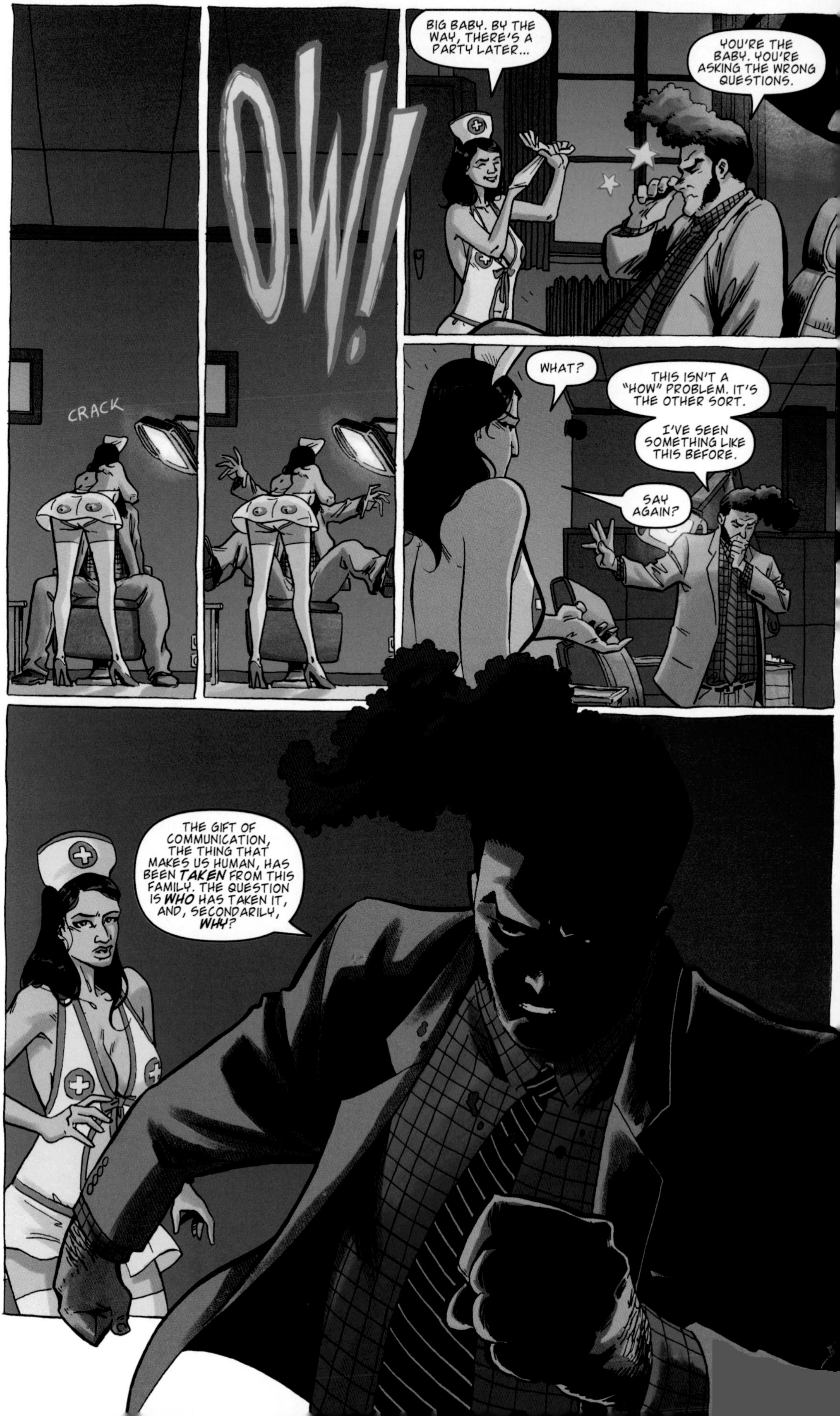
CRACK
OW!
BIG BABY. BY THE WAY, THERE'S A PARTY LATER...
YOU'RE THE BABY. YOU'RE ASKING THE WRONG QUESTIONS.
WHAT?
THIS ISN'T A "HOW" PROBLEM. IT'S THE OTHER SORT.
I'VE SEEN SOMETHING LIKE THIS BEFORE.
SAY AGAIN?
THE GIFT OF COMMUNICATION, THE THING THAT MAKES US HUMAN, HAS BEEN *TAKEN* FROM THIS FAMILY. THE QUESTION IS *WHO* HAS TAKEN IT, AND, SECONDARILY, *WHY*?

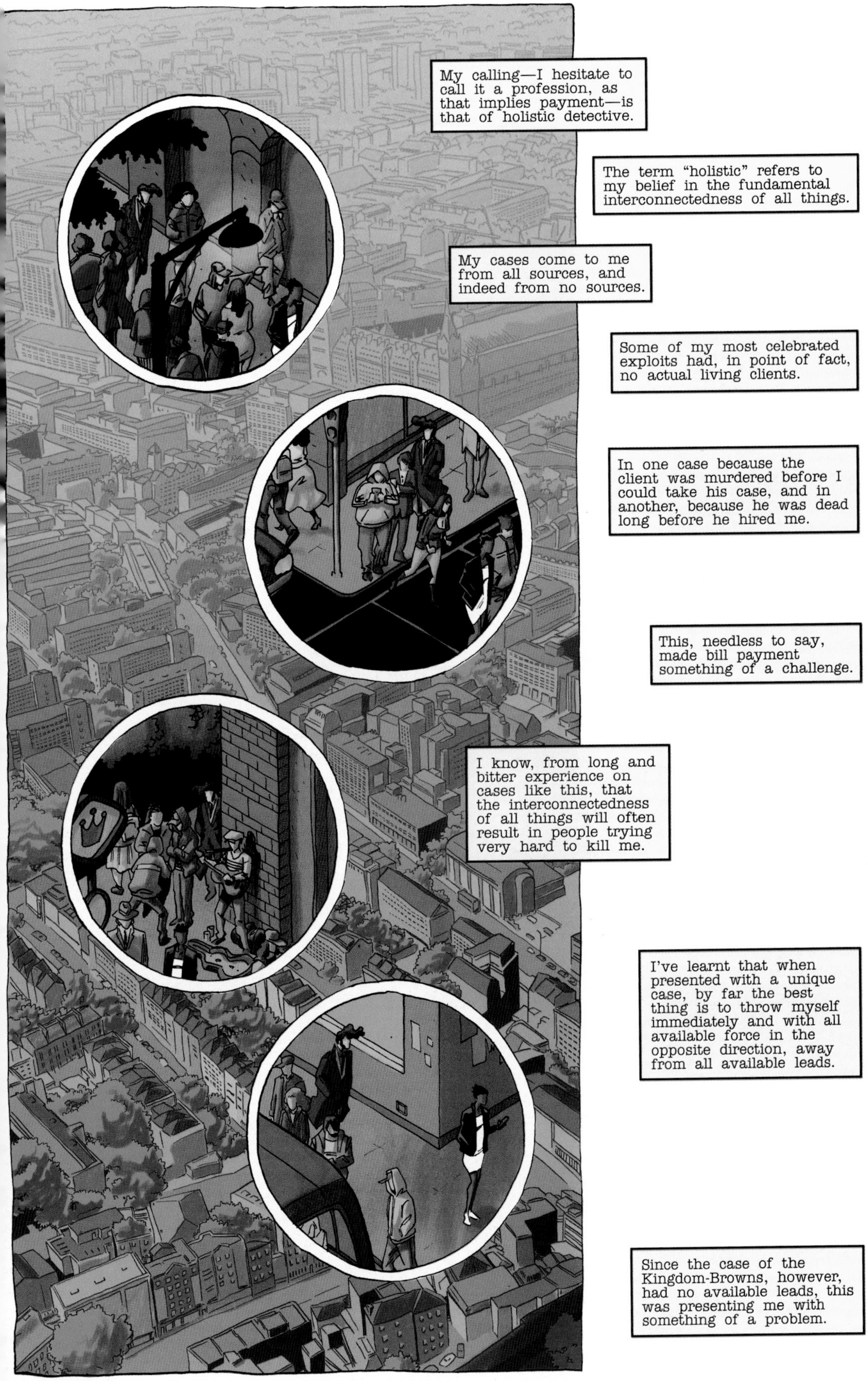
My calling—I hesitate to call it a profession, as that implies payment—is that of holistic detective.
The term "holistic" refers to my belief in the fundamental interconnectedness of all things.
My cases come to me from all sources, and indeed from no sources.
Some of my most celebrated exploits had, in point of fact, no actual living clients.
In one case because the client was murdered before I could take his case, and in another, because he was dead long before he hired me.
This, needless to say, made bill payment something of a challenge.
I know, from long and bitter experience on cases like this, that the interconnectedness of all things will often result in people trying very hard to kill me.
I've learnt that when presented with a unique case, by far the best thing is to throw myself immediately and with all available force in the opposite direction, away from all available leads.
Since the case of the Kingdom-Browns, however, had no available leads, this was presenting me with something of a problem.

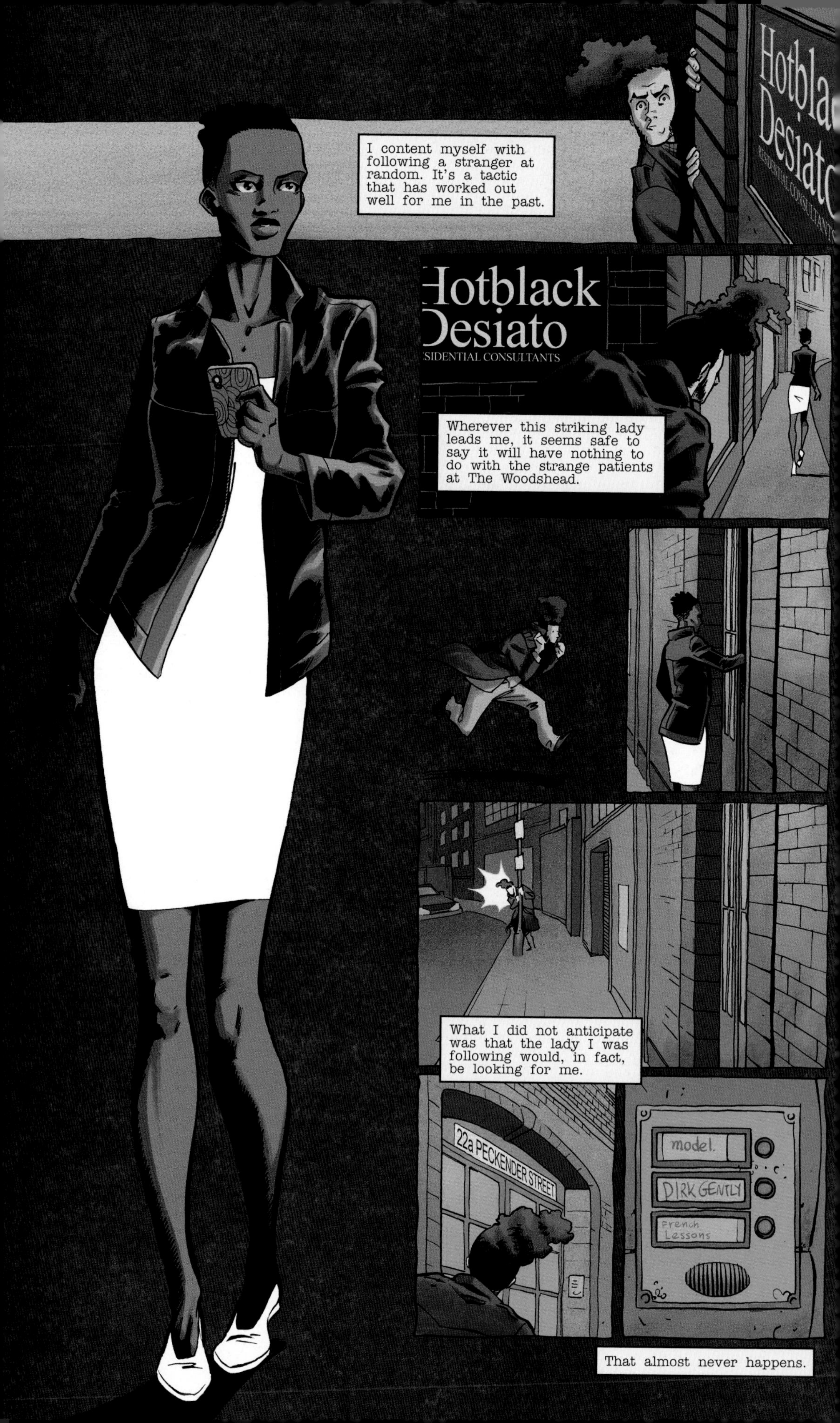
Hotblack Desiato
RESIDENTIAL CONSULTANTS
I content myself with following a stranger at random. It's a tactic that has worked out well for me in the past.
Hotblack Desiato
RESIDENTIAL CONSULTANTS
Wherever this striking lady leads me, it seems safe to say it will have nothing to do with the strange patients at The Woodshead.
What I did not anticipate was that the lady I was following would, in fact, be looking for me.
22a PECKENDER STREET
model.
DIRK GENTLY
French Lessons
That almost never happens.

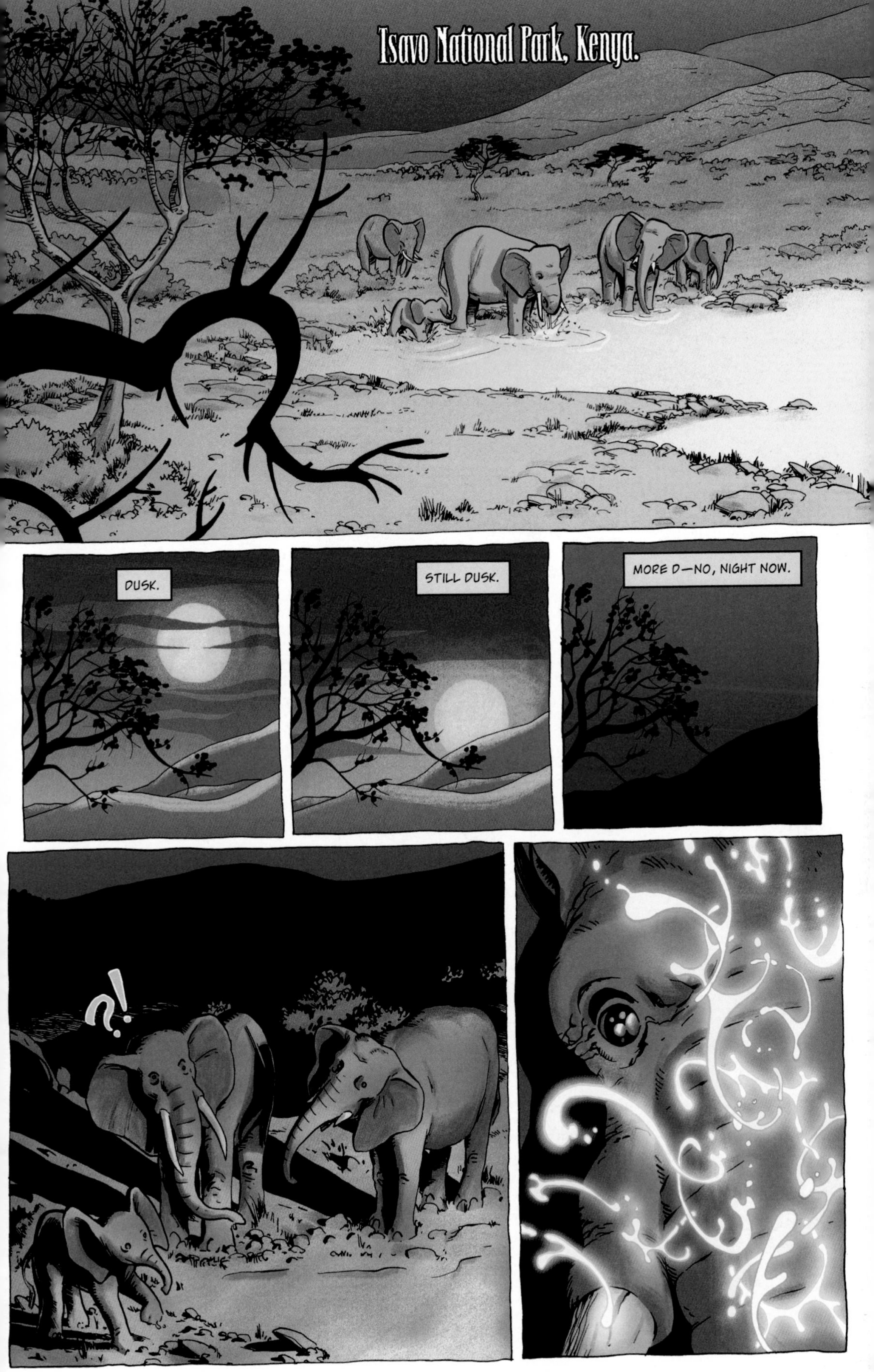
Isavo National Park, Kenya.
DUSK.
STILL DUSK.
MORE D—NO, NIGHT NOW.
?!

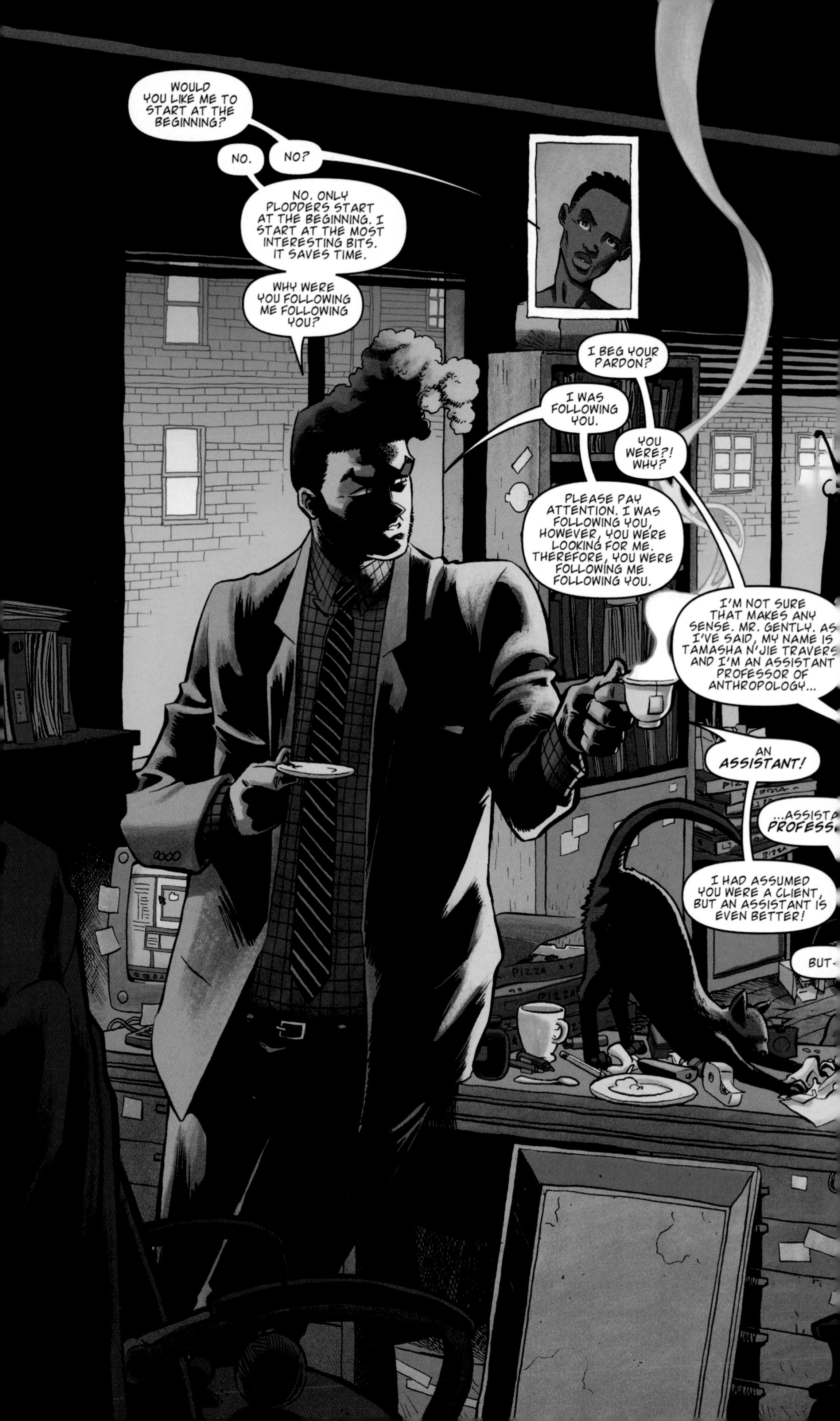
WOULD YOU LIKE ME TO START AT THE BEGINNING?
NO?
NO.
NO. ONLY PLODDERS START AT THE BEGINNING. I START AT THE MOST INTERESTING BITS. IT SAVES TIME.
WHY WERE YOU FOLLOWING ME FOLLOWING YOU?
I BEG YOUR PARDON?
I WAS FOLLOWING YOU.
YOU WERE?! WHY?
PLEASE PAY ATTENTION. I WAS FOLLOWING YOU, HOWEVER, YOU WERE LOOKING FOR ME. THEREFORE, YOU WERE FOLLOWING ME FOLLOWING YOU.
I'M NOT SURE THAT MAKES ANY SENSE. MR. GENTLY. AS I'VE SAID, MY NAME IS TAMASHA N'JIE TRAVERS AND I'M AN ASSISTANT PROFESSOR OF ANTHROPOLOGY...
AN ASSISTANT!
...ASSISTA PROFESS
I HAD ASSUMED YOU WERE A CLIENT, BUT AN ASSISTANT IS EVEN BETTER!
BUT-

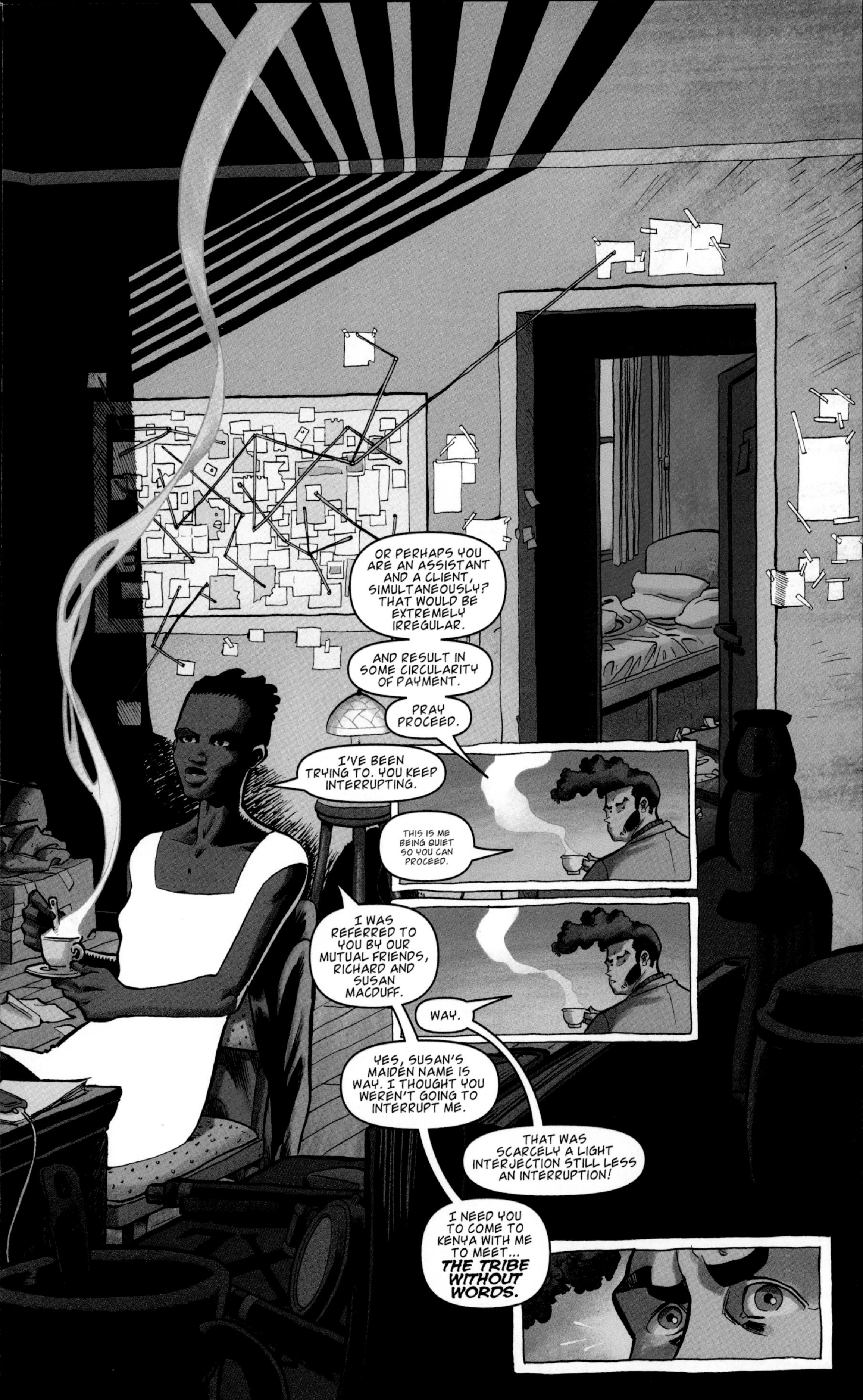

OR PERHAPS YOU ARE AN ASSISTANT AND A CLIENT, SIMULTANEOUSLY? THAT WOULD BE EXTREMELY IRREGULAR.
AND RESULT IN SOME CIRCULARITY OF PAYMENT.
PRAY PROCEED.
I'VE BEEN TRYING TO. YOU KEEP INTERRUPTING.
THIS IS ME BEING QUIET SO YOU CAN PROCEED.
I WAS REFERRED TO YOU BY OUR MUTUAL FRIENDS, RICHARD AND SUSAN MACDUFF.
WAY.
YES, SUSAN'S MAIDEN NAME IS WAY. I THOUGHT YOU WEREN'T GOING TO INTERRUPT ME.
THAT WAS SCARCELY A LIGHT INTERJECTION STILL LESS AN INTERRUPTION!
I NEED YOU TO COME TO KENYA WITH ME TO MEET... ***THE TRIBE WITHOUT WORDS.***

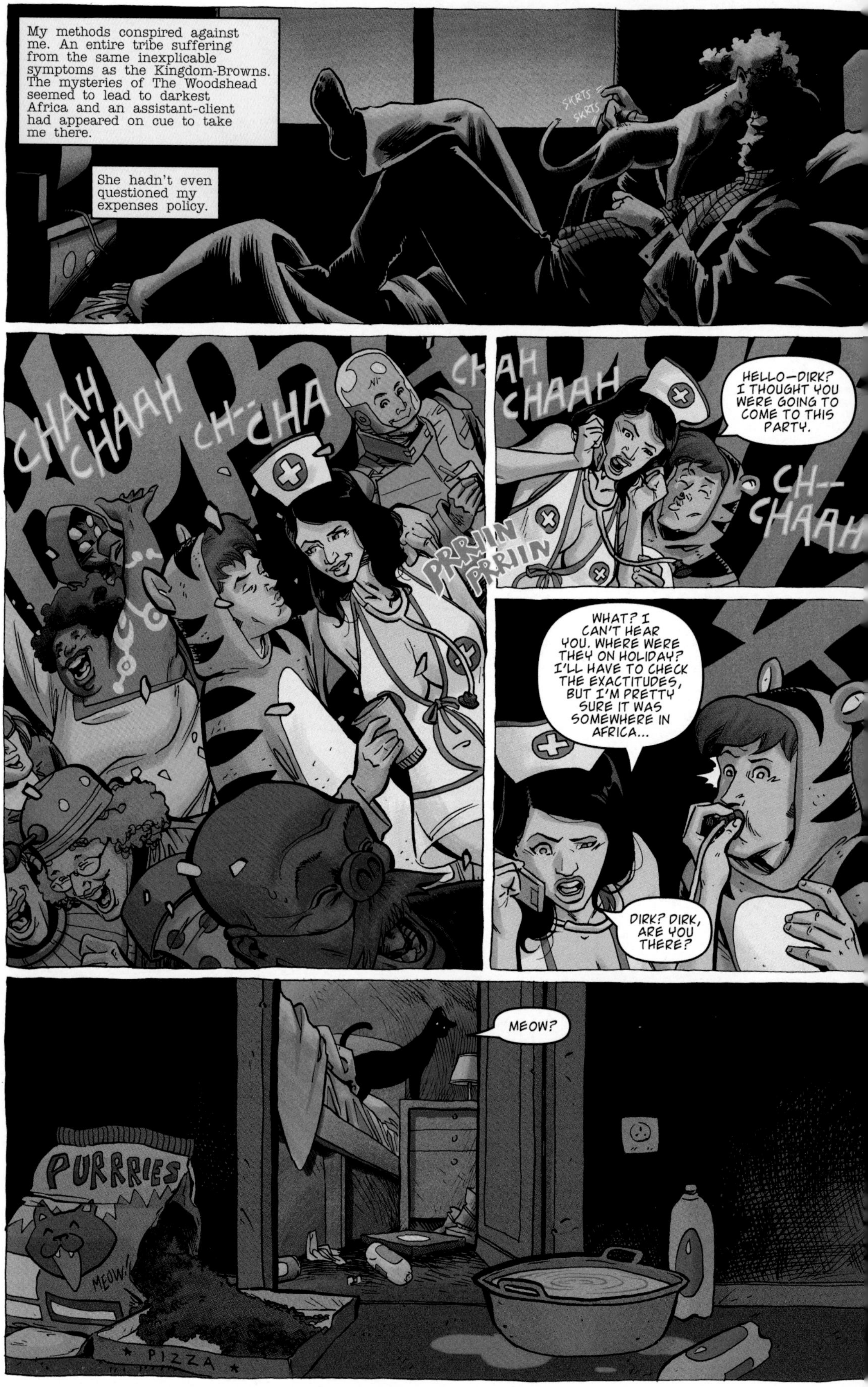
My methods conspired against me. An entire tribe suffering from the same inexplicable symptoms as the Kingdom-Browns. The mysteries of The Woodshead seemed to lead to darkest Africa and an assistant-client had appeared on cue to take me there.
She hadn't even questioned my expenses policy.
SKRTS SKRTS
CHAH CHAAH CH-CHA
PRRIIN PRRIIN
CHAH CHAAH
HELLO—DIRK? I THOUGHT YOU WERE GOING TO COME TO THIS PARTY.
CH-CHAAH
WHAT? I CAN'T HEAR YOU. WHERE WERE THEY ON HOLIDAY? I'LL HAVE TO CHECK THE EXACTITUDES, BUT I'M PRETTY SURE IT WAS SOMEWHERE IN AFRICA...
DIRK? DIRK, ARE YOU THERE?
MEOW?
PURRRIES
MEOW!
PIZZA

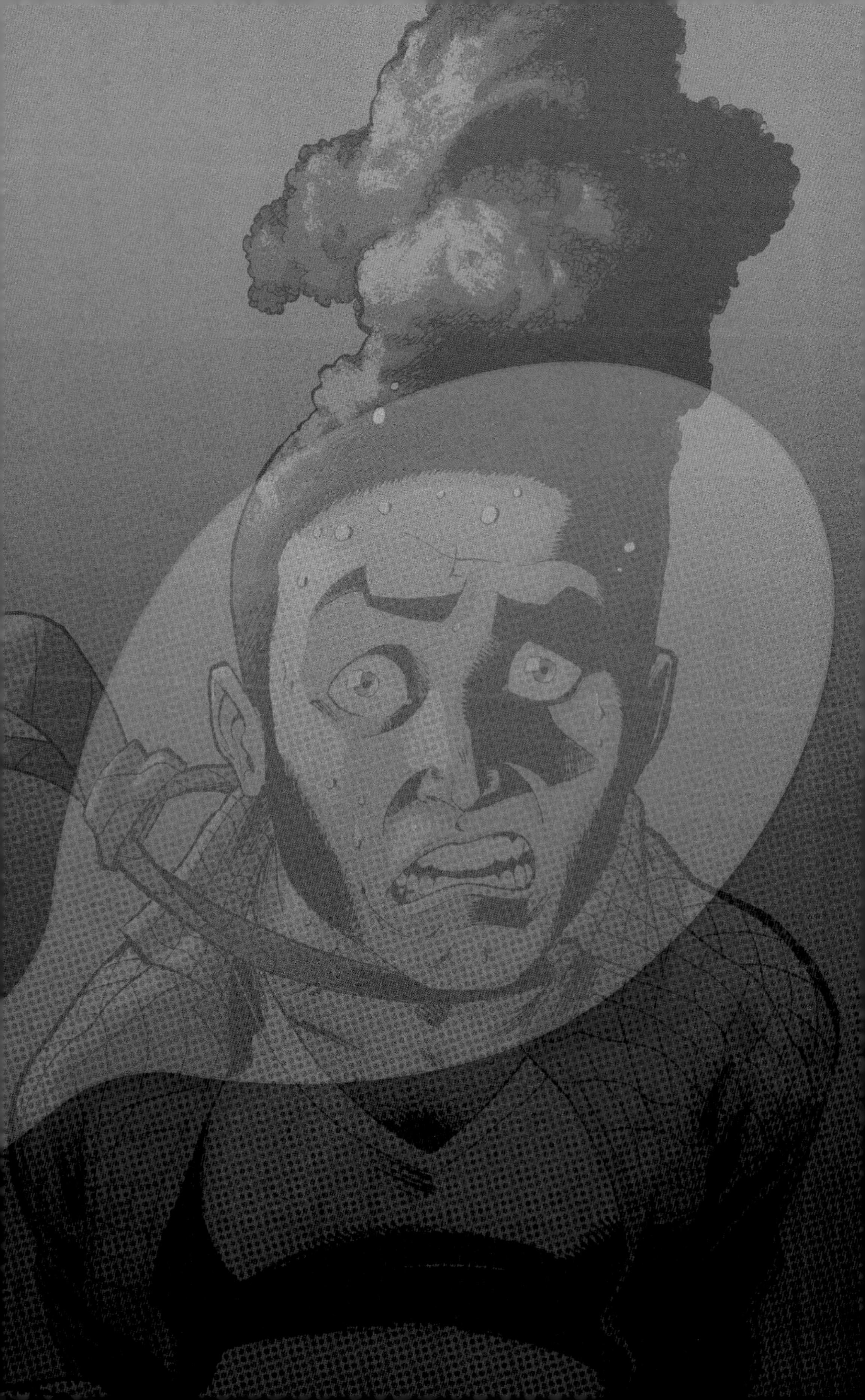

CHAPTER
TWO

Cover Art by **ILIAS KYRIAZIS**

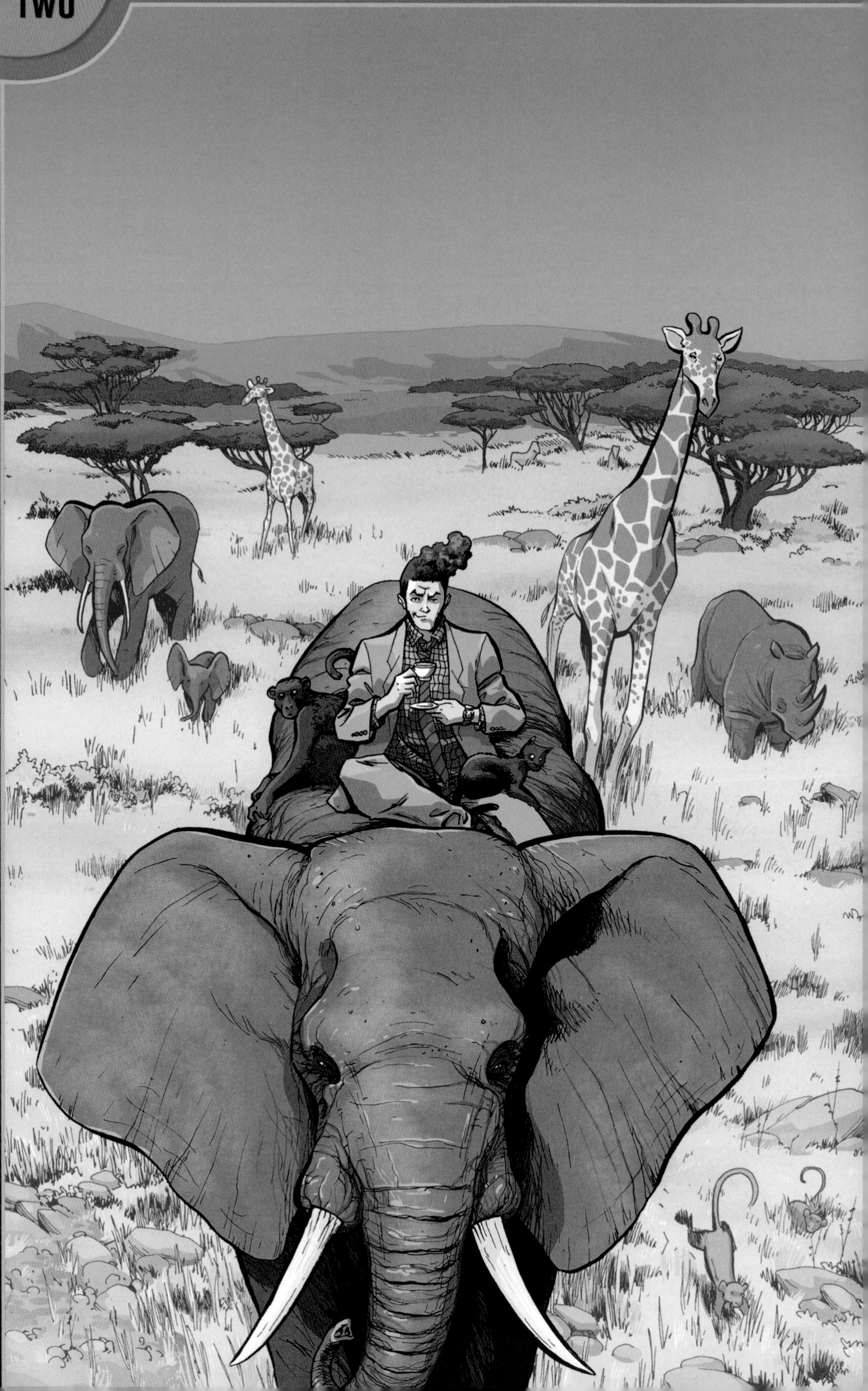

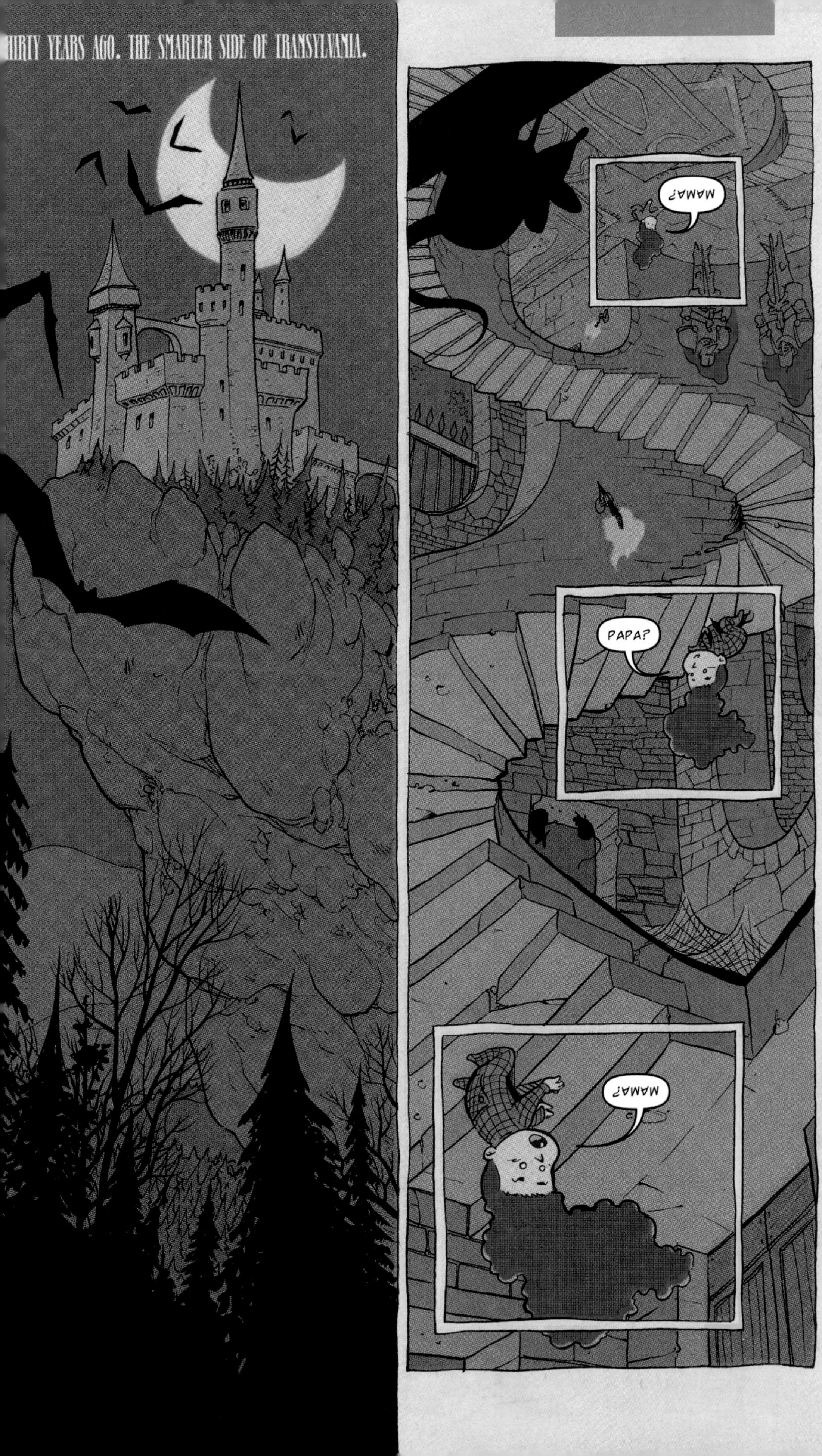
HIRTY YEARS AGO. THE SMARTER SIDE OF TRANSYLVANIA.
MAMA?
PAPA?
MAMA?

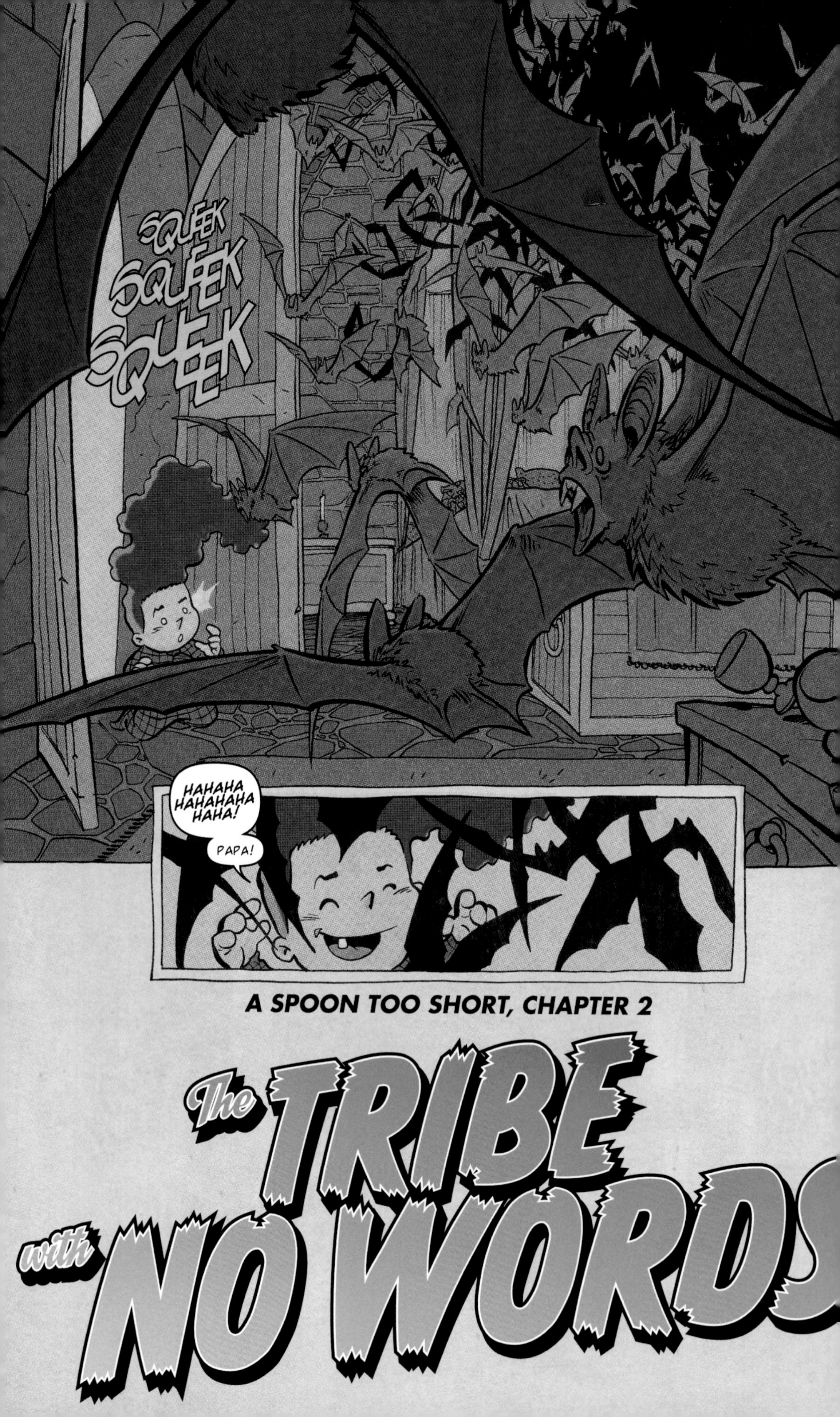
SQUEEK
SQUEEK
SQUEEK
HAHAHA HAHAHAHA HAHA!
PAPA!

A SPOON TOO SHORT, CHAPTER 2

The TRIBE with NO WORDS

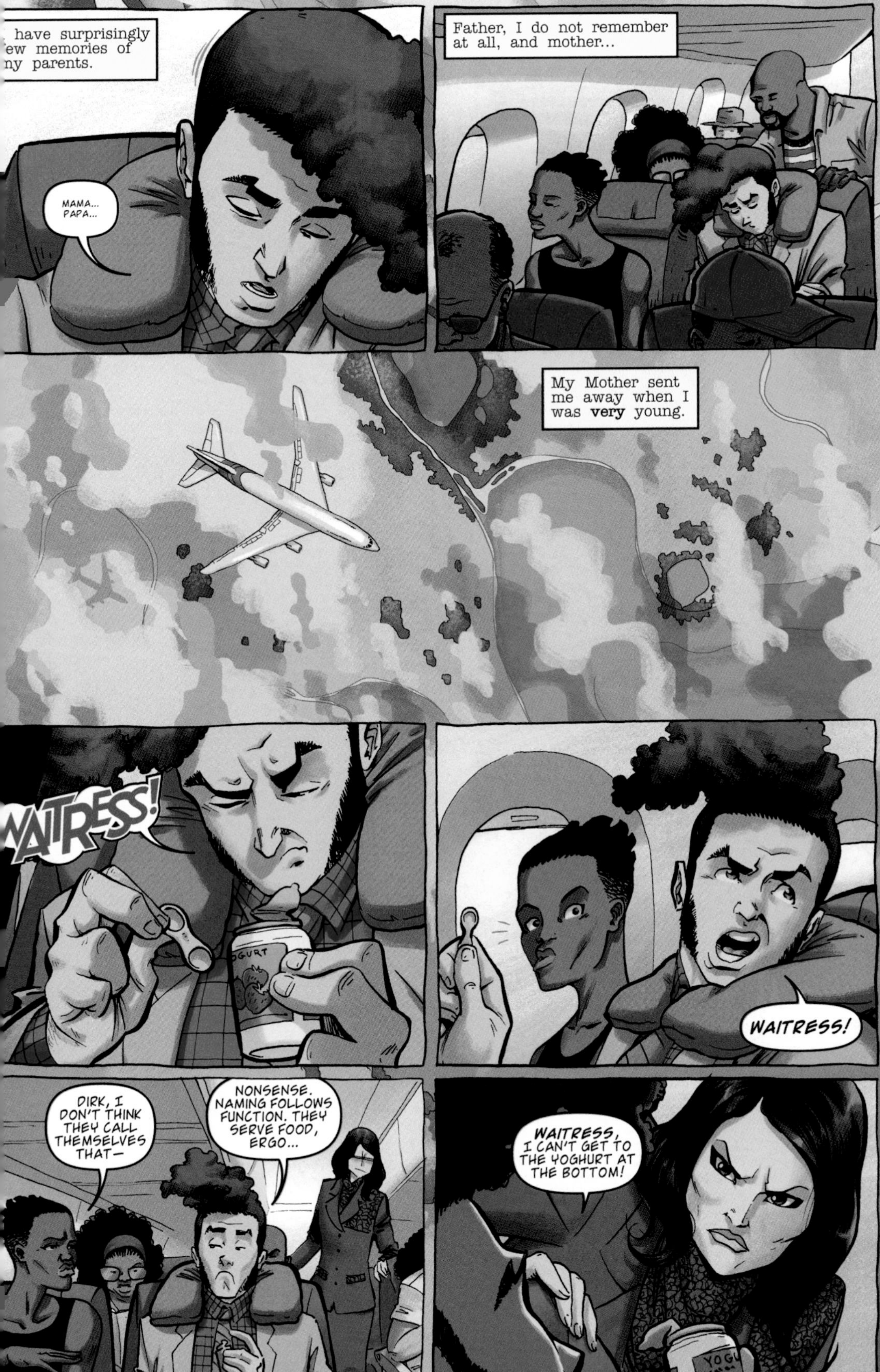

have surprisingly
ew memories of
ny parents.
MAMA...
PAPA...
Father, I do not remember at all, and mother...
My Mother sent me away when I was **very** young.
WAITRESS!
OGURT
WAITRESS!
DIRK, I DON'T THINK THEY CALL THEMSELVES THAT—
NONSENSE. NAMING FOLLOWS FUNCTION. THEY SERVE FOOD, ERGO...
WAITRESS, I CAN'T GET TO THE YOGHURT AT THE BOTTOM!

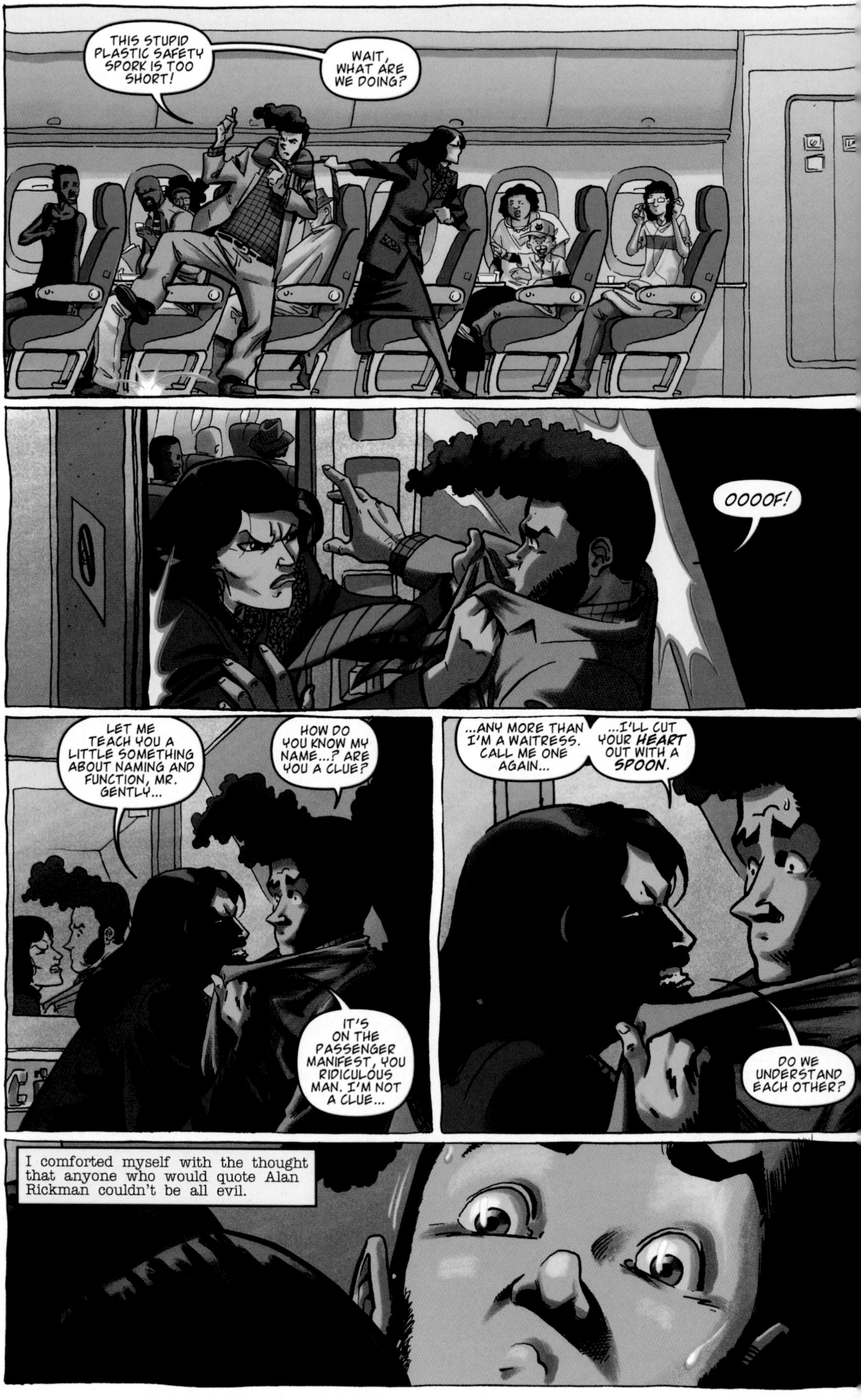
THIS STUPID PLASTIC SAFETY SPORK IS TOO SHORT!
WAIT, WHAT ARE WE DOING?
OOOOF!
LET ME TEACH YOU A LITTLE SOMETHING ABOUT NAMING AND FUNCTION, MR. GENTLY...
HOW DO YOU KNOW MY NAME...? ARE YOU A CLUE?
IT'S ON THE PASSENGER MANIFEST, YOU RIDICULOUS MAN. I'M NOT A CLUE...
...ANY MORE THAN I'M A WAITRESS. CALL ME ONE AGAIN...
...I'LL CUT YOUR HEART OUT WITH A SPOON.
DO WE UNDERSTAND EACH OTHER?
I comforted myself with the thought that anyone who would quote Alan Rickman couldn't be all evil.

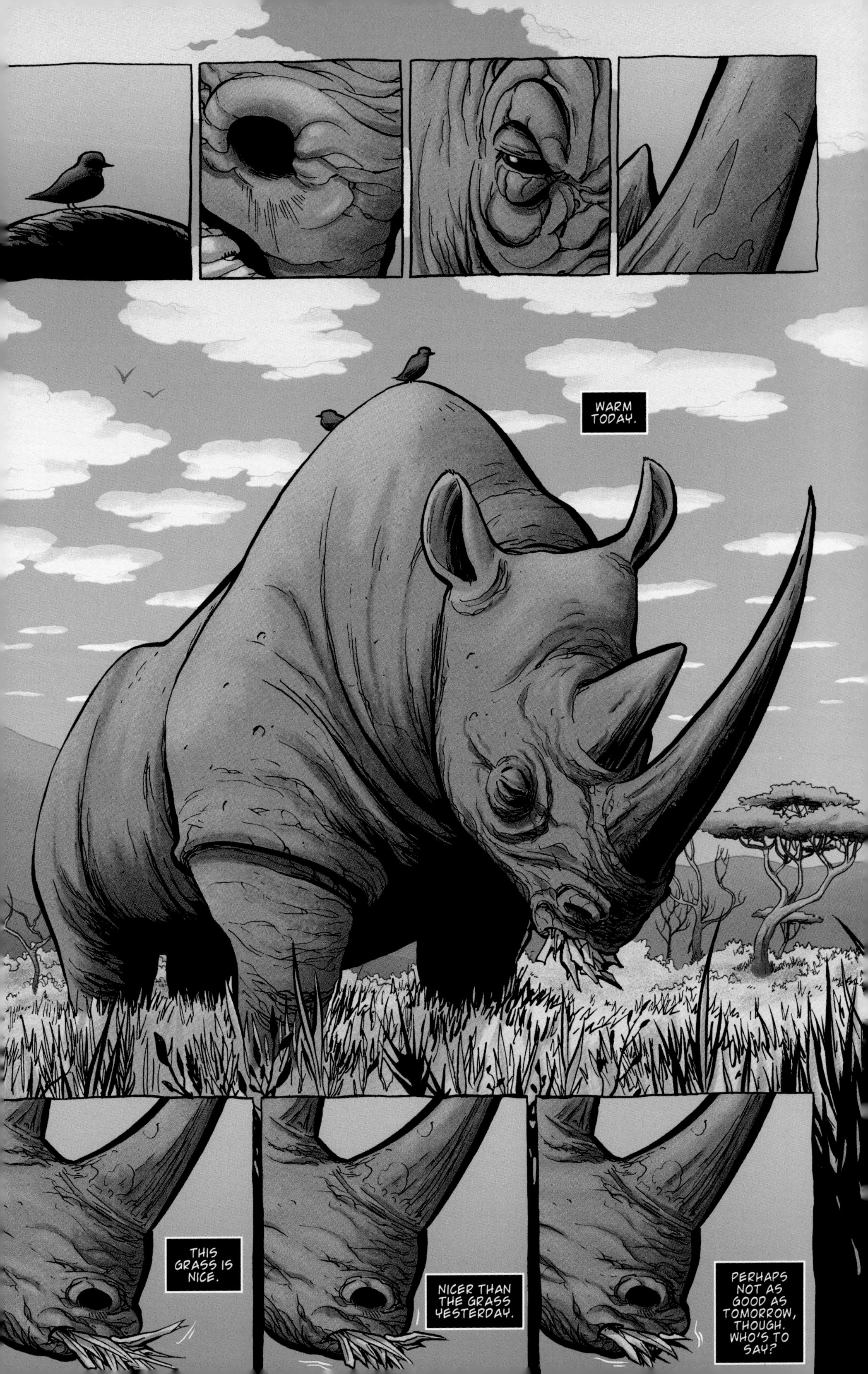
WARM TODAY.
THIS GRASS IS NICE.
NICER THAN THE GRASS YESTERDAY.
PERHAPS NOT AS GOOD AS TOMORROW, THOUGH. WHO'S TO SAY?

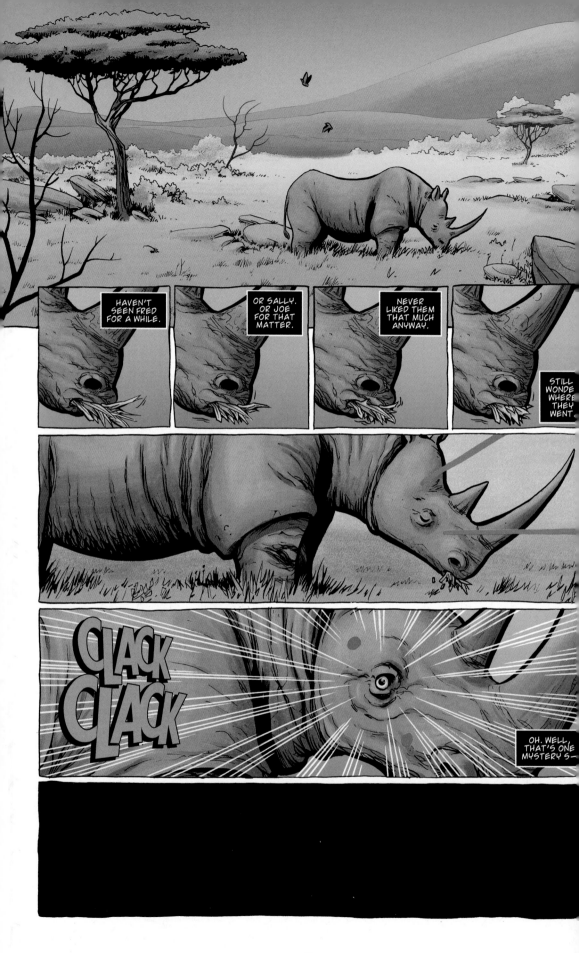

HAVEN'T SEEN FRED FOR A WHILE.

OR SALLY. OR JOE FOR THAT MATTER.

NEVER LIKED THEM THAT MUCH ANYWAY.

STILL WONDE WHERE THEY WENT.

CLACK CLACK

OH. WELL THAT'S ONE MYSTERY S—

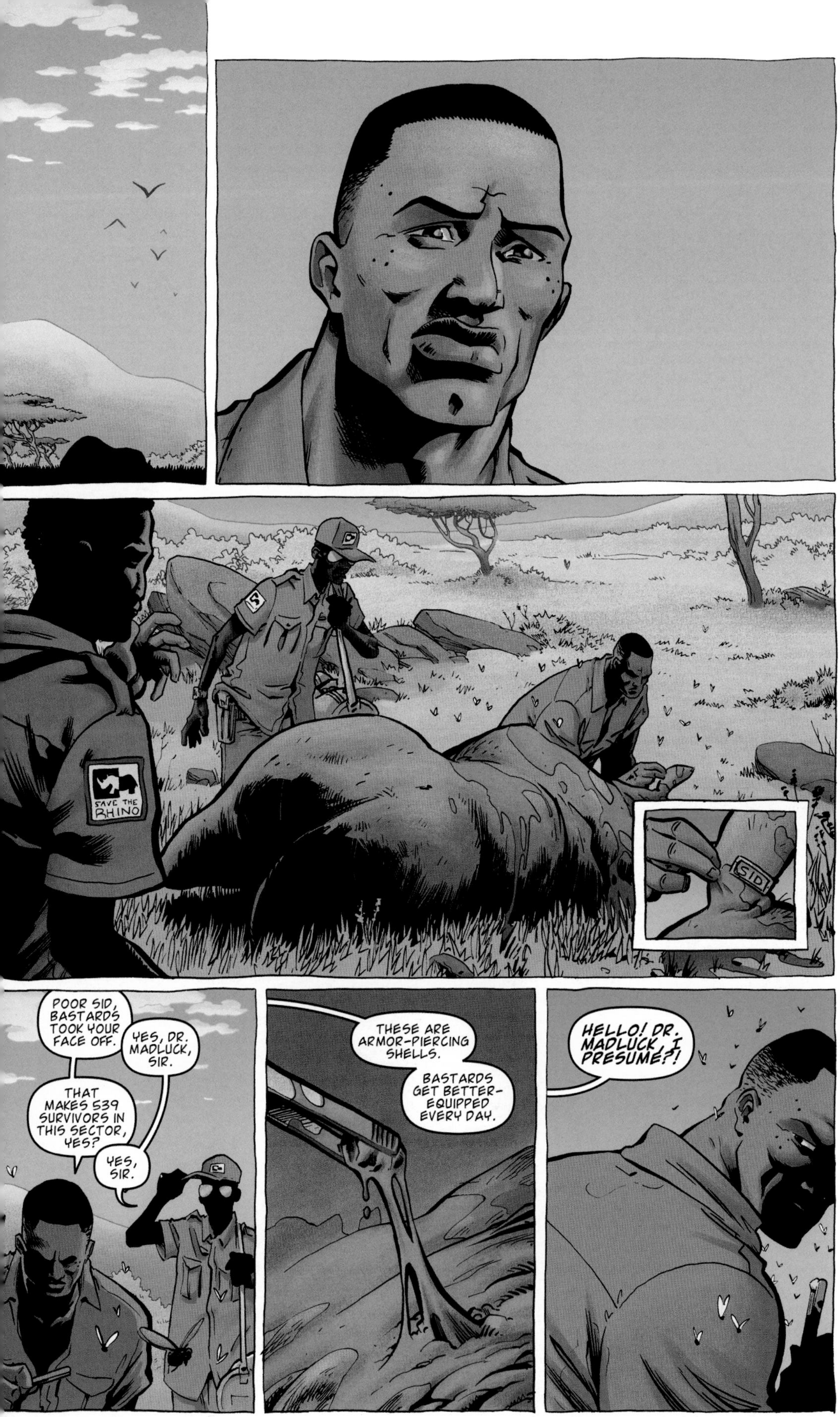
SAVE THE RHINO
SID
POOR SID, BASTARDS TOOK YOUR FACE OFF.
YES, DR. MADLUCK, SIR.
THAT MAKES 539 SURVIVORS IN THIS SECTOR, YES?
YES, SIR.
THESE ARE ARMOR-PIERCING SHELLS.
BASTARDS GET BETTER-EQUIPPED EVERY DAY.
HELLO! DR. MADLUCK, I PRESUME?!

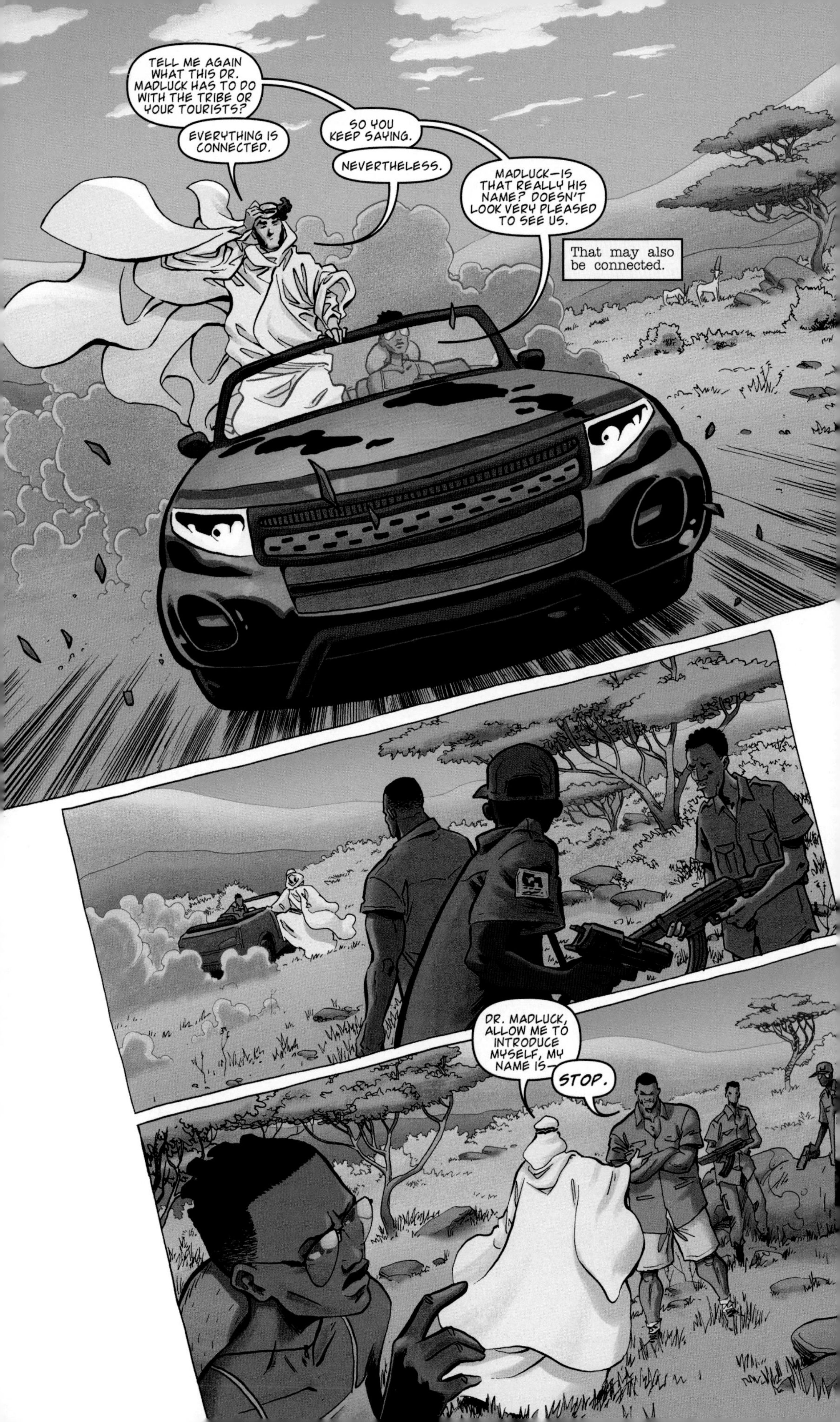
TELL ME AGAIN WHAT THIS DR. MADLUCK HAS TO DO WITH THE TRIBE OR YOUR TOURISTS?
EVERYTHING IS CONNECTED.
SO YOU KEEP SAYING.
NEVERTHELESS.
MADLUCK—IS THAT REALLY HIS NAME? DOESN'T LOOK VERY PLEASED TO SEE US.
That may also be connected.
DR. MADLUCK, ALLOW ME TO INTRODUCE MYSELF, MY NAME IS—
STOP.

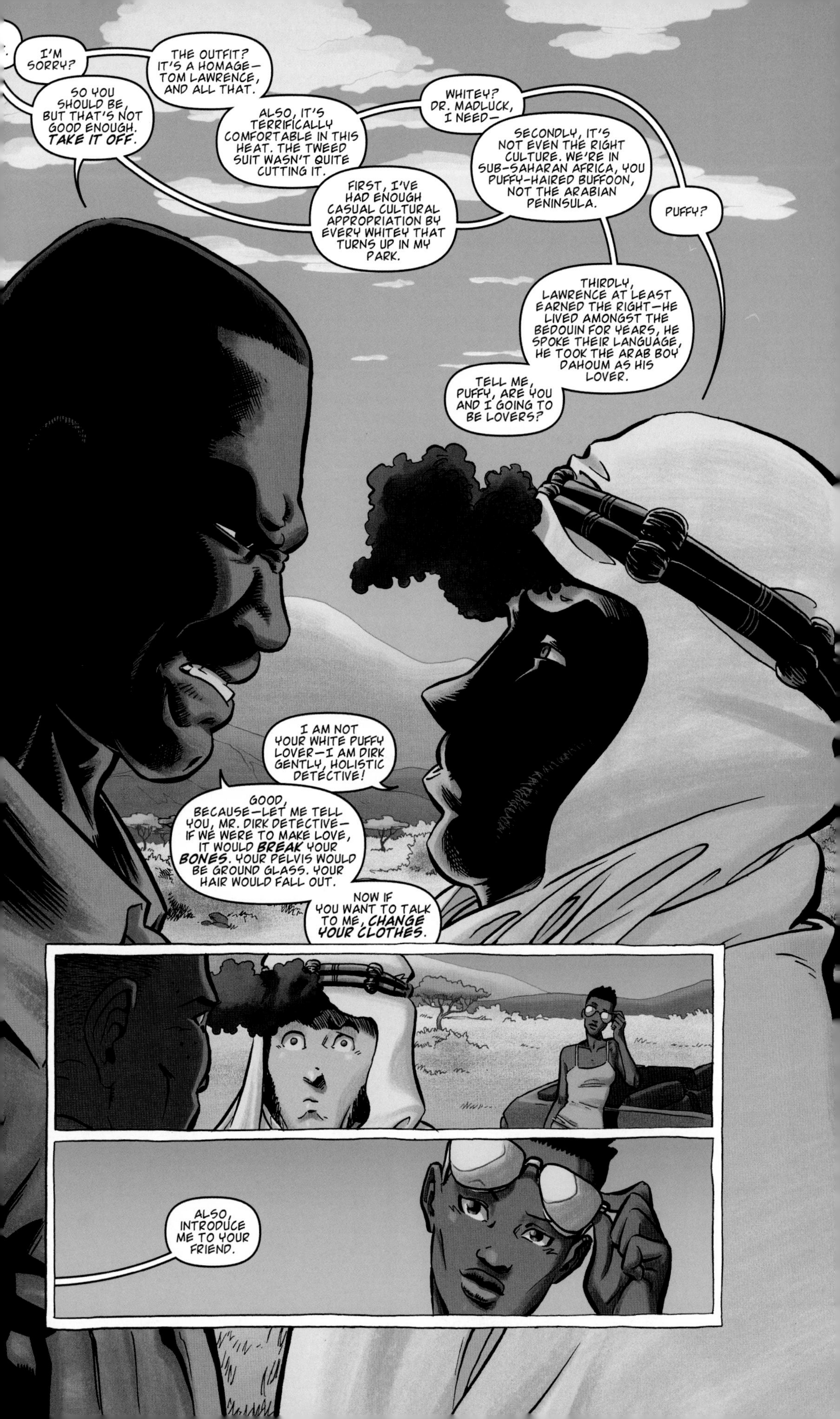
I'M SORRY?
THE OUTFIT? IT'S A HOMAGE—TOM LAWRENCE, AND ALL THAT.
SO YOU SHOULD BE, BUT THAT'S NOT GOOD ENOUGH. TAKE IT OFF.
ALSO, IT'S TERRIFICALLY COMFORTABLE IN THIS HEAT. THE TWEED SUIT WASN'T QUITE CUTTING IT.
WHITEY? DR. MADLUCK, I NEED—
FIRST, I'VE HAD ENOUGH CASUAL CULTURAL APPROPRIATION BY EVERY WHITEY THAT TURNS UP IN MY PARK.
SECONDLY, IT'S NOT EVEN THE RIGHT CULTURE. WE'RE IN SUB-SAHARAN AFRICA, YOU PUFFY-HAIRED BUFFOON, NOT THE ARABIAN PENINSULA.
PUFFY?
THIRDLY, LAWRENCE AT LEAST EARNED THE RIGHT—HE LIVED AMONGST THE BEDOUIN FOR YEARS, HE SPOKE THEIR LANGUAGE, HE TOOK THE ARAB BOY DAHOUM AS HIS LOVER.
TELL ME, PUFFY, ARE YOU AND I GOING TO BE LOVERS?
I AM NOT YOUR WHITE PUFFY LOVER—I AM DIRK GENTLY, HOLISTIC DETECTIVE!
GOOD, BECAUSE—LET ME TELL YOU, MR. DIRK DETECTIVE—IF WE WERE TO MAKE LOVE, IT WOULD BREAK YOUR BONES. YOUR PELVIS WOULD BE GROUND GLASS. YOUR HAIR WOULD FALL OUT.
NOW IF YOU WANT TO TALK TO ME, CHANGE YOUR CLOTHES.
ALSO, INTRODUCE ME TO YOUR FRIEND.

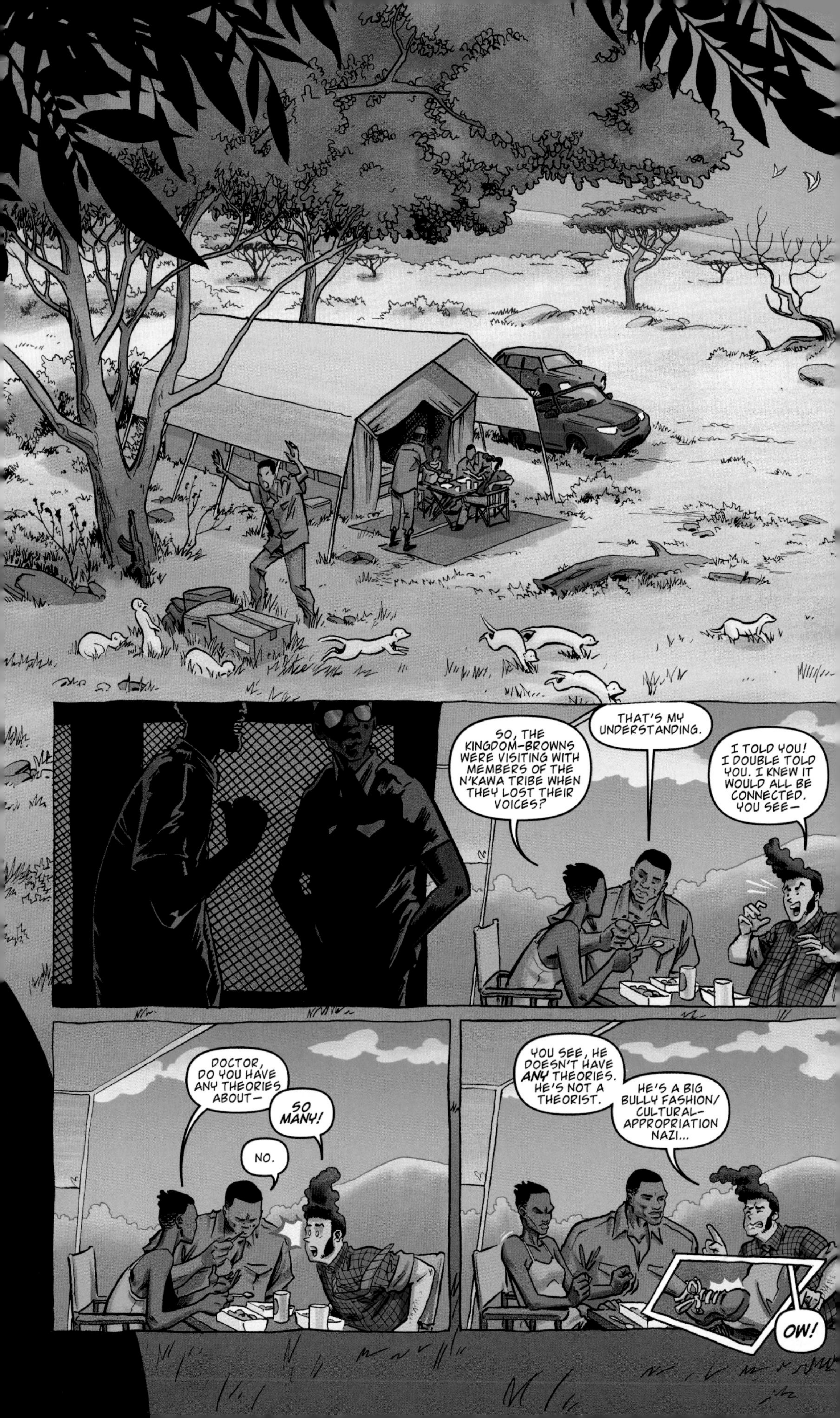
SO, THE KINGDOM-BROWNS WERE VISITING WITH MEMBERS OF THE N'KAWA TRIBE WHEN THEY LOST THEIR VOICES?
THAT'S MY UNDERSTANDING.
I TOLD YOU! I DOUBLE TOLD YOU. I KNEW IT WOULD ALL BE CONNECTED. YOU SEE—
DOCTOR, DO YOU HAVE ANY THEORIES ABOUT—
SO MANY!
NO.
YOU SEE, HE DOESN'T HAVE ANY THEORIES. HE'S NOT A THEORIST.
HE'S A BIG BULLY FASHION/ CULTURAL-APPROPRIATION NAZI...
OW!

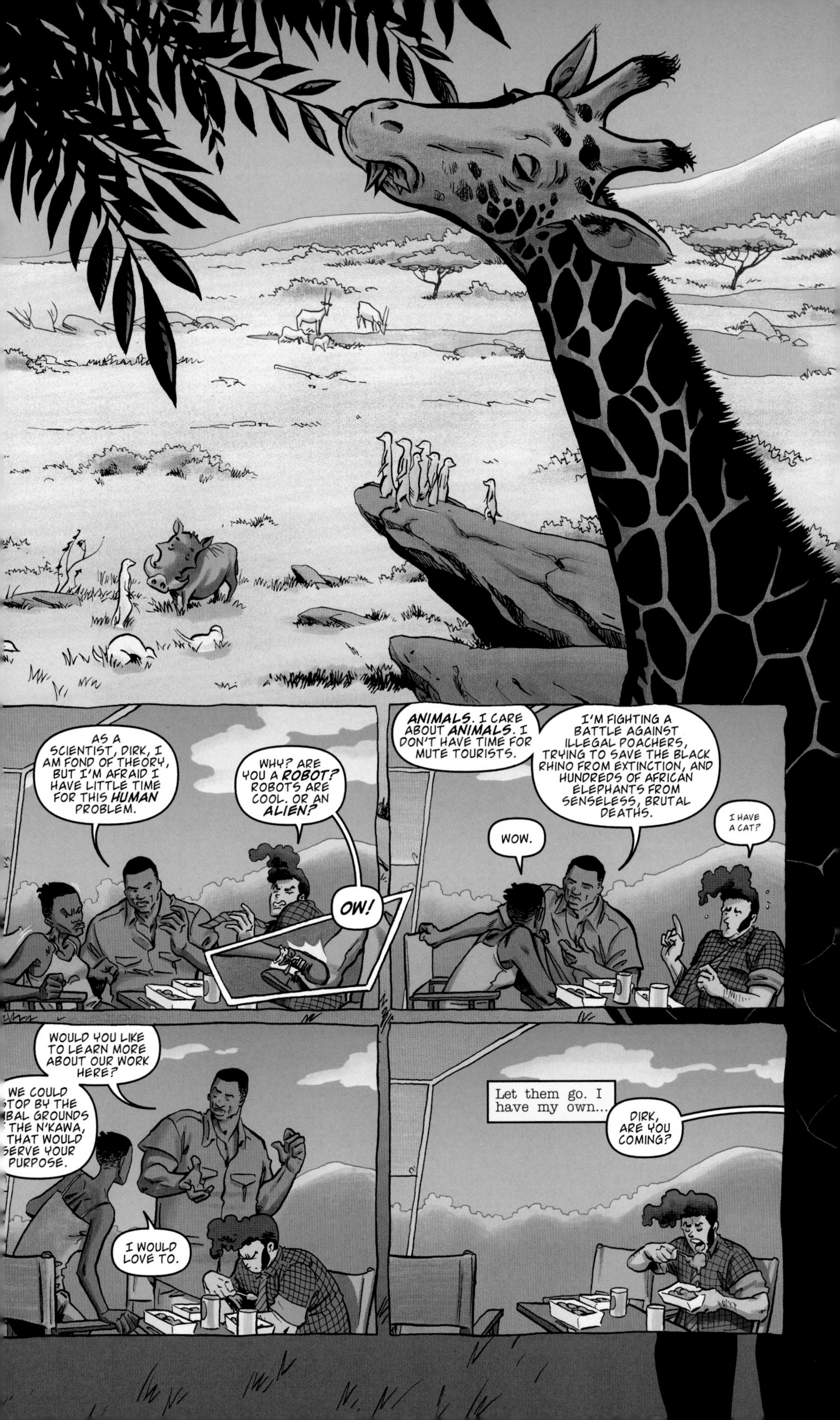

AS A SCIENTIST, DIRK, I AM FOND OF THEORY, BUT I'M AFRAID I HAVE LITTLE TIME FOR THIS HUMAN PROBLEM.
WHY? ARE YOU A ROBOT? ROBOTS ARE COOL. OR AN ALIEN?
OW!
ANIMALS. I CARE ABOUT ANIMALS. I DON'T HAVE TIME FOR MUTE TOURISTS.
I'M FIGHTING A BATTLE AGAINST ILLEGAL POACHERS, TRYING TO SAVE THE BLACK RHINO FROM EXTINCTION, AND HUNDREDS OF AFRICAN ELEPHANTS FROM SENSELESS, BRUTAL DEATHS.
WOW.
I HAVE A CAT?
WOULD YOU LIKE TO LEARN MORE ABOUT OUR WORK HERE?
WE COULD STOP BY THE BAL GROUNDS THE N'KAWA, THAT WOULD SERVE YOUR PURPOSE.
I WOULD LOVE TO.
Let them go. I have my own...
DIRK, ARE YOU COMING?

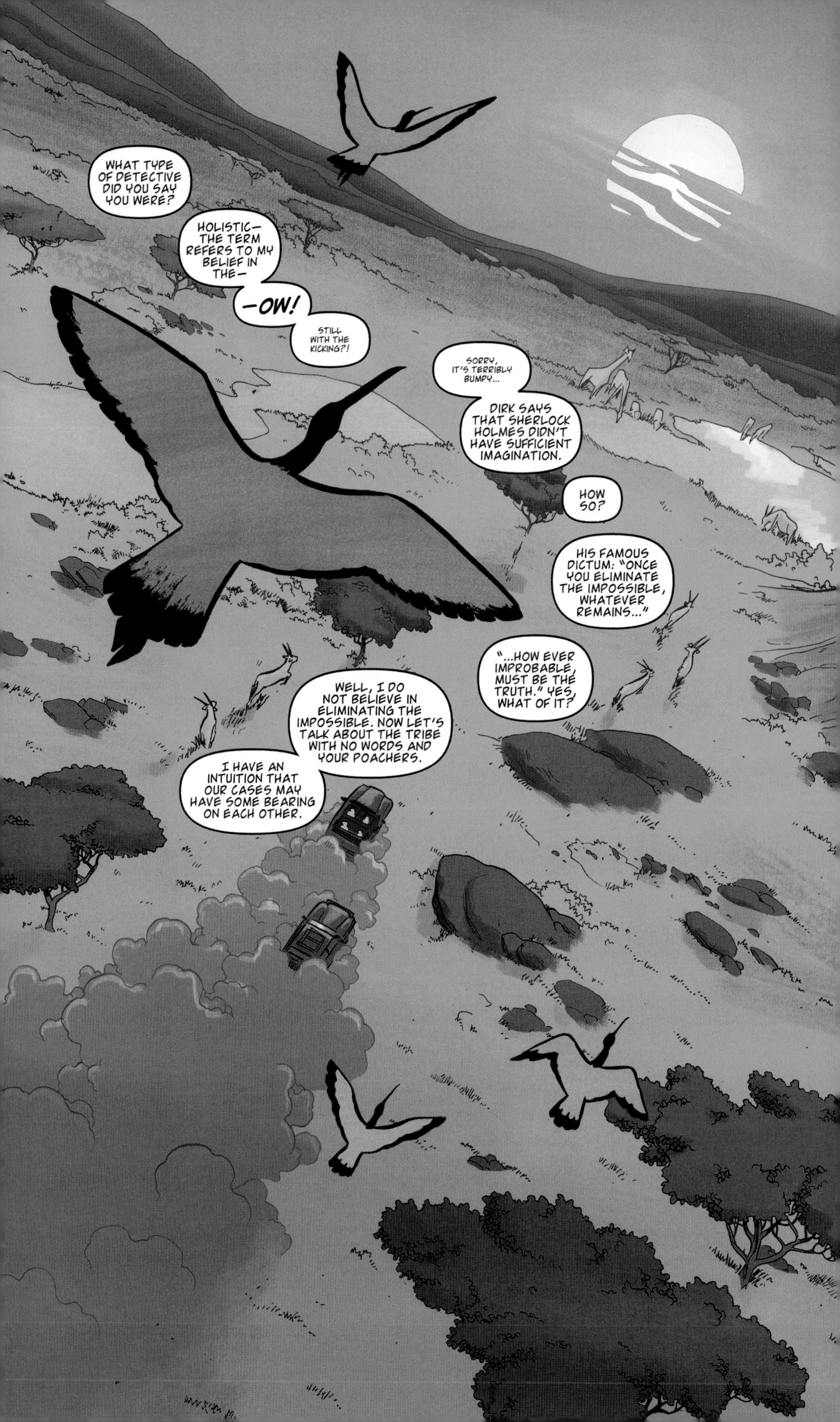
WHAT TYPE OF DETECTIVE DID YOU SAY YOU WERE?
HOLISTIC— THE TERM REFERS TO MY BELIEF IN THE—
—OW!
STILL WITH THE KICKING?!
SORRY, IT'S TERRIBLY BUMPY...
DIRK SAYS THAT SHERLOCK HOLMES DIDN'T HAVE SUFFICIENT IMAGINATION.
HOW SO?
HIS FAMOUS DICTUM: "ONCE YOU ELIMINATE THE IMPOSSIBLE, WHATEVER REMAINS..."
"...HOW EVER IMPROBABLE, MUST BE THE TRUTH." YES, WHAT OF IT?
WELL, I DO NOT BELIEVE IN ELIMINATING THE IMPOSSIBLE. NOW LET'S TALK ABOUT THE TRIBE WITH NO WORDS AND YOUR POACHERS.
I HAVE AN INTUITION THAT OUR CASES MAY HAVE SOME BEARING ON EACH OTHER.

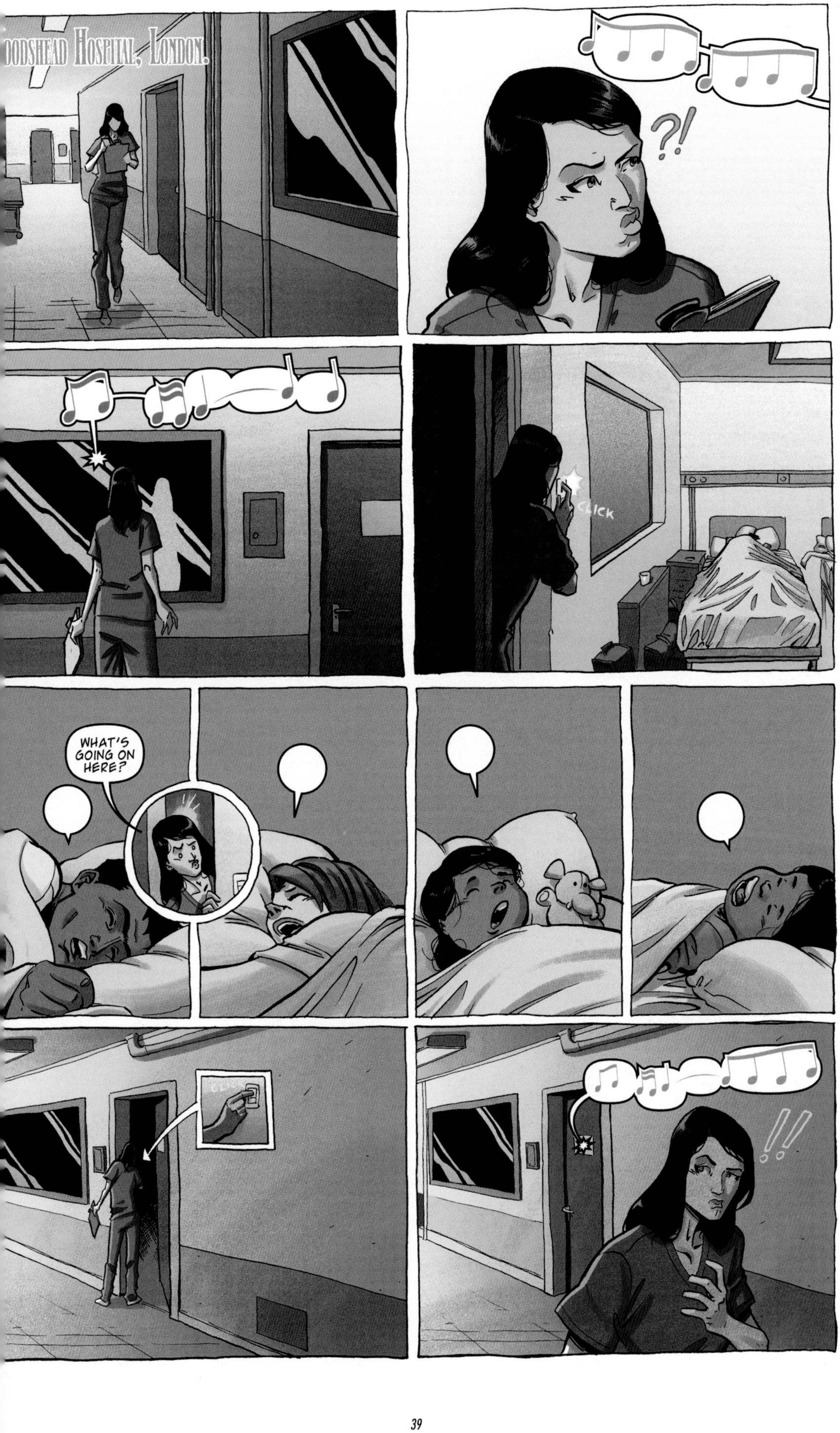
OODSHEAD HOSPITAL, LONDON.
?!
CLICK
WHAT'S GOING ON HERE?
!
CLICK
!!

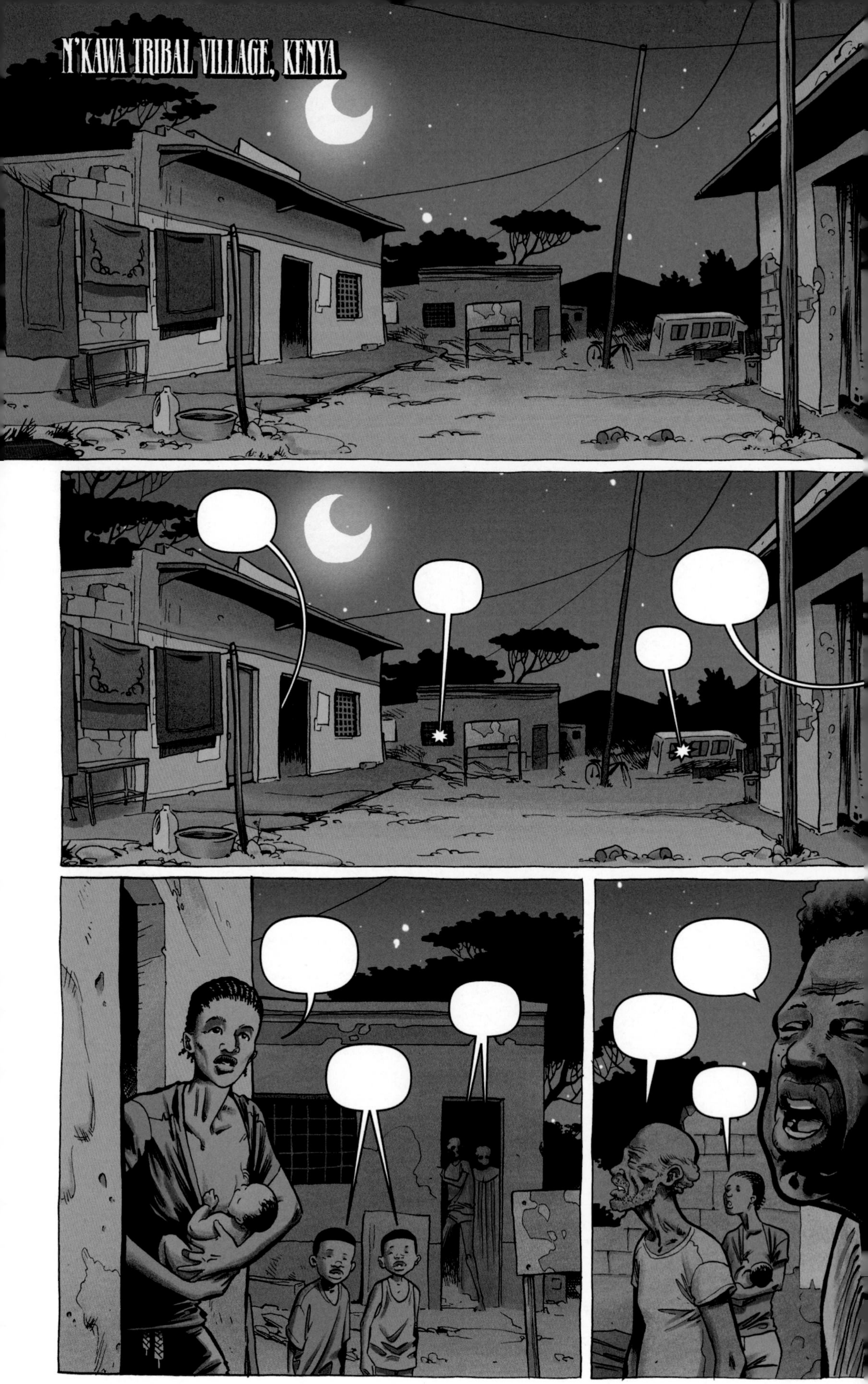
N'KAWA TRIBAL VILLAGE, KENYA.

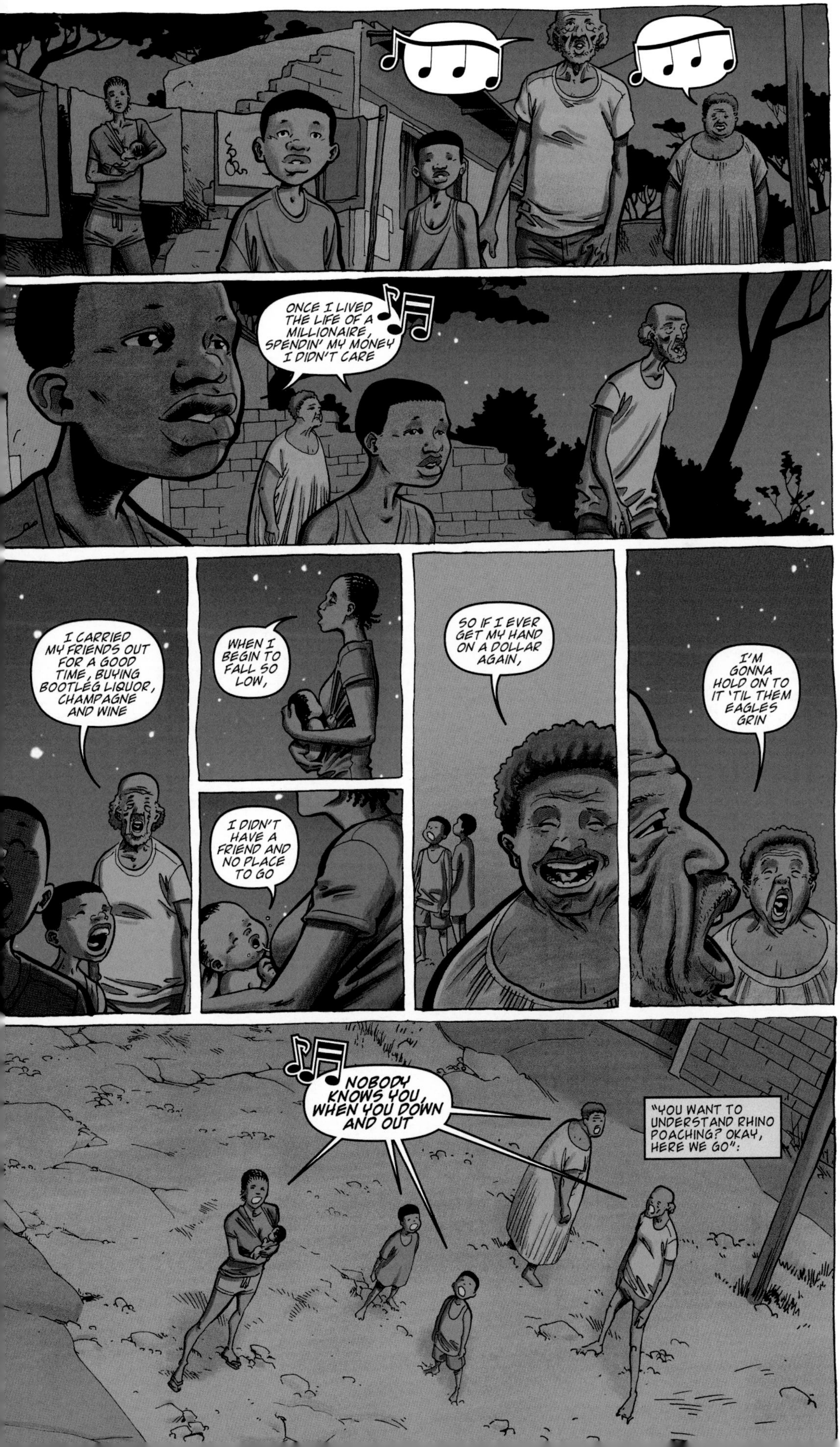
ONCE I LIVED THE LIFE OF A MILLIONAIRE, SPENDIN' MY MONEY I DIDN'T CARE
I CARRIED MY FRIENDS OUT FOR A GOOD TIME, BUYING BOOTLEG LIQUOR, CHAMPAGNE AND WINE
WHEN I BEGIN TO FALL SO LOW,
I DIDN'T HAVE A FRIEND AND NO PLACE TO GO
SO IF I EVER GET MY HAND ON A DOLLAR AGAIN,
I'M GONNA HOLD ON TO IT 'TIL THEM EAGLES GRIN
NOBODY KNOWS YOU, WHEN YOU DOWN AND OUT
"YOU WANT TO UNDERSTAND RHINO POACHING? OKAY, HERE WE GO":

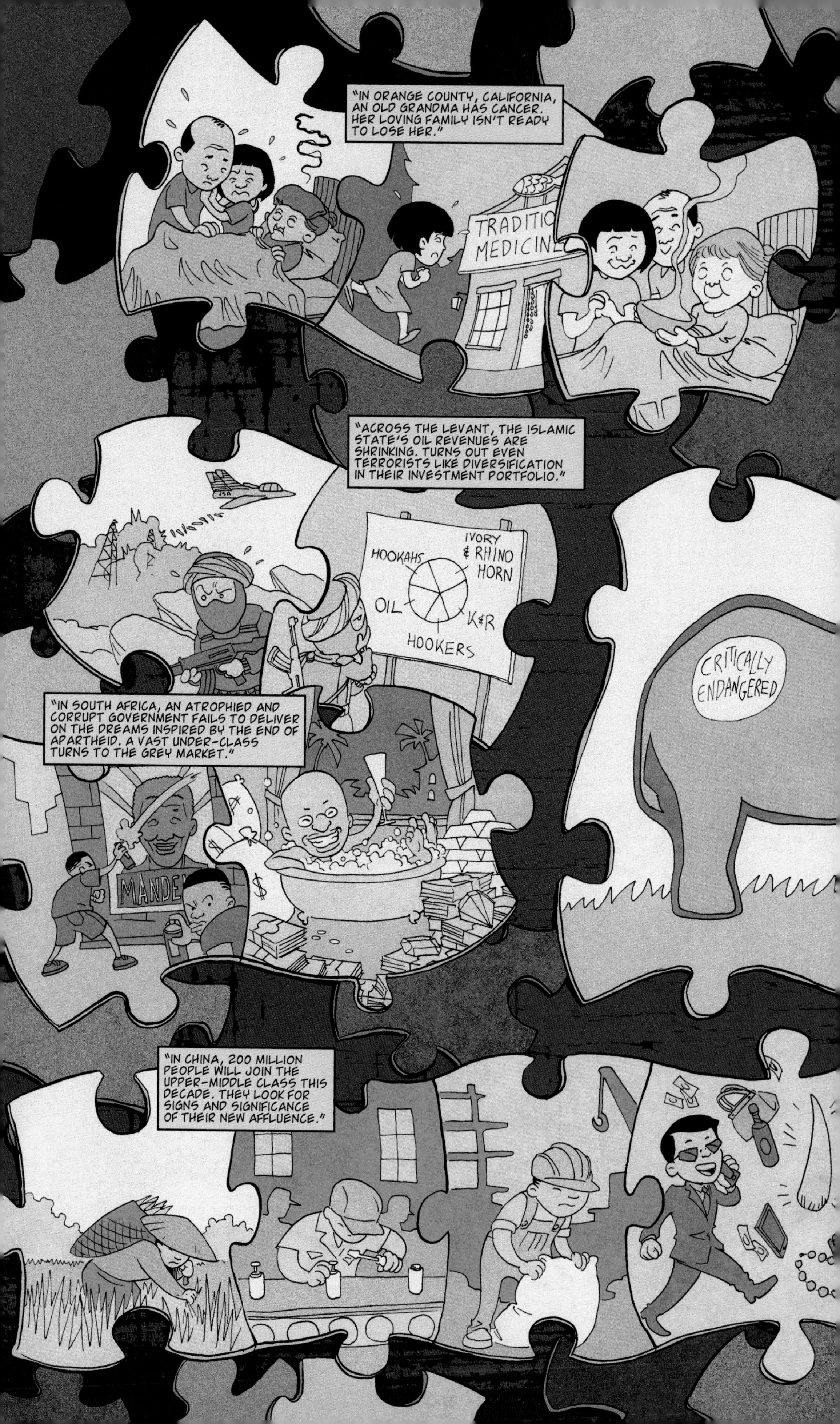
"IN ORANGE COUNTY, CALIFORNIA, AN OLD GRANDMA HAS CANCER. HER LOVING FAMILY ISN'T READY TO LOSE HER."
TRADITIO
MEDICINE
"ACROSS THE LEVANT, THE ISLAMIC STATE'S OIL REVENUES ARE SHRINKING. TURNS OUT EVEN TERRORISTS LIKE DIVERSIFICATION IN THEIR INVESTMENT PORTFOLIO."
USA
HOOKAHS
IVORY & RHINO HORN
OIL
K&R
HOOKERS
CRITICALLY ENDANGERED
"IN SOUTH AFRICA, AN ATROPHIED AND CORRUPT GOVERNMENT FAILS TO DELIVER ON THE DREAMS INSPIRED BY THE END OF APARTHEID. A VAST UNDER-CLASS TURNS TO THE GREY MARKET."
MANDE
"IN CHINA, 200 MILLION PEOPLE WILL JOIN THE UPPER-MIDDLE CLASS THIS DECADE. THEY LOOK FOR SIGNS AND SIGNIFICANCE OF THEIR NEW AFFLUENCE."

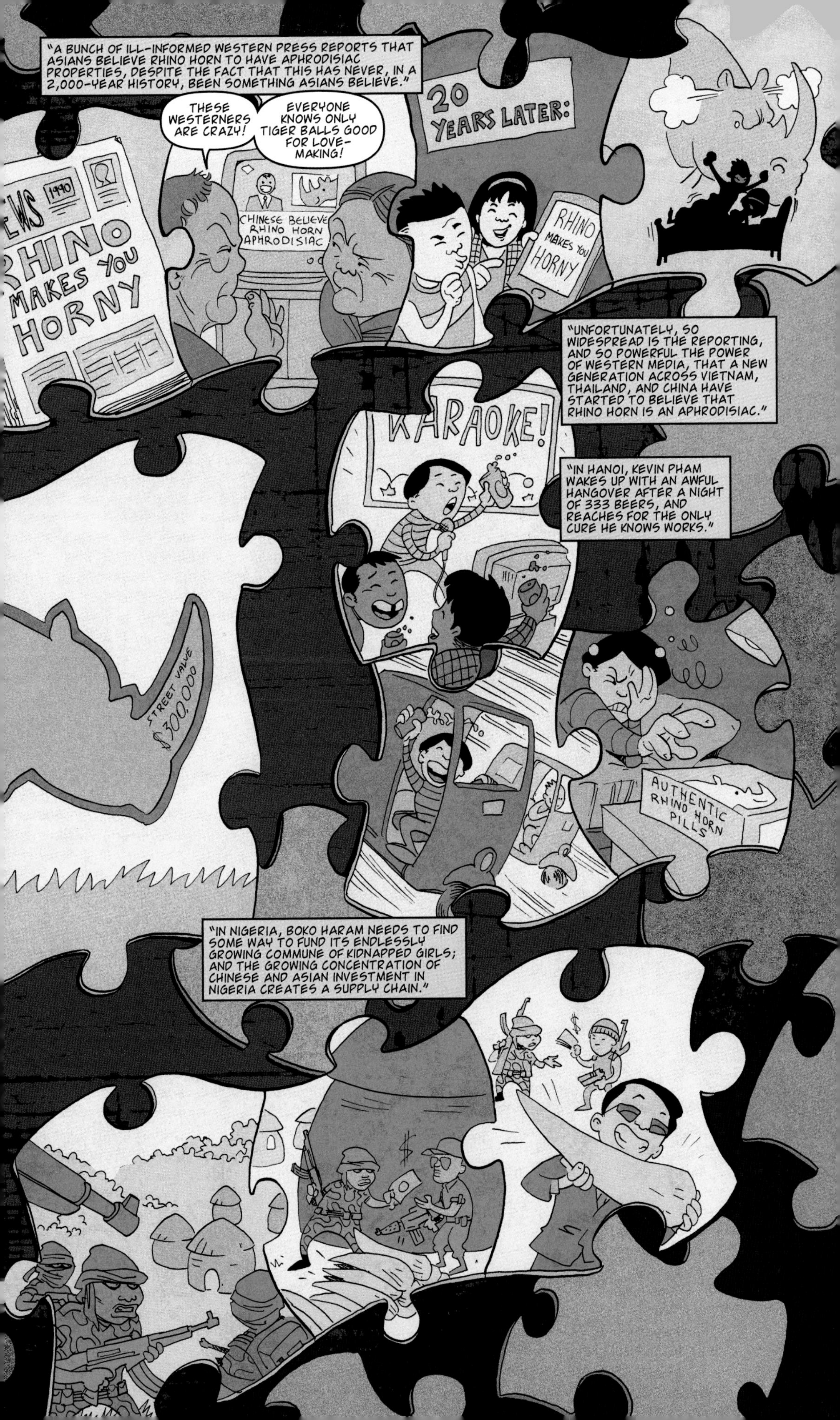
"A BUNCH OF ILL-INFORMED WESTERN PRESS REPORTS THAT ASIANS BELIEVE RHINO HORN TO HAVE APHRODISIAC PROPERTIES, DESPITE THE FACT THAT THIS HAS NEVER, IN A 2,000-YEAR HISTORY, BEEN SOMETHING ASIANS BELIEVE."
NEWS 1990
RHINO MAKES YOU HORNY
THESE WESTERNERS ARE CRAZY!
EVERYONE KNOWS ONLY TIGER BALLS GOOD FOR LOVE-MAKING!
CHINESE BELIEVE RHINO HORN APHRODISIAC
20 YEARS LATER:
RHINO MAKES YOU HORNY
"UNFORTUNATELY, SO WIDESPREAD IS THE REPORTING, AND SO POWERFUL THE POWER OF WESTERN MEDIA, THAT A NEW GENERATION ACROSS VIETNAM, THAILAND, AND CHINA HAVE STARTED TO BELIEVE THAT RHINO HORN IS AN APHRODISIAC."
KARAOKE!
"IN HANOI, KEVIN PHAM WAKES UP WITH AN AWFUL HANGOVER AFTER A NIGHT OF 333 BEERS, AND REACHES FOR THE ONLY CURE HE KNOWS WORKS."
STREET VALUE $300,000
AUTHENTIC RHINO HORN PILLS
"IN NIGERIA, BOKO HARAM NEEDS TO FIND SOME WAY TO FUND ITS ENDLESSLY GROWING COMMUNE OF KIDNAPPED GIRLS; AND THE GROWING CONCENTRATION OF CHINESE AND ASIAN INVESTMENT IN NIGERIA CREATES A SUPPLY CHAIN."

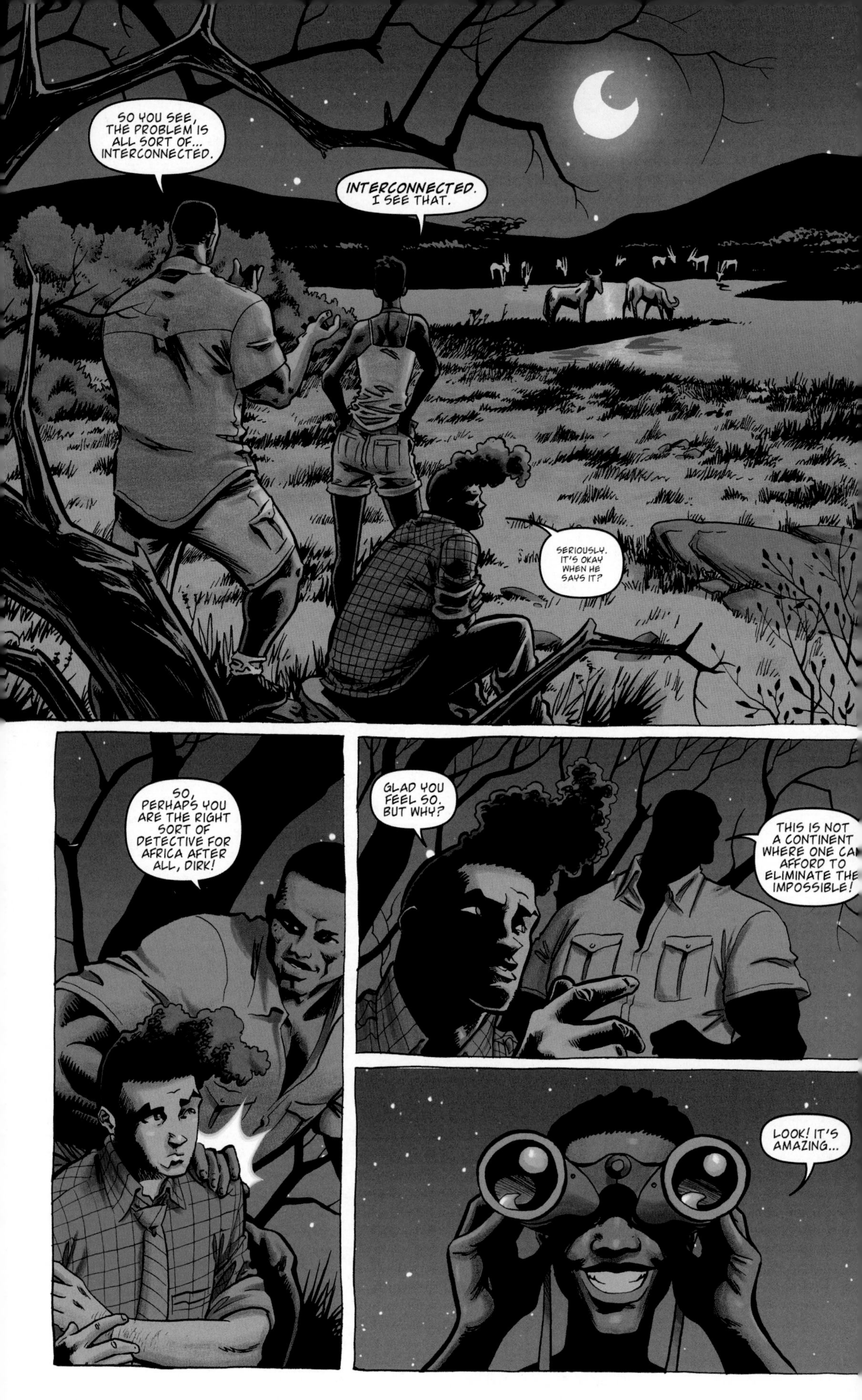
SO YOU SEE, THE PROBLEM IS ALL SORT OF... INTERCONNECTED.
INTERCONNECTED. I SEE THAT.
SERIOUSLY. IT'S OKAY WHEN HE SAYS IT?
SO, PERHAPS YOU ARE THE RIGHT SORT OF DETECTIVE FOR AFRICA AFTER ALL, DIRK!
GLAD YOU FEEL SO. BUT WHY?
THIS IS NOT A CONTINENT WHERE ONE CA AFFORD TO ELIMINATE THE IMPOSSIBLE!
LOOK! IT'S AMAZING...

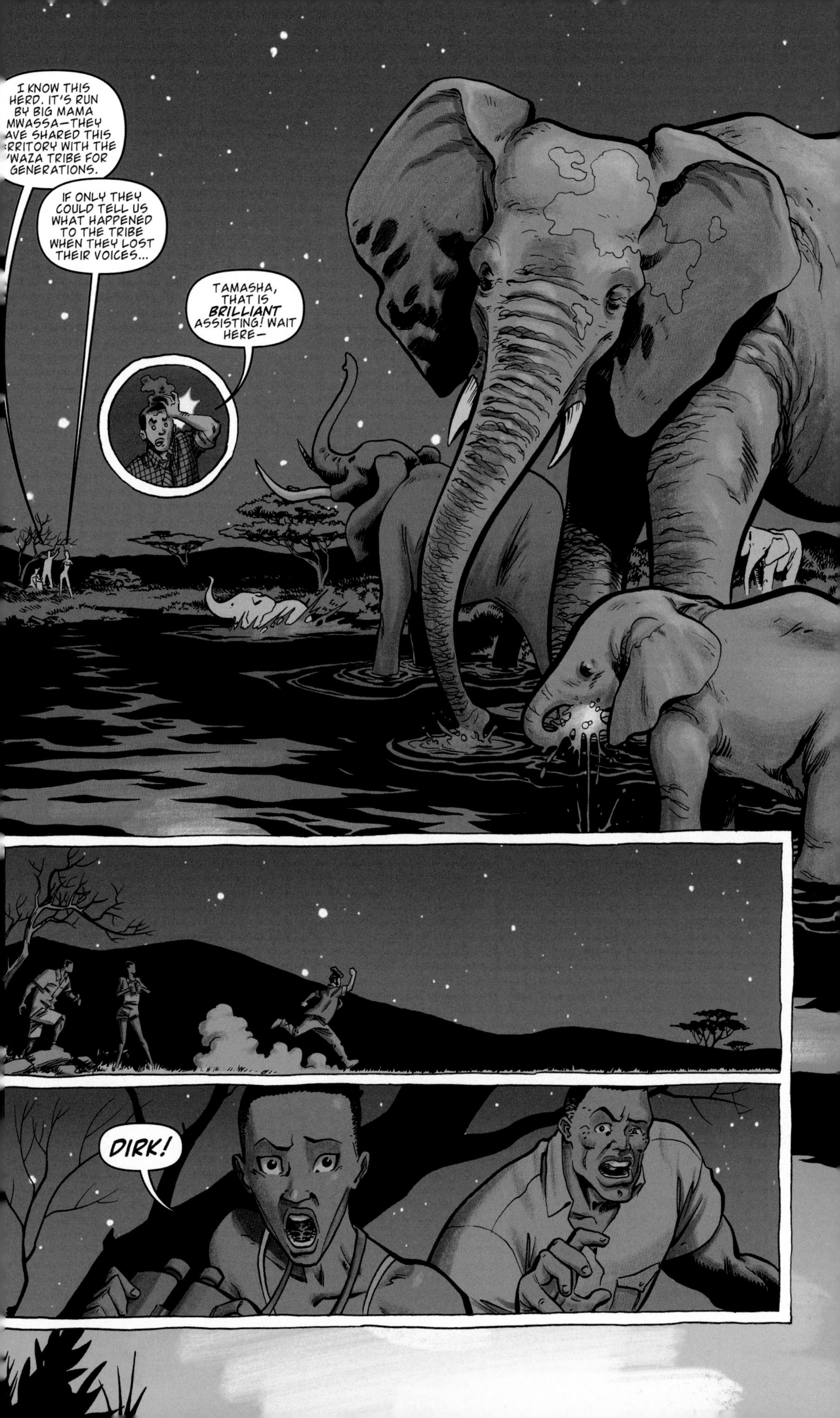
I KNOW THIS HERD. IT'S RUN BY BIG MAMA MWASSA—THEY AVE SHARED THIS ERRITORY WITH THE 'WAZA TRIBE FOR GENERATIONS.
IF ONLY THEY COULD TELL US WHAT HAPPENED TO THE TRIBE WHEN THEY LOST THEIR VOICES...
TAMASHA, THAT IS BRILLIANT ASSISTING! WAIT HERE—
DIRK!

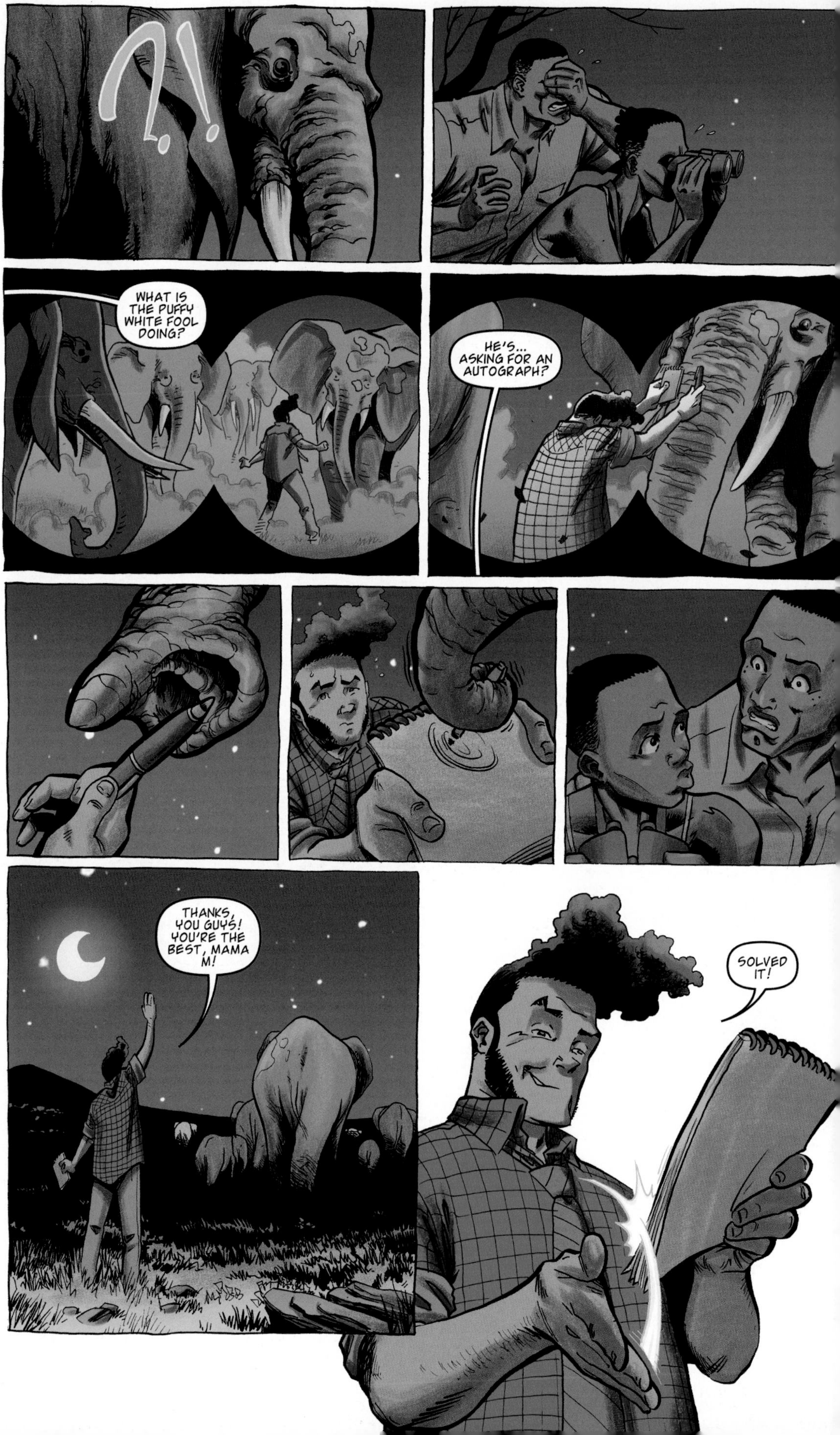
?!
WHAT IS THE PUFFY WHITE FOOL DOING?
HE'S... ASKING FOR AN AUTOGRAPH?
THANKS, YOU GUYS! YOU'RE THE BEST, MAMA M!
SOLVED IT!

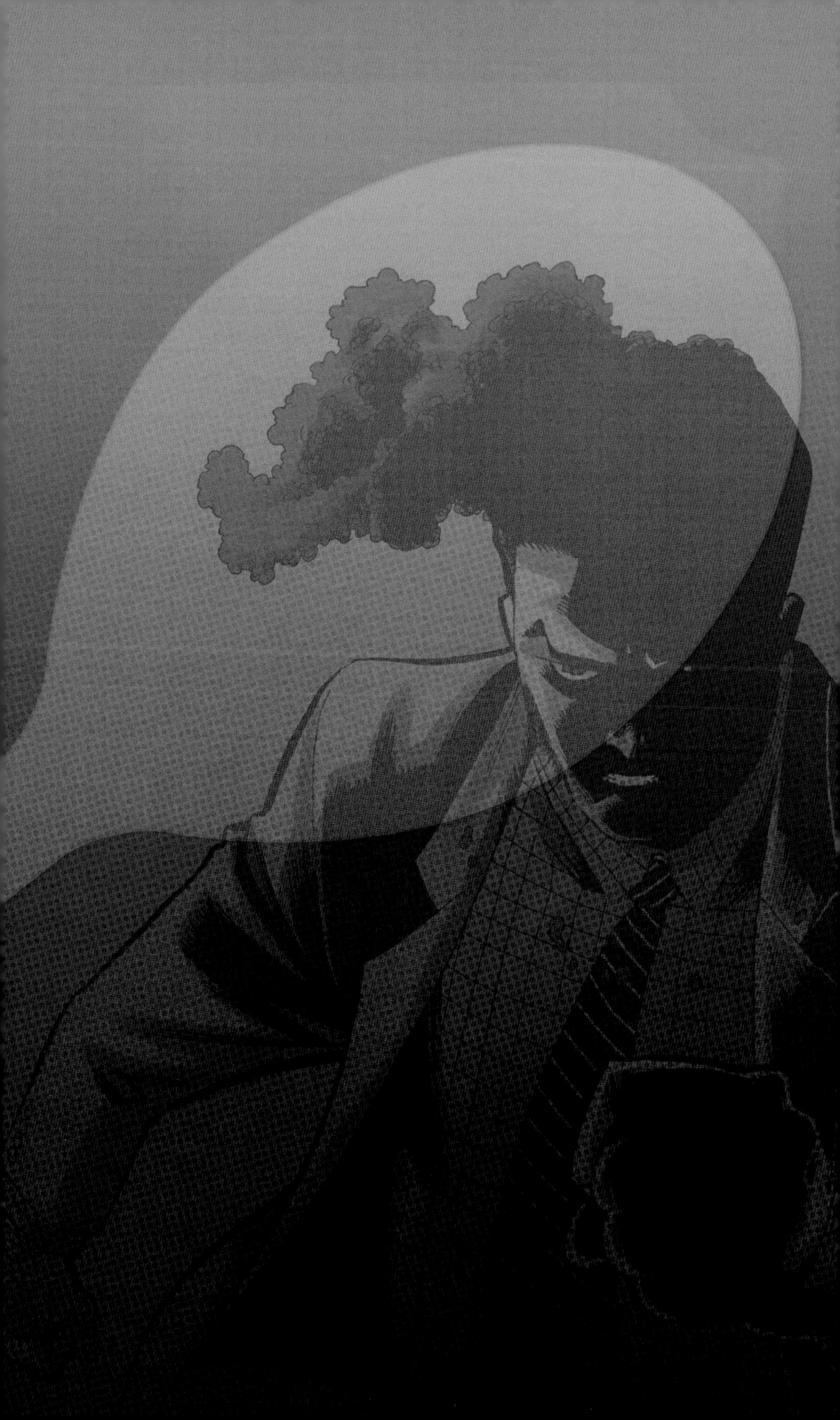

Cover Art by **ILIAS KYRIAZIS**

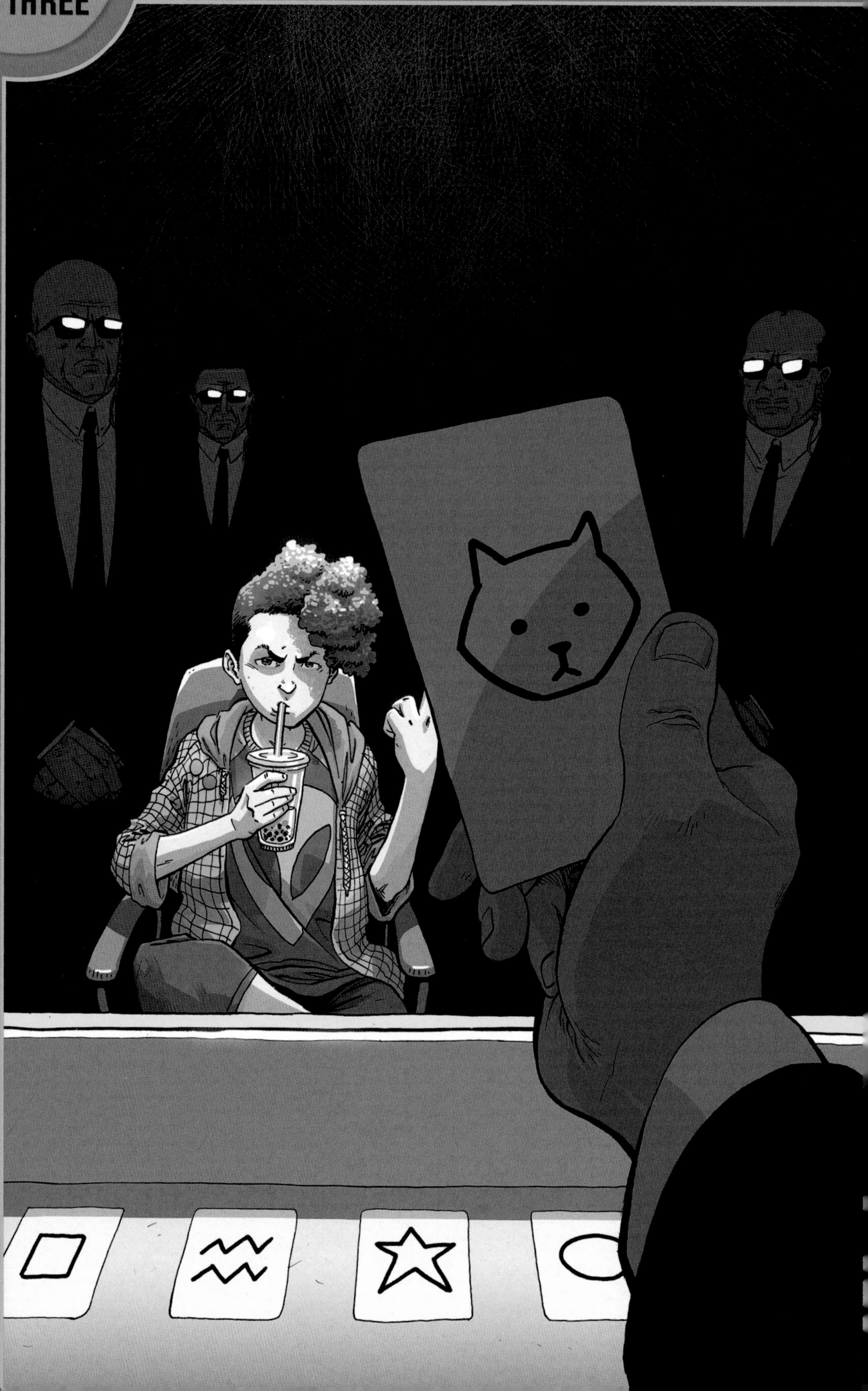

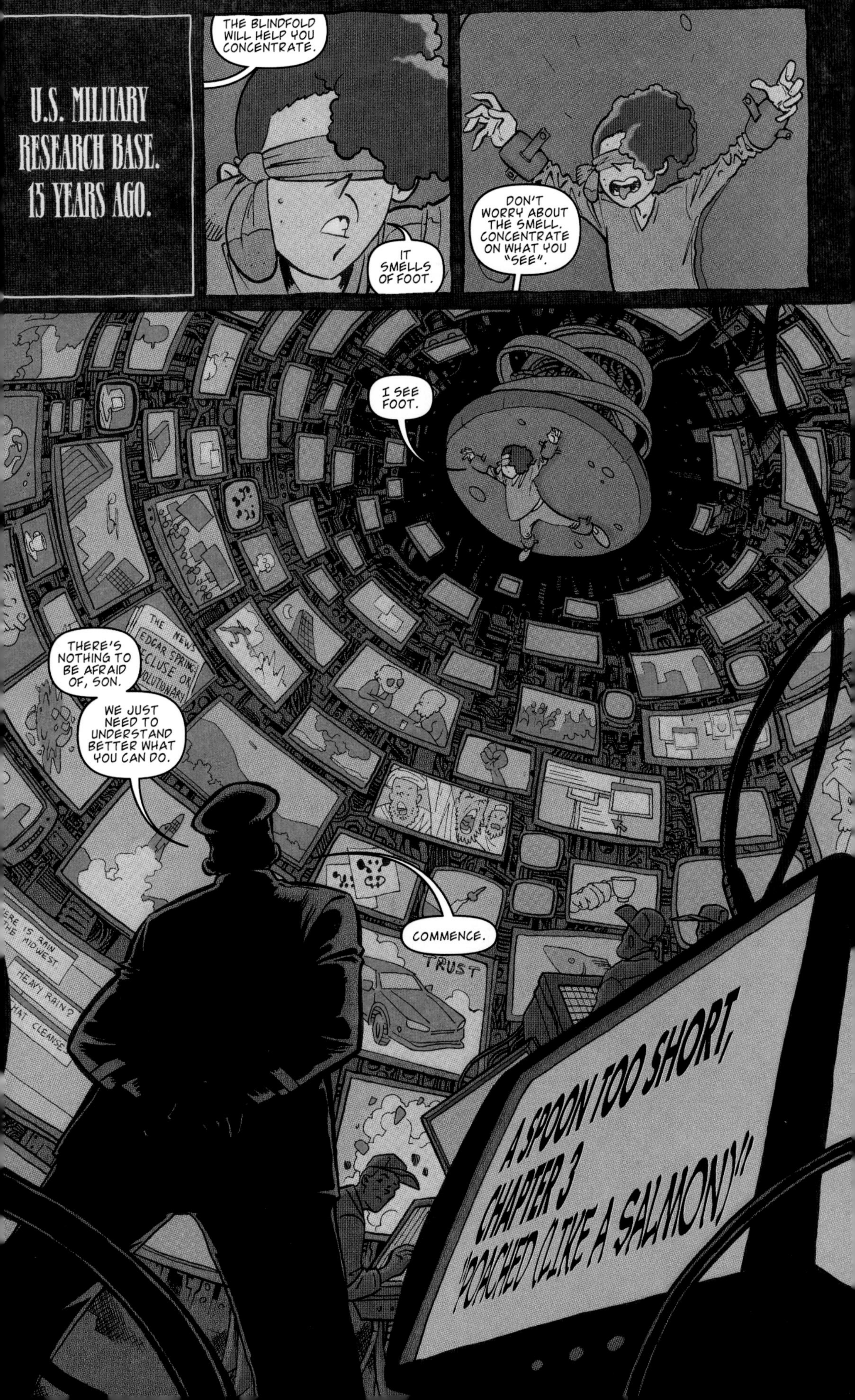
U.S. MILITARY RESEARCH BASE. 15 YEARS AGO.
THE BLINDFOLD WILL HELP YOU CONCENTRATE.
IT SMELLS OF FOOT.
DON'T WORRY ABOUT THE SMELL. CONCENTRATE ON WHAT YOU "SEE".
I SEE FOOT.
THERE'S NOTHING TO BE AFRAID OF, SON.
WE JUST NEED TO UNDERSTAND BETTER WHAT YOU CAN DO.
COMMENCE.
TRUST
HEAVY RAIN?
A SPOON TOO SHORT, CHAPTER 3 "POACHED (LIKE A SALMON)"

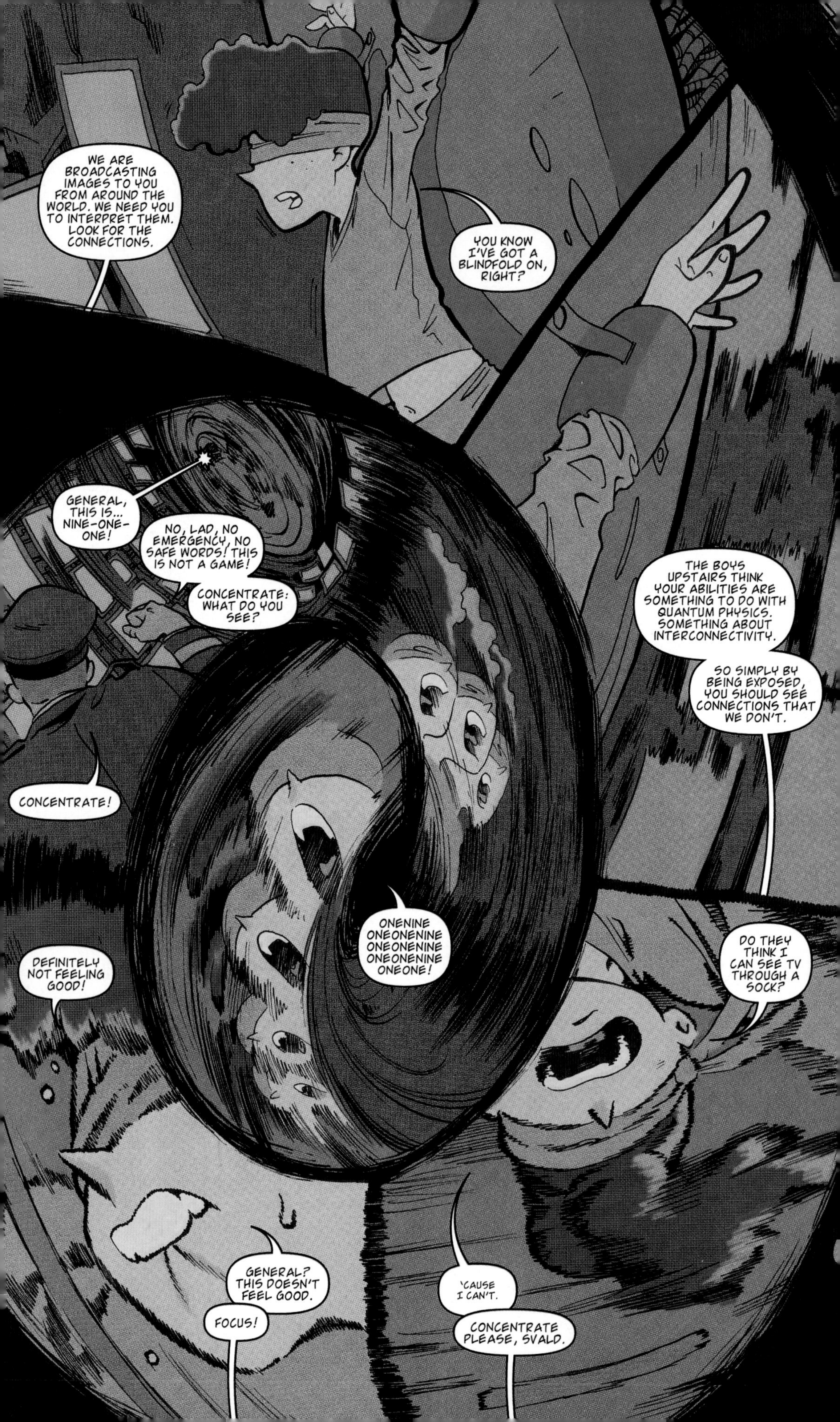
WE ARE BROADCASTING IMAGES TO YOU FROM AROUND THE WORLD. WE NEED YOU TO INTERPRET THEM. LOOK FOR THE CONNECTIONS.
YOU KNOW I'VE GOT A BLINDFOLD ON, RIGHT?
GENERAL, THIS IS... NINE-ONE-ONE!
NO, LAD, NO EMERGENCY, NO SAFE WORDS! THIS IS NOT A GAME!
CONCENTRATE: WHAT DO YOU SEE?
THE BOYS UPSTAIRS THINK YOUR ABILITIES ARE SOMETHING TO DO WITH QUANTUM PHYSICS. SOMETHING ABOUT INTERCONNECTIVITY.
SO SIMPLY BY BEING EXPOSED, YOU SHOULD SEE CONNECTIONS THAT WE DON'T.
CONCENTRATE!
ONENINE ONEONENINE ONEONENINE ONEONENINE ONEONE!
DEFINITELY NOT FEELING GOOD!
DO THEY THINK I CAN SEE TV THROUGH A SOCK?
GENERAL? THIS DOESN'T FEEL GOOD.
FOCUS!
'CAUSE I CAN'T.
CONCENTRATE PLEASE, SVALD.

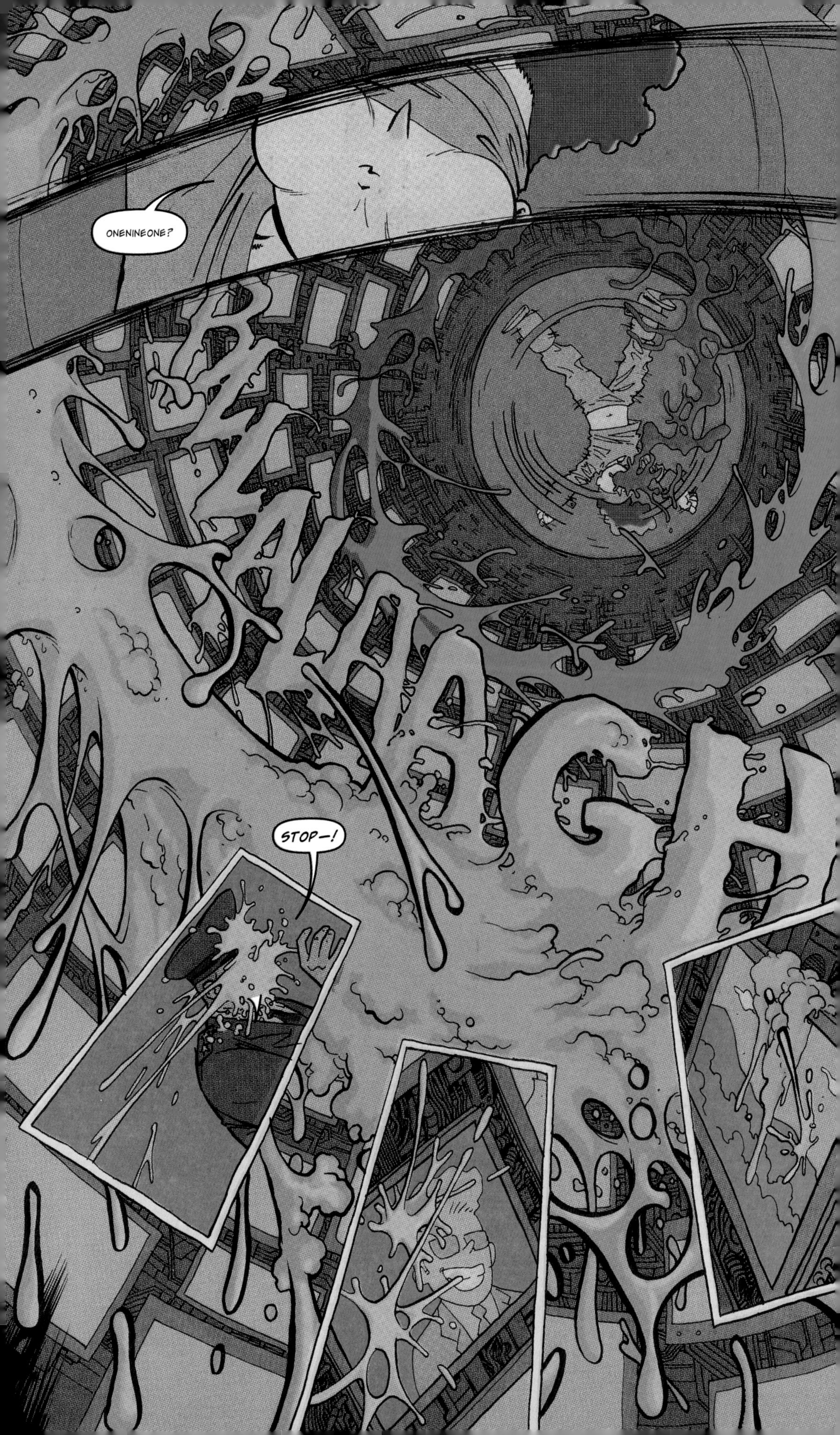
ONENINEONE?
STOP—!

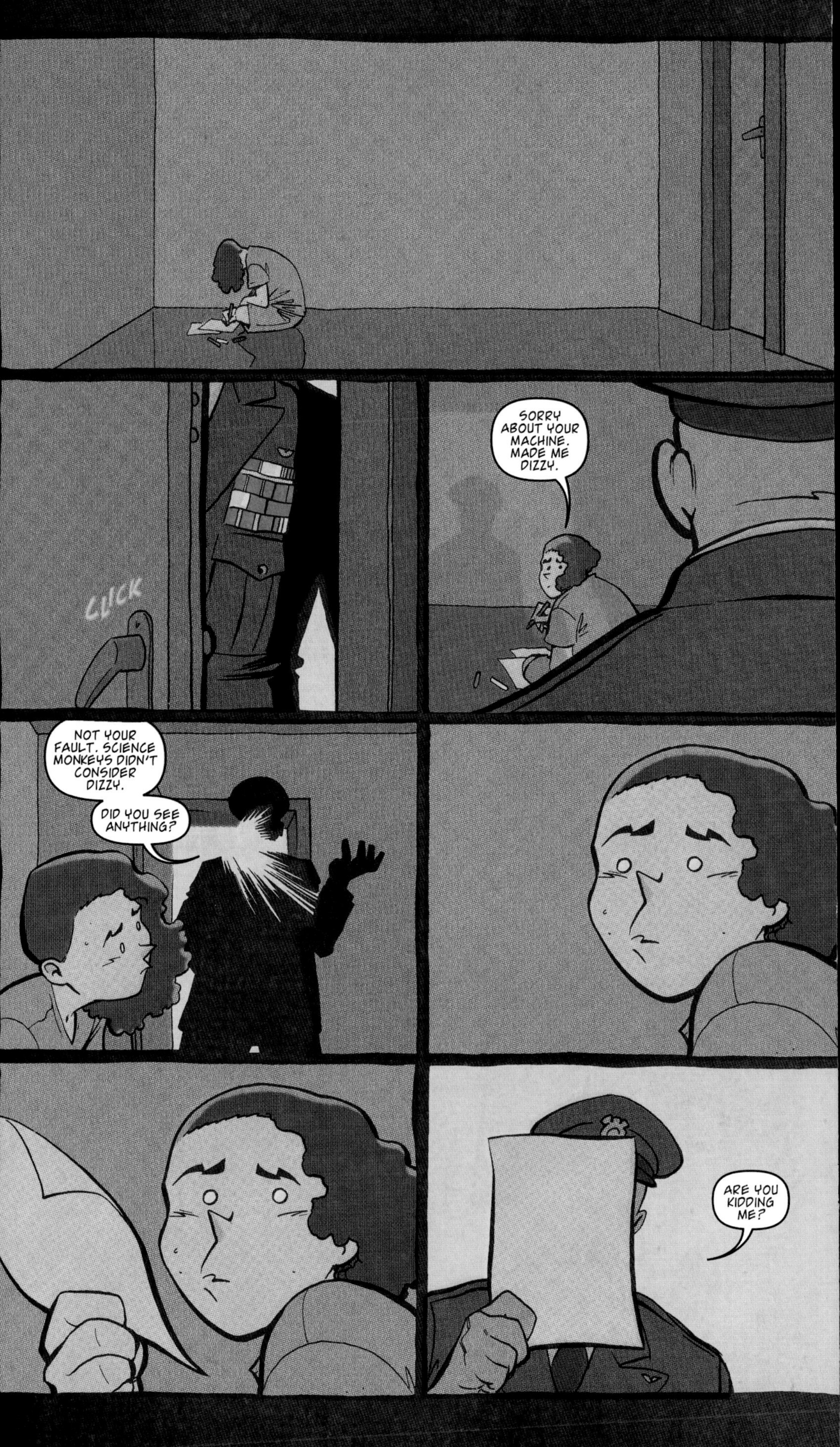
CLICK
SORRY ABOUT YOUR MACHINE. MADE ME DIZZY.
NOT YOUR FAULT. SCIENCE MONKEYS DIDN'T CONSIDER DIZZY.
DID YOU SEE ANYTHING?
ARE YOU KIDDING ME?

ENYA. TODAY.

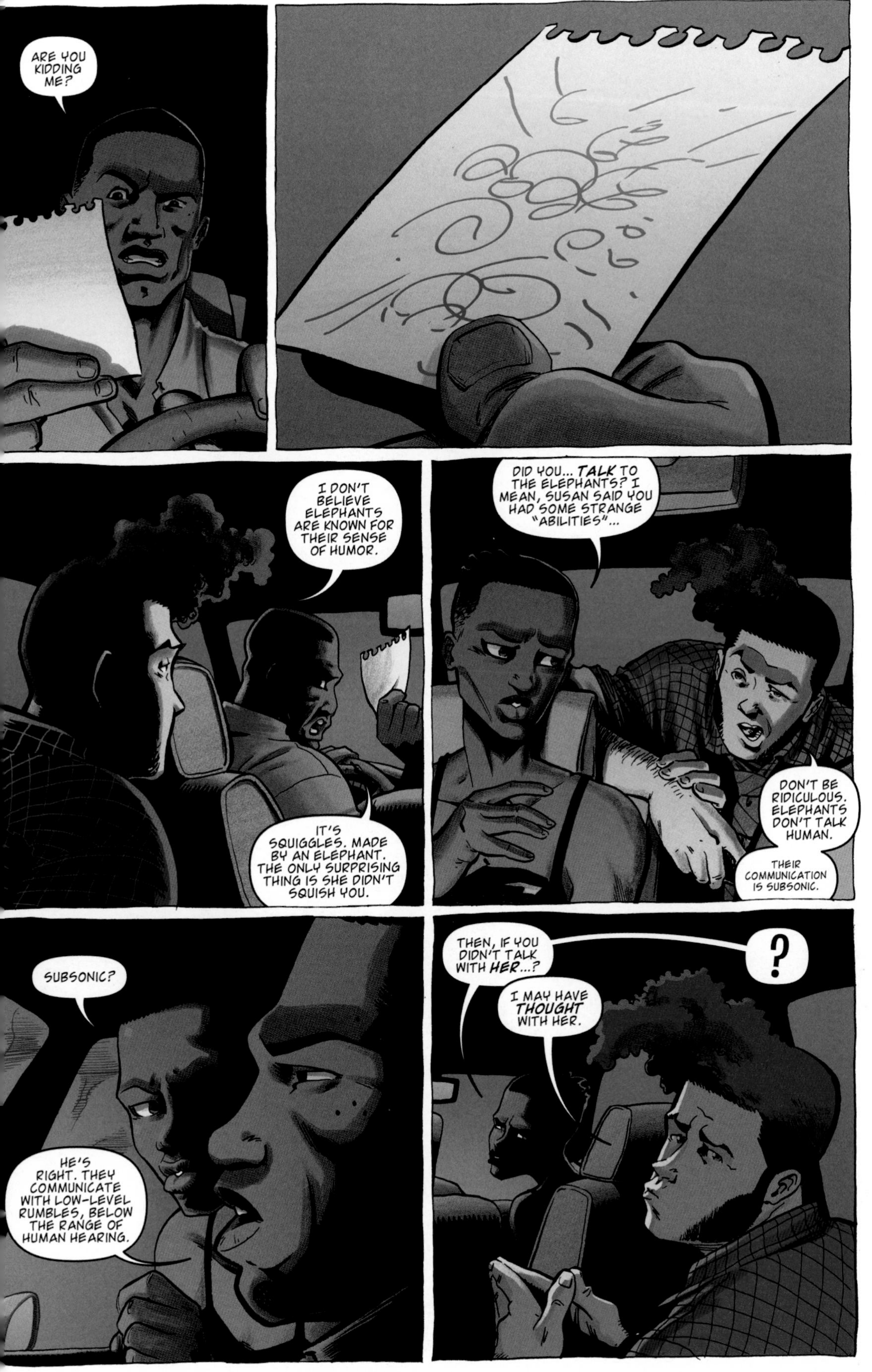
ARE YOU KIDDING ME?
I DON'T BELIEVE ELEPHANTS ARE KNOWN FOR THEIR SENSE OF HUMOR.
IT'S SQUIGGLES. MADE BY AN ELEPHANT. THE ONLY SURPRISING THING IS SHE DIDN'T SQUISH YOU.
DID YOU... TALK TO THE ELEPHANTS? I MEAN, SUSAN SAID YOU HAD SOME STRANGE "ABILITIES"...
DON'T BE RIDICULOUS. ELEPHANTS DON'T TALK HUMAN.
THEIR COMMUNICATION IS SUBSONIC.
SUBSONIC?
HE'S RIGHT. THEY COMMUNICATE WITH LOW-LEVEL RUMBLES, BELOW THE RANGE OF HUMAN HEARING.
THEN, IF YOU DIDN'T TALK WITH HER...?
?
I MAY HAVE THOUGHT WITH HER.

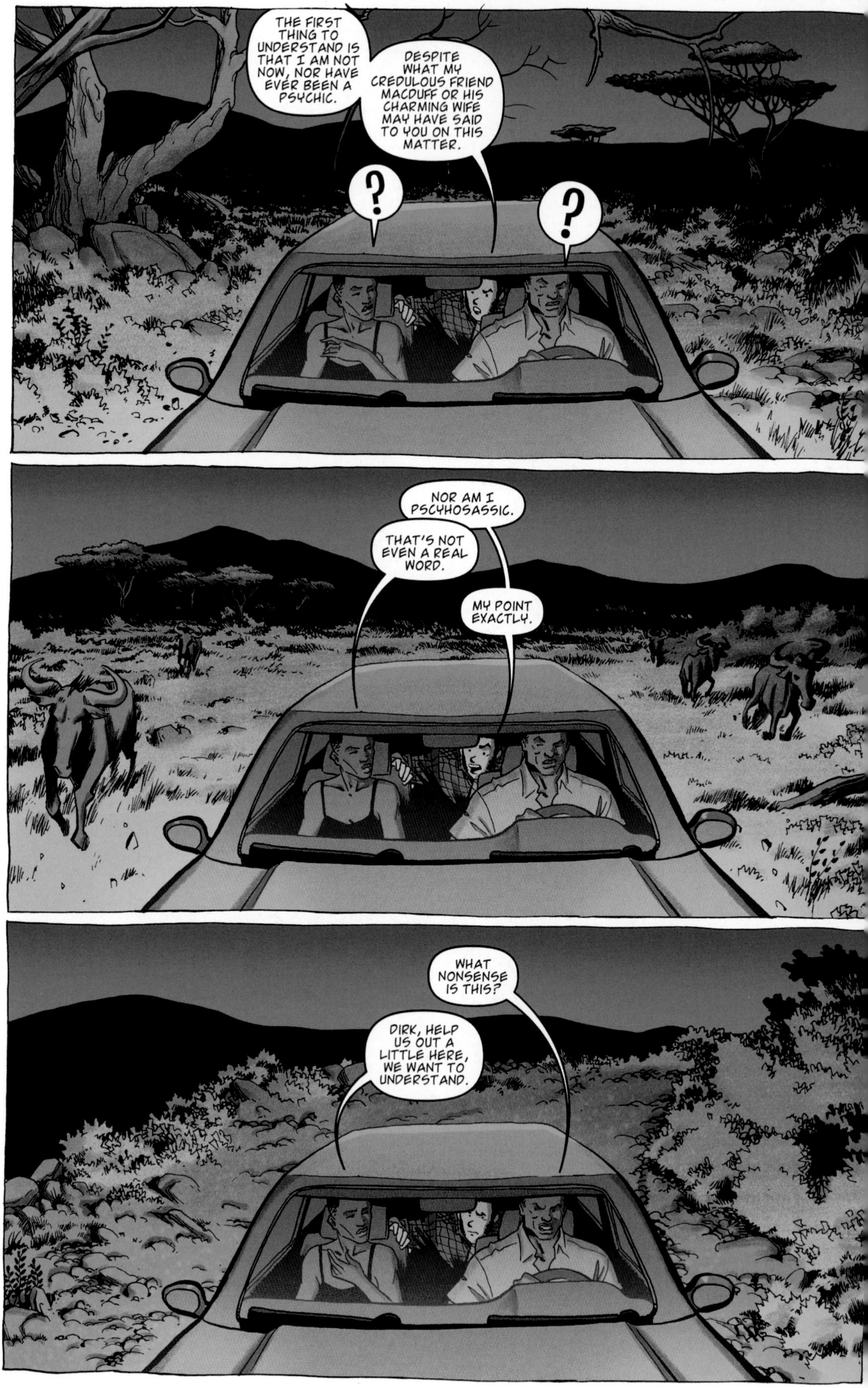
THE FIRST THING TO UNDERSTAND IS THAT I AM NOT NOW, NOR HAVE EVER BEEN A PSYCHIC.
DESPITE WHAT MY CREDULOUS FRIEND MACDUFF OR HIS CHARMING WIFE MAY HAVE SAID TO YOU ON THIS MATTER.
?
?
NOR AM I PSCYHOSASSIC.
THAT'S NOT EVEN A REAL WORD.
MY POINT EXACTLY.
WHAT NONSENSE IS THIS?
DIRK, HELP US OUT A LITTLE HERE, WE WANT TO UNDERSTAND.

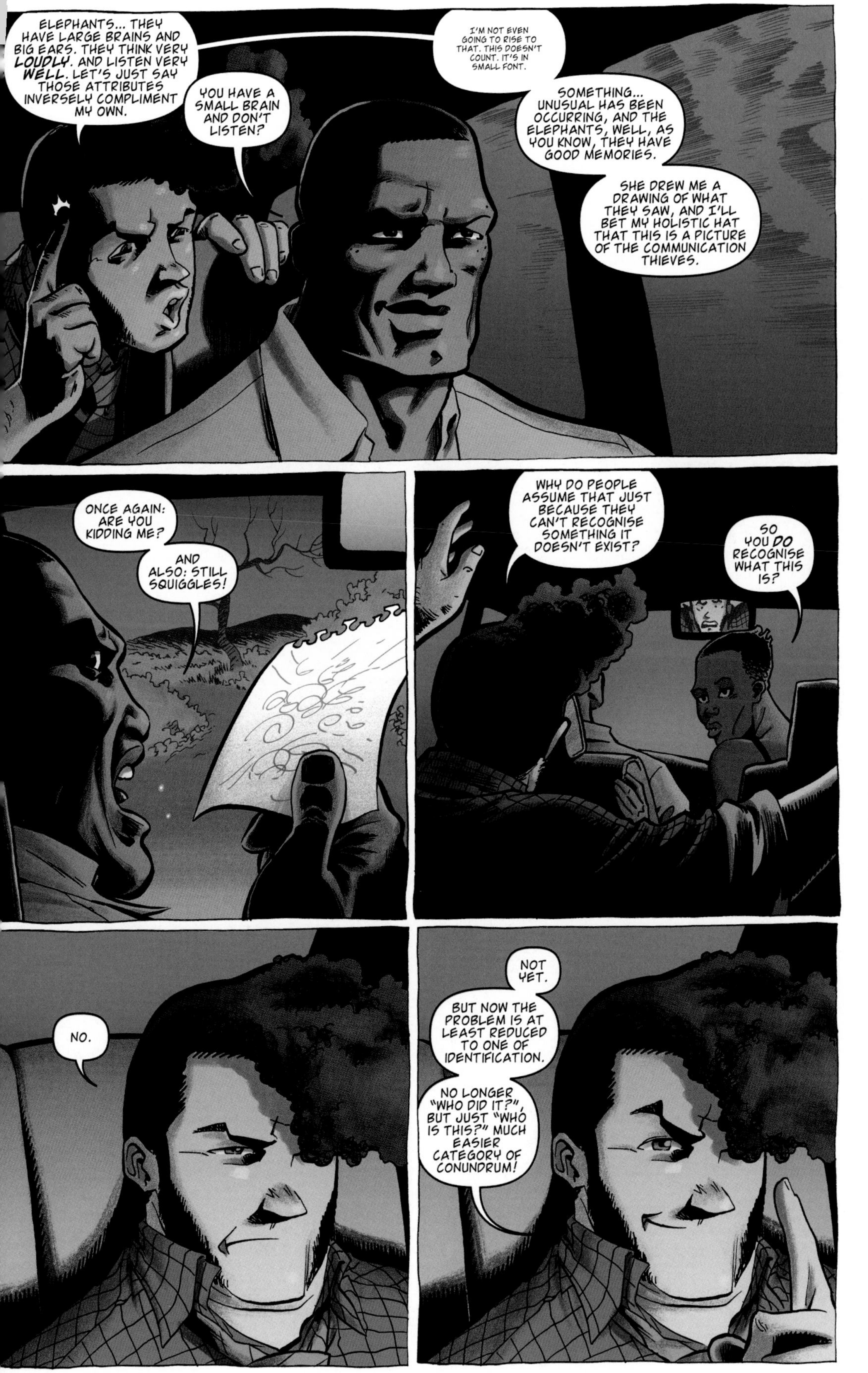
ELEPHANTS... THEY HAVE LARGE BRAINS AND BIG EARS. THEY THINK VERY LOUDLY. AND LISTEN VERY WELL. LET'S JUST SAY THOSE ATTRIBUTES INVERSELY COMPLIMENT MY OWN.
YOU HAVE A SMALL BRAIN AND DON'T LISTEN?
I'M NOT EVEN GOING TO RISE TO THAT. THIS DOESN'T COUNT. IT'S IN SMALL FONT.
SOMETHING... UNUSUAL HAS BEEN OCCURRING, AND THE ELEPHANTS, WELL, AS YOU KNOW, THEY HAVE GOOD MEMORIES.
SHE DREW ME A DRAWING OF WHAT THEY SAW, AND I'LL BET MY HOLISTIC HAT THAT THIS IS A PICTURE OF THE COMMUNICATION THIEVES.
ONCE AGAIN: ARE YOU KIDDING ME?
AND ALSO: STILL SQUIGGLES!
WHY DO PEOPLE ASSUME THAT JUST BECAUSE THEY CAN'T RECOGNISE SOMETHING IT DOESN'T EXIST?
SO YOU DO RECOGNISE WHAT THIS IS?
NO.
NOT YET.
BUT NOW THE PROBLEM IS AT LEAST REDUCED TO ONE OF IDENTIFICATION.
NO LONGER "WHO DID IT?", BUT JUST "WHO IS THIS?" MUCH EASIER CATEGORY OF CONUNDRUM!

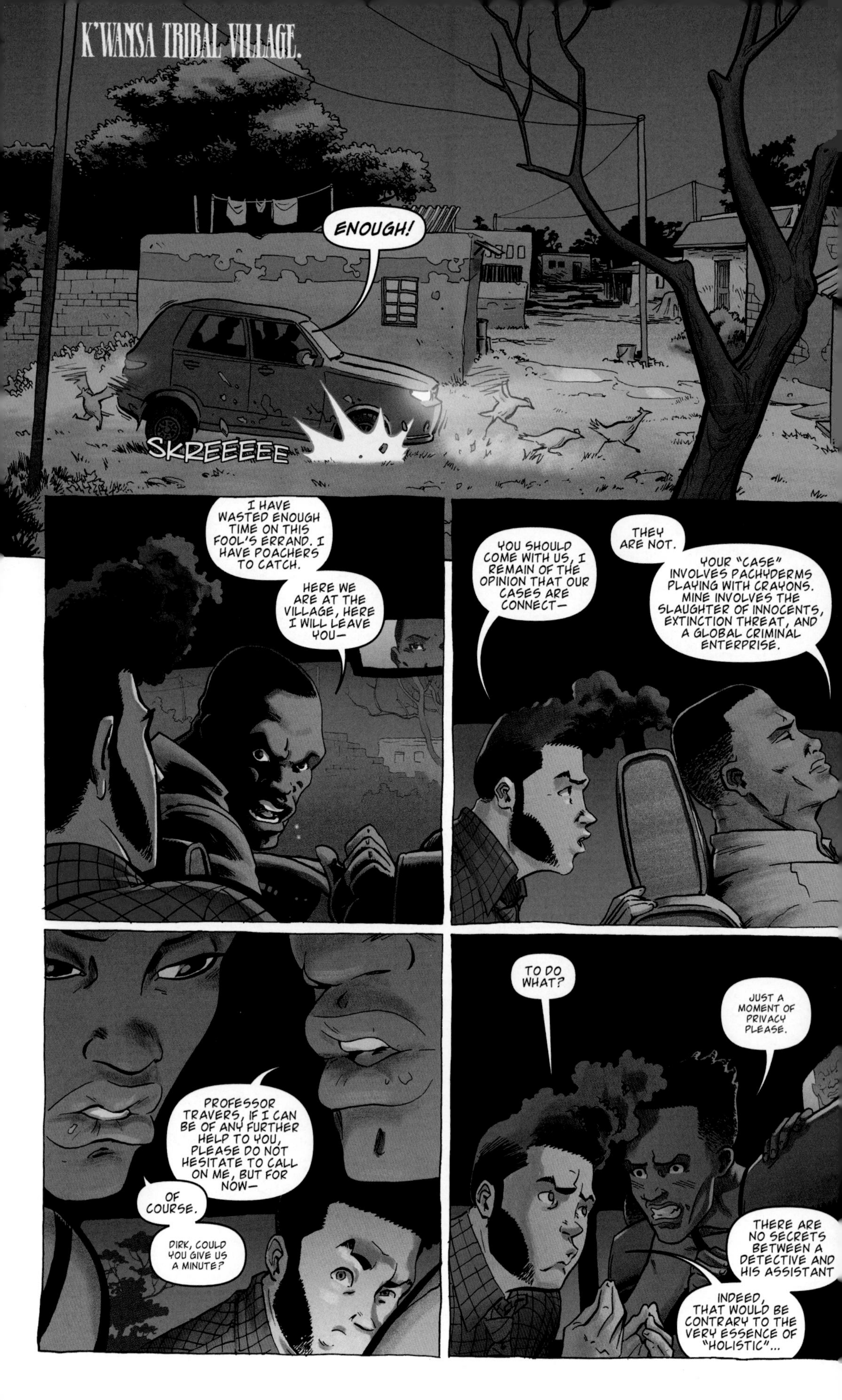
K'WANSA TRIBAL VILLAGE.
ENOUGH!
SKREEEEEE
I HAVE WASTED ENOUGH TIME ON THIS FOOL'S ERRAND. I HAVE POACHERS TO CATCH.
HERE WE ARE AT THE VILLAGE, HERE I WILL LEAVE YOU—
YOU SHOULD COME WITH US, I REMAIN OF THE OPINION THAT OUR CASES ARE CONNECT—
THEY ARE NOT.
YOUR "CASE" INVOLVES PACHYDERMS PLAYING WITH CRAYONS. MINE INVOLVES THE SLAUGHTER OF INNOCENTS, EXTINCTION THREAT, AND A GLOBAL CRIMINAL ENTERPRISE.
PROFESSOR TRAVERS, IF I CAN BE OF ANY FURTHER HELP TO YOU, PLEASE DO NOT HESITATE TO CALL ON ME, BUT FOR NOW—
OF COURSE.
DIRK, COULD YOU GIVE US A MINUTE?
TO DO WHAT?
JUST A MOMENT OF PRIVACY PLEASE.
THERE ARE NO SECRETS BETWEEN A DETECTIVE AND HIS ASSISTANT
INDEED, THAT WOULD BE CONTRARY TO THE VERY ESSENCE OF "HOLISTIC"...

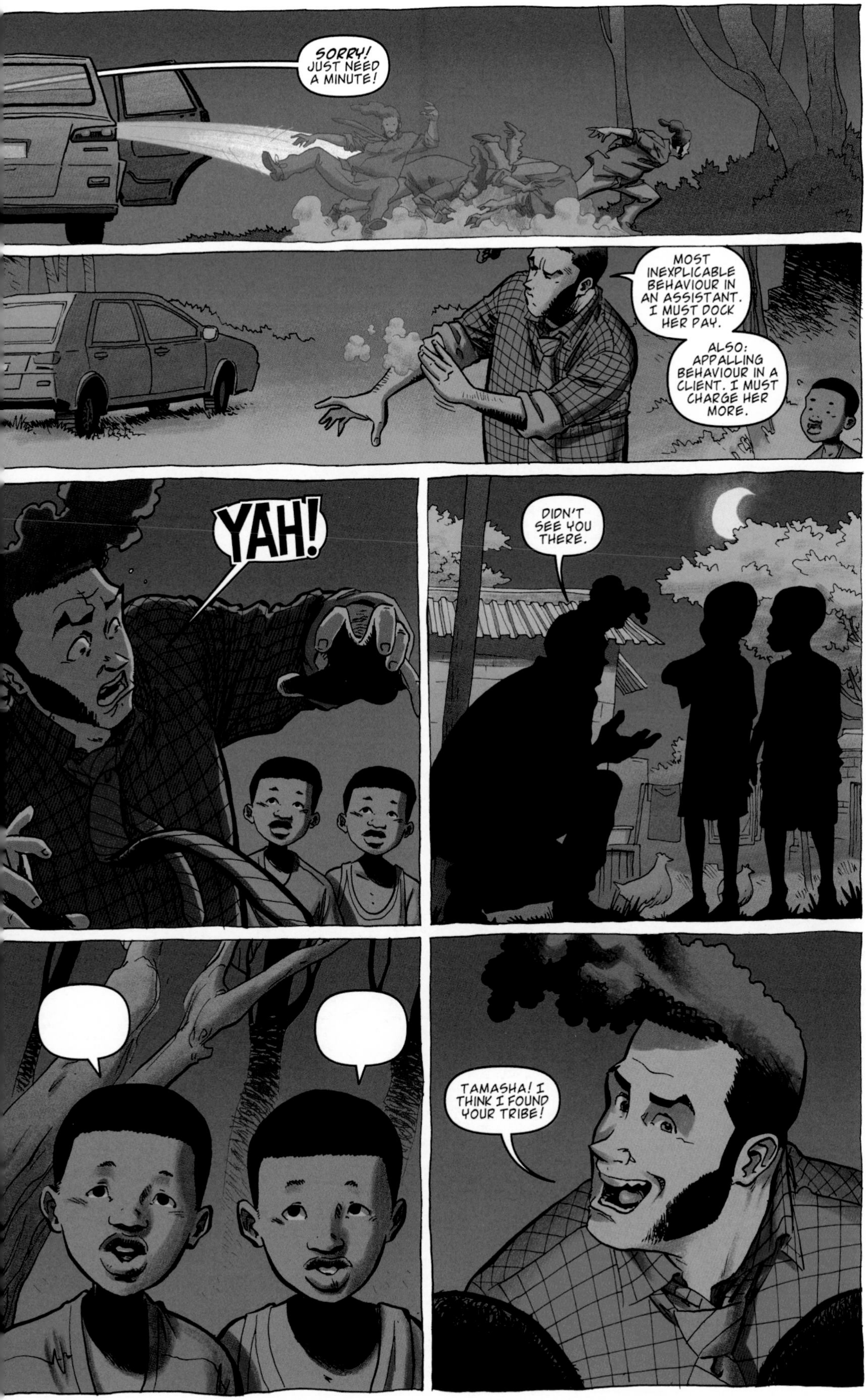
SORRY! JUST NEED A MINUTE!
MOST INEXPLICABLE BEHAVIOUR IN AN ASSISTANT. I MUST DOCK HER PAY.
ALSO: APPALLING BEHAVIOUR IN A CLIENT. I MUST CHARGE HER MORE.
YAH!
DIDN'T SEE YOU THERE.
TAMASHA! I THINK I FOUND YOUR TRIBE!

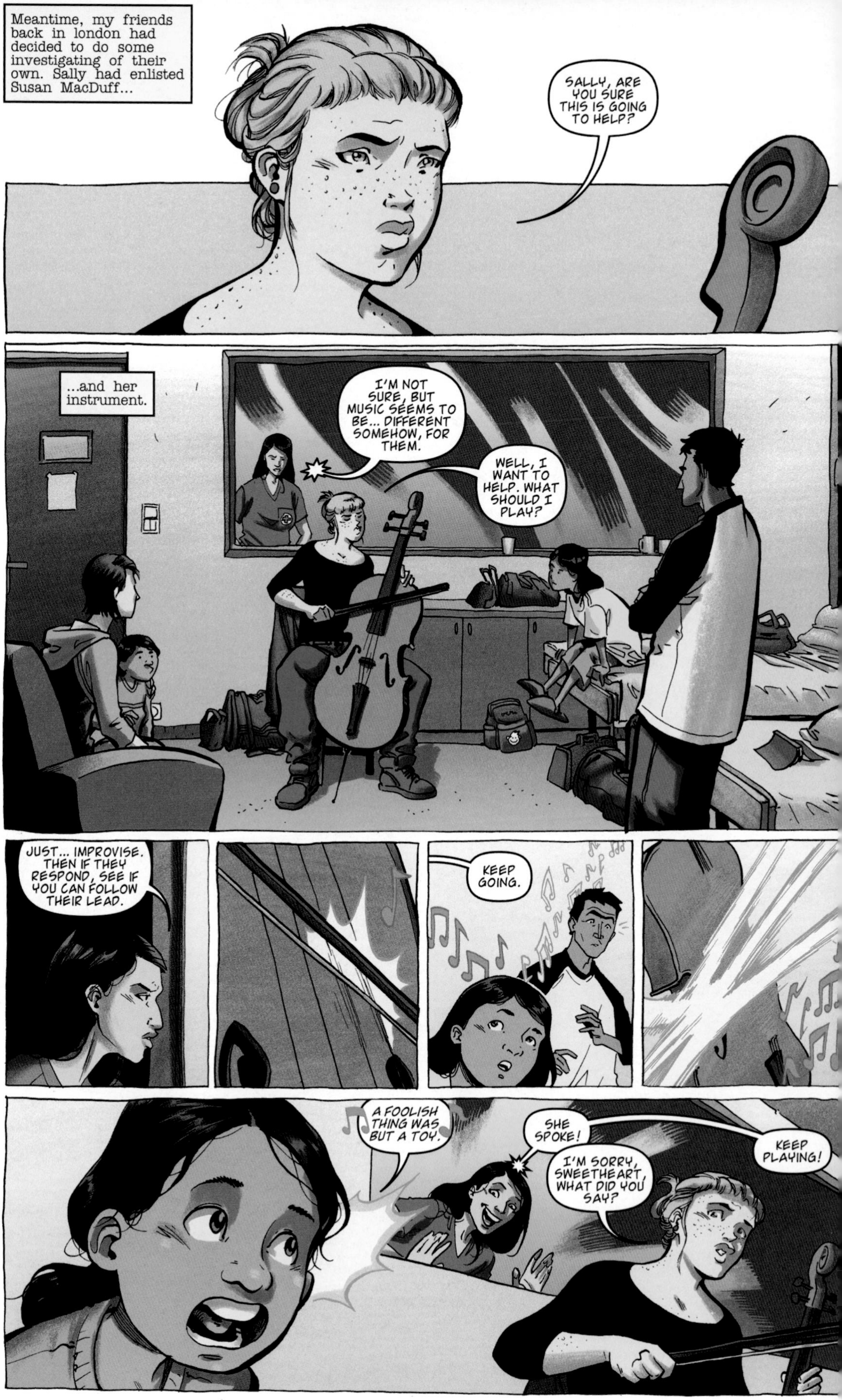

Meantime, my friends back in london had decided to do some investigating of their own. Sally had enlisted Susan MacDuff...
SALLY, ARE YOU SURE THIS IS GOING TO HELP?
...and her instrument.
I'M NOT SURE, BUT MUSIC SEEMS TO BE... DIFFERENT SOMEHOW, FOR THEM.
WELL, I WANT TO HELP. WHAT SHOULD I PLAY?
JUST... IMPROVISE. THEN IF THEY RESPOND, SEE IF YOU CAN FOLLOW THEIR LEAD.
KEEP GOING.
A FOOLISH THING WAS BUT A TOY.
SHE SPOKE!
I'M SORRY, SWEETHEART, WHAT DID YOU SAY?
KEEP PLAYING!

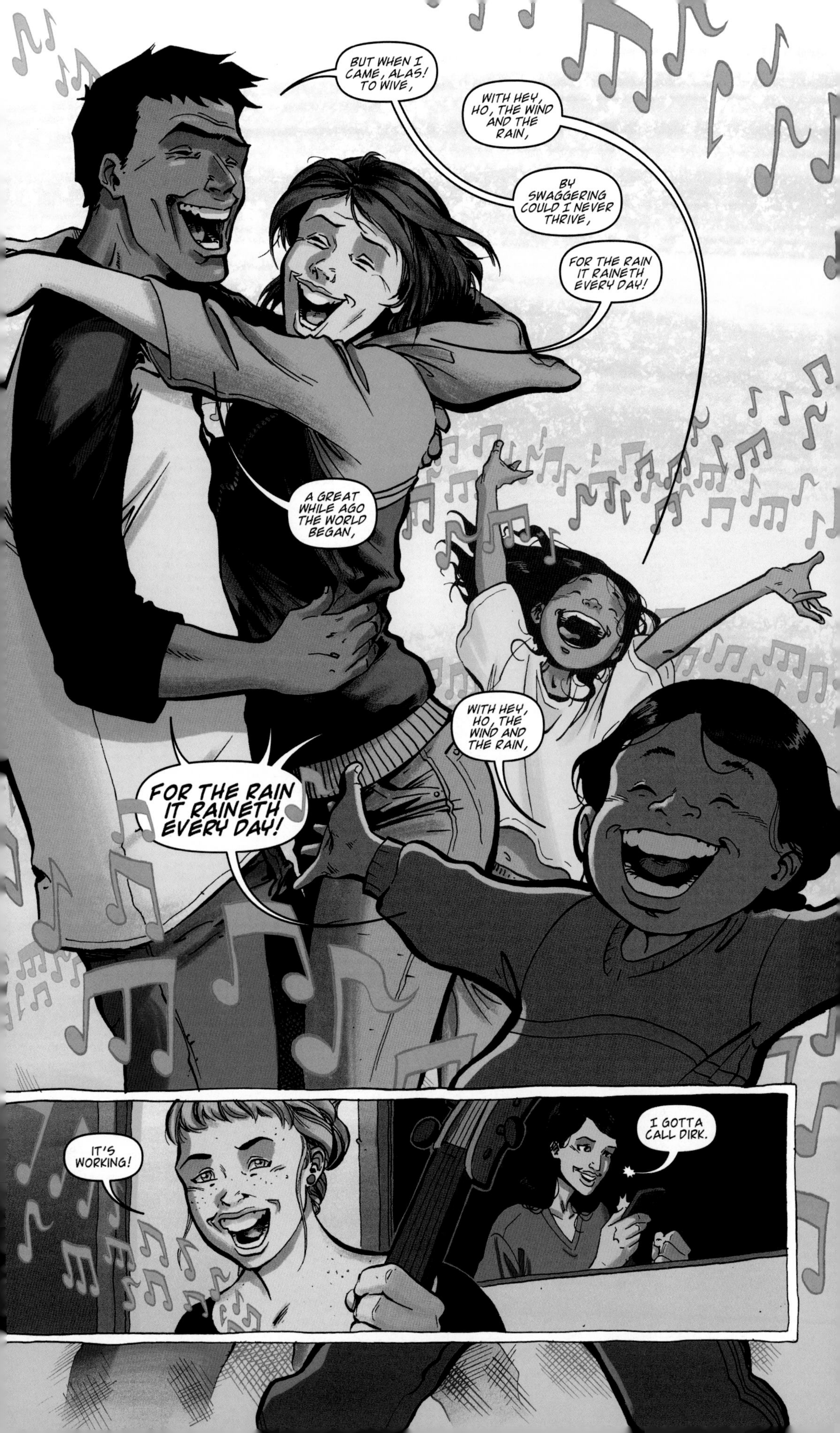
BUT WHEN I CAME, ALAS! TO WIVE,
WITH HEY, HO, THE WIND AND THE RAIN,
BY SWAGGERING COULD I NEVER THRIVE,
FOR THE RAIN IT RAINETH EVERY DAY!
A GREAT WHILE AGO THE WORLD BEGAN,
WITH HEY, HO, THE WIND AND THE RAIN,
FOR THE RAIN IT RAINETH EVERY DAY!
IT'S WORKING!
I GOTTA CALL DIRK.

Meantime, with the K'wansa, our own breakthrough had not yet broken... *uh*... through.

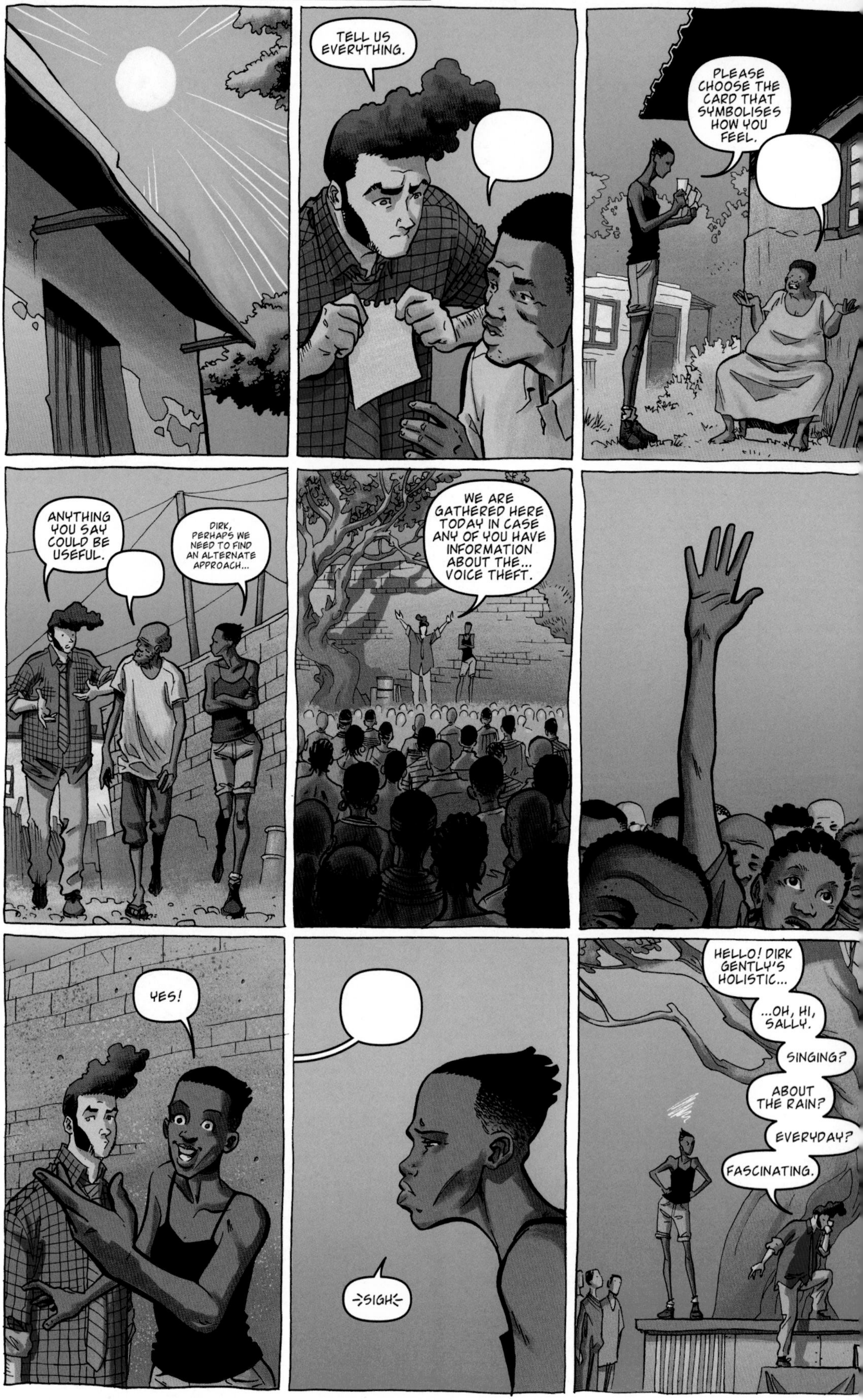

TELL US EVERYTHING.
PLEASE CHOOSE THE CARD THAT SYMBOLISES HOW YOU FEEL.
ANYTHING YOU SAY COULD BE USEFUL.
DIRK, PERHAPS WE NEED TO FIND AN ALTERNATE APPROACH...
WE ARE GATHERED HERE TODAY IN CASE ANY OF YOU HAVE INFORMATION ABOUT THE... VOICE THEFT.
YES!
⁼SIGH⁼
HELLO! DIRK GENTLY'S HOLISTIC...
...OH, HI, SALLY.
SINGING?
ABOUT THE RAIN?
EVERYDAY?
FASCINATING.

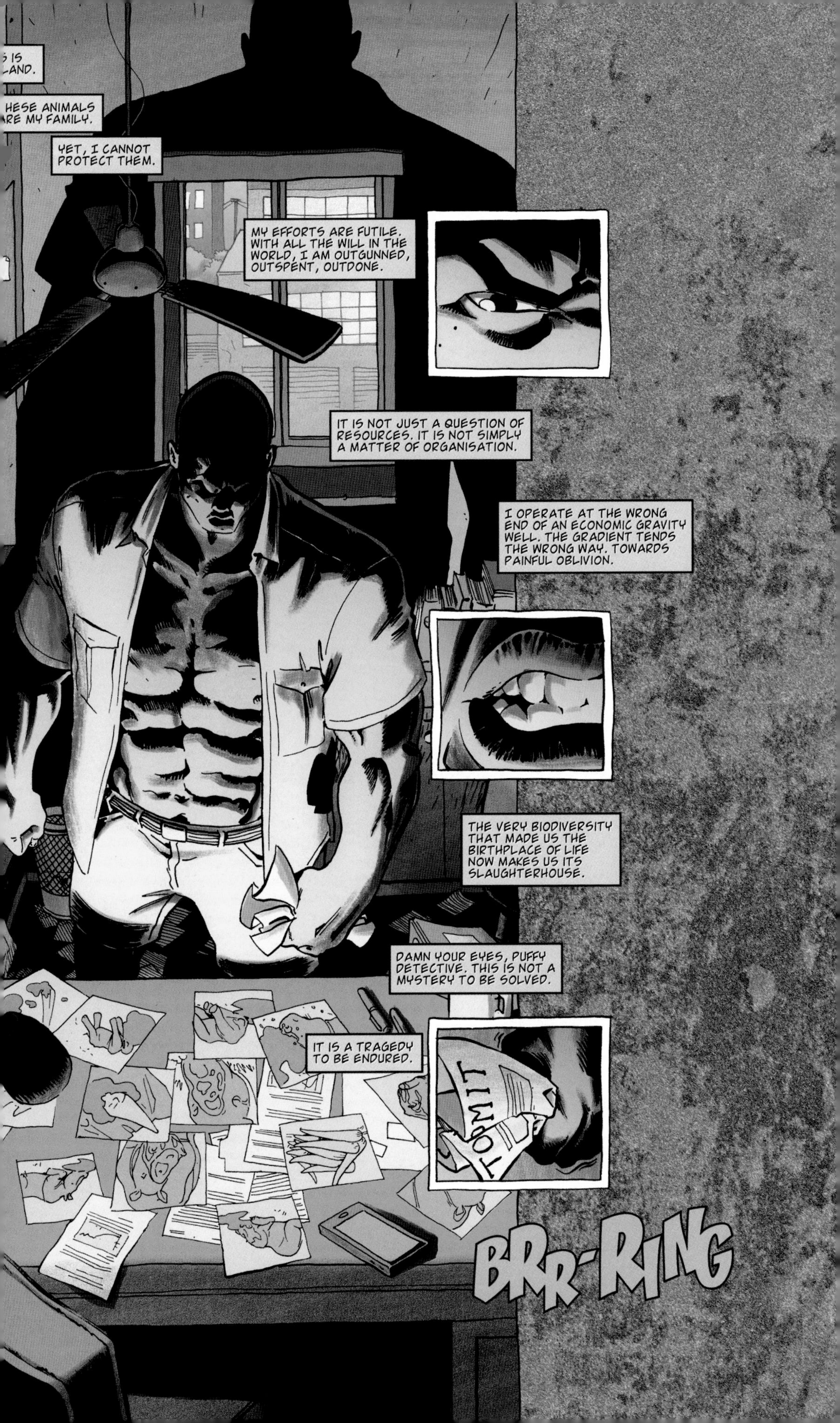

S IS
LAND.
HESE ANIMALS
RE MY FAMILY.
YET, I CANNOT PROTECT THEM.
MY EFFORTS ARE FUTILE. WITH ALL THE WILL IN THE WORLD, I AM OUTGUNNED, OUTSPENT, OUTDONE.
IT IS NOT JUST A QUESTION OF RESOURCES. IT IS NOT SIMPLY A MATTER OF ORGANISATION.
I OPERATE AT THE WRONG END OF AN ECONOMIC GRAVITY WELL. THE GRADIENT TENDS THE WRONG WAY. TOWARDS PAINFUL OBLIVION.
THE VERY BIODIVERSITY THAT MADE US THE BIRTHPLACE OF LIFE NOW MAKES US ITS SLAUGHTERHOUSE.
DAMN YOUR EYES, PUFFY DETECTIVE. THIS IS NOT A MYSTERY TO BE SOLVED.
IT IS A TRAGEDY TO BE ENDURED.
BRR-RING

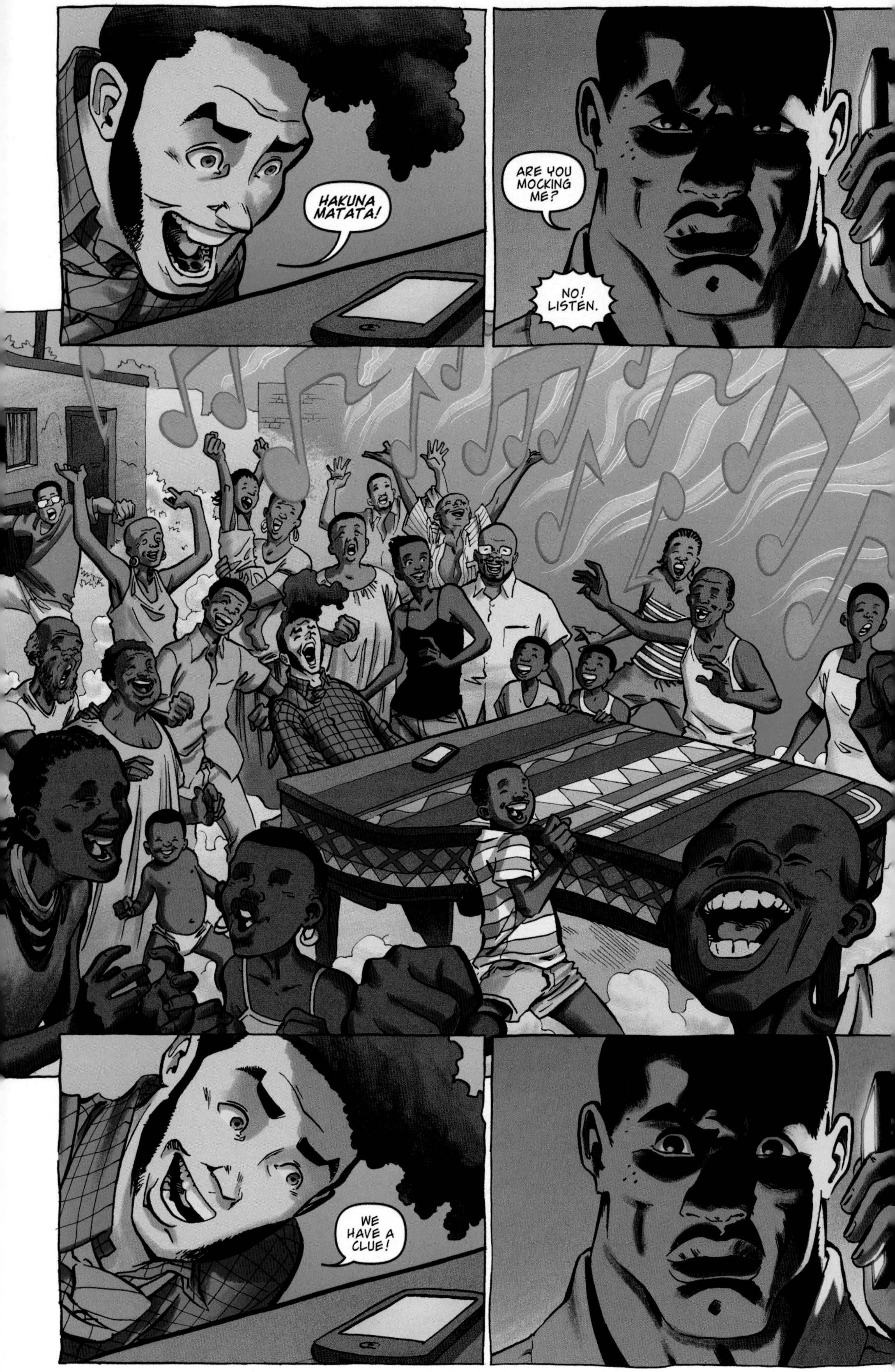
HAKUNA MATATA!
ARE YOU MOCKING ME?
NO! LISTEN.
WE HAVE A CLUE!

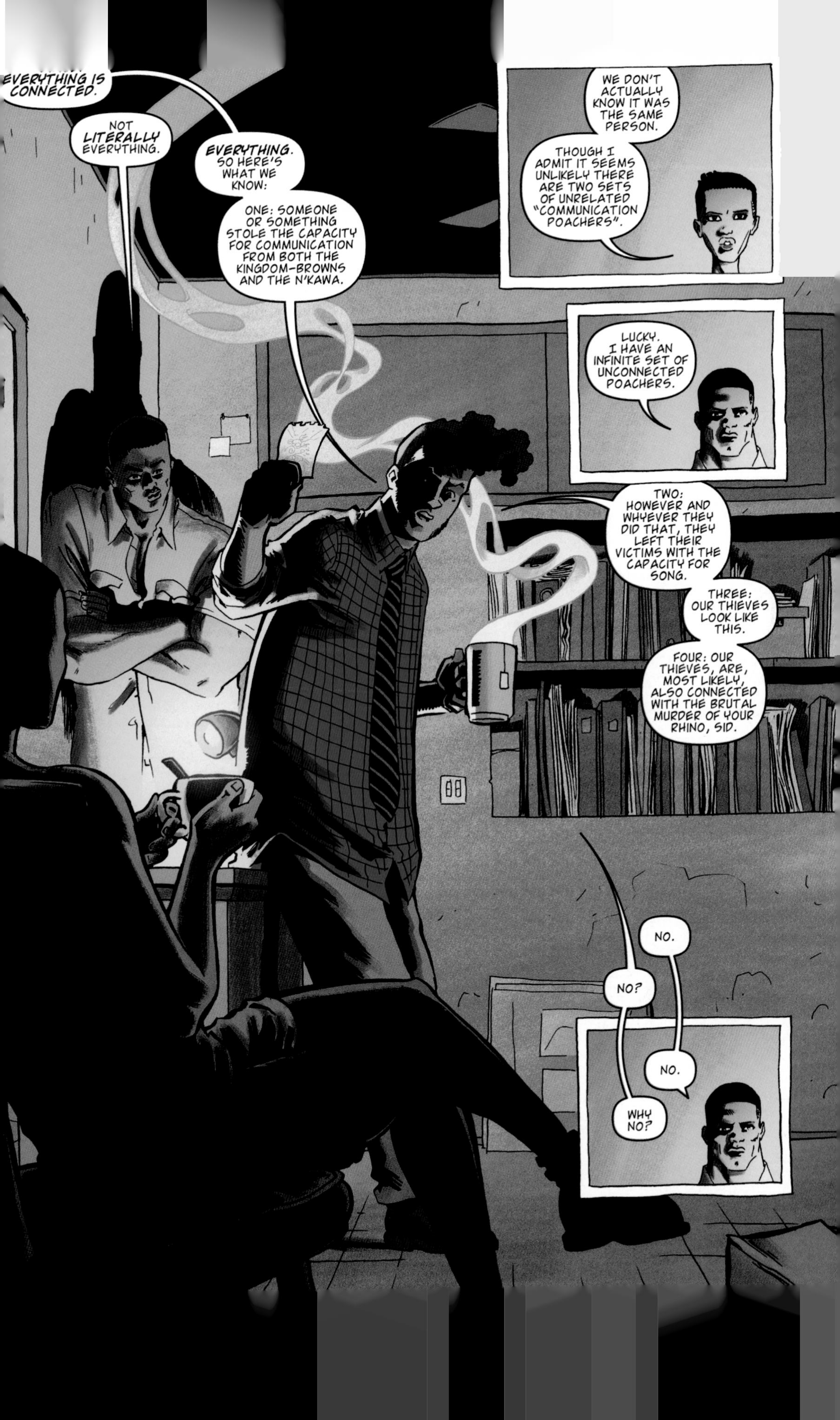
EVERYTHING IS CONNECTED.
NOT LITERALLY EVERYTHING.
EVERYTHING. SO HERE'S WHAT WE KNOW:
ONE: SOMEONE OR SOMETHING STOLE THE CAPACITY FOR COMMUNICATION FROM BOTH THE KINGDOM-BROWNS AND THE N'KAWA.
WE DON'T ACTUALLY KNOW IT WAS THE SAME PERSON.
THOUGH I ADMIT IT SEEMS UNLIKELY THERE ARE TWO SETS OF UNRELATED "COMMUNICATION POACHERS".
LUCKY. I HAVE AN INFINITE SET OF UNCONNECTED POACHERS.
TWO: HOWEVER AND WHYEVER THEY DID THAT, THEY LEFT THEIR VICTIMS WITH THE CAPACITY FOR SONG.
THREE: OUR THIEVES LOOK LIKE THIS.
FOUR: OUR THIEVES, ARE, MOST LIKELY, ALSO CONNECTED WITH THE BRUTAL MURDER OF YOUR RHINO, SID.
NO?
NO.
WHY NO?
NO.

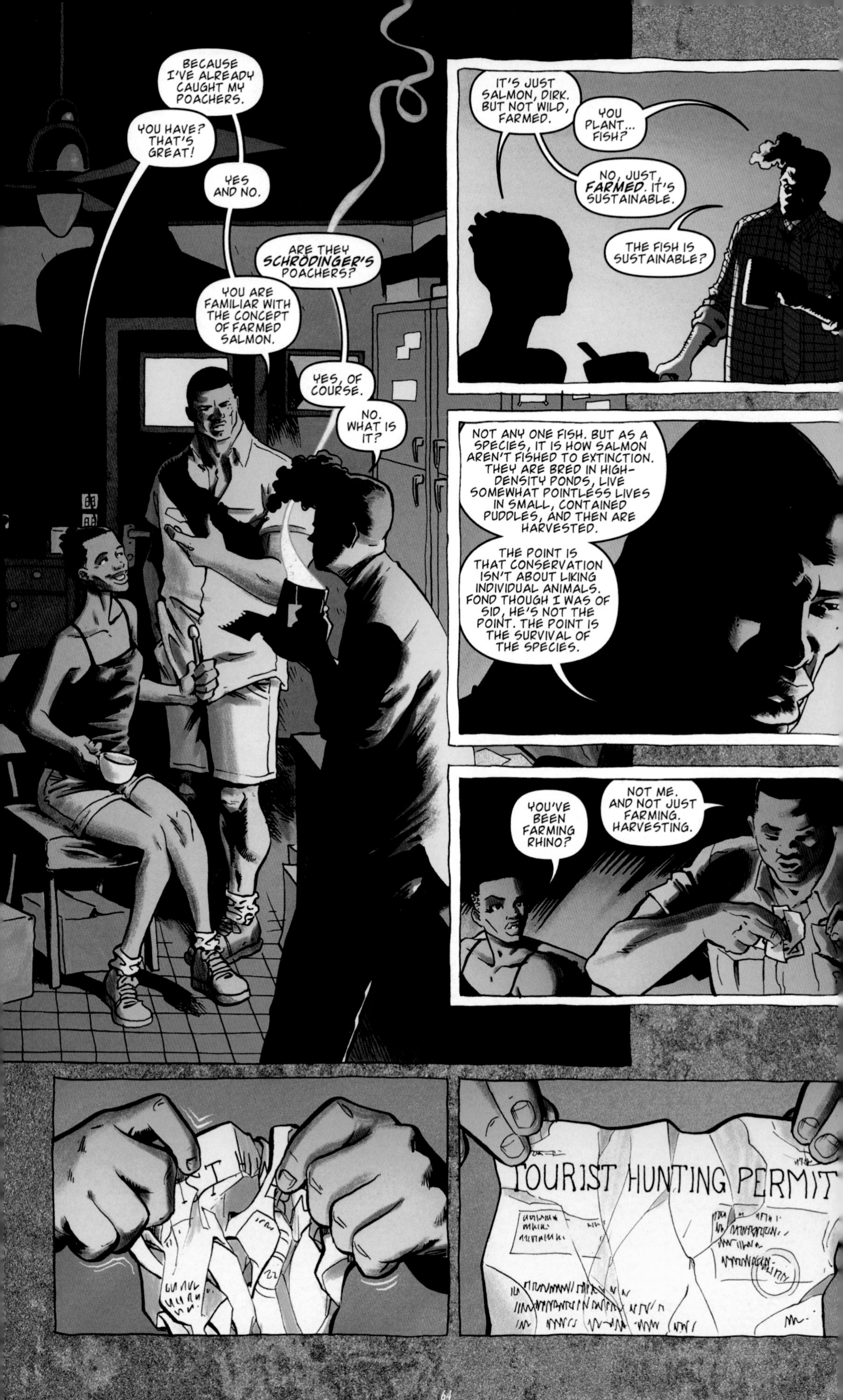

BECAUSE I'VE ALREADY CAUGHT MY POACHERS.
YOU HAVE? THAT'S GREAT!
YES AND NO.
ARE THEY SCHRÖDINGER'S POACHERS?
YOU ARE FAMILIAR WITH THE CONCEPT OF FARMED SALMON.
YES, OF COURSE.
NO. WHAT IS IT?
IT'S JUST SALMON, DIRK. BUT NOT WILD, FARMED.
YOU PLANT... FISH?
NO, JUST, FARMED. IT'S SUSTAINABLE.
THE FISH IS SUSTAINABLE?
NOT ANY ONE FISH. BUT AS A SPECIES, IT IS HOW SALMON AREN'T FISHED TO EXTINCTION. THEY ARE BRED IN HIGH-DENSITY PONDS, LIVE SOMEWHAT POINTLESS LIVES IN SMALL, CONTAINED PUDDLES, AND THEN ARE HARVESTED.
THE POINT IS THAT CONSERVATION ISN'T ABOUT LIKING INDIVIDUAL ANIMALS. FOND THOUGH I WAS OF SID, HE'S NOT THE POINT. THE POINT IS THE SURVIVAL OF THE SPECIES.
YOU'VE BEEN FARMING RHINO?
NOT ME. AND NOT JUST FARMING. HARVESTING.
TOURIST HUNTING PERMIT

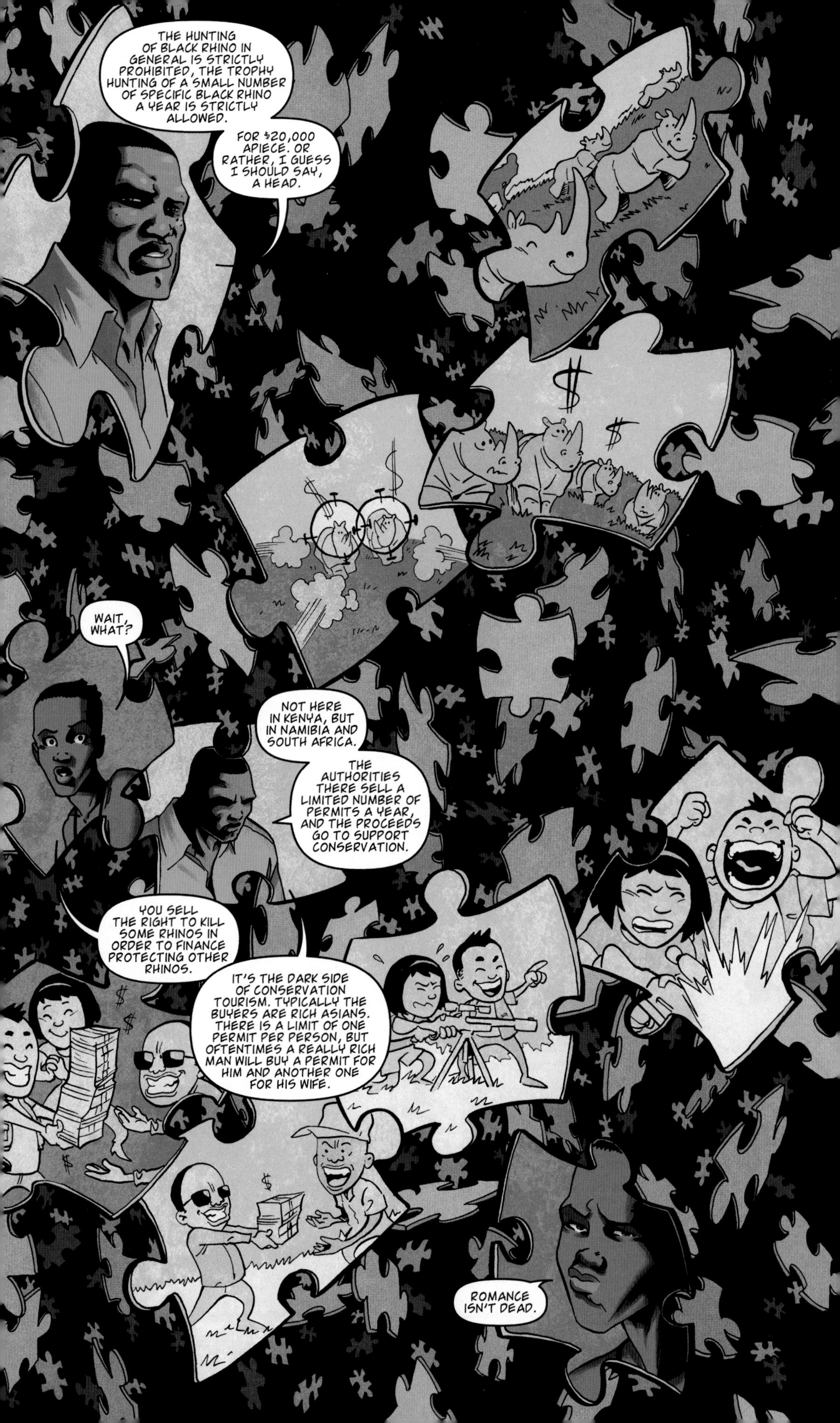
THE HUNTING OF BLACK RHINO IN GENERAL IS STRICTLY PROHIBITED, THE TROPHY HUNTING OF A SMALL NUMBER OF SPECIFIC BLACK RHINO A YEAR IS STRICTLY ALLOWED.
FOR $20,000 APIECE. OR RATHER, I GUESS I SHOULD SAY, A HEAD.
WAIT, WHAT?
NOT HERE IN KENYA, BUT IN NAMIBIA AND SOUTH AFRICA.
THE AUTHORITIES THERE SELL A LIMITED NUMBER OF PERMITS A YEAR, AND THE PROCEEDS GO TO SUPPORT CONSERVATION.
YOU SELL THE RIGHT TO KILL SOME RHINOS IN ORDER TO FINANCE PROTECTING OTHER RHINOS.
IT'S THE DARK SIDE OF CONSERVATION TOURISM. TYPICALLY THE BUYERS ARE RICH ASIANS. THERE IS A LIMIT OF ONE PERMIT PER PERSON, BUT OFTENTIMES A REALLY RICH MAN WILL BUY A PERMIT FOR HIM AND ANOTHER ONE FOR HIS WIFE.
ROMANCE ISN'T DEAD.

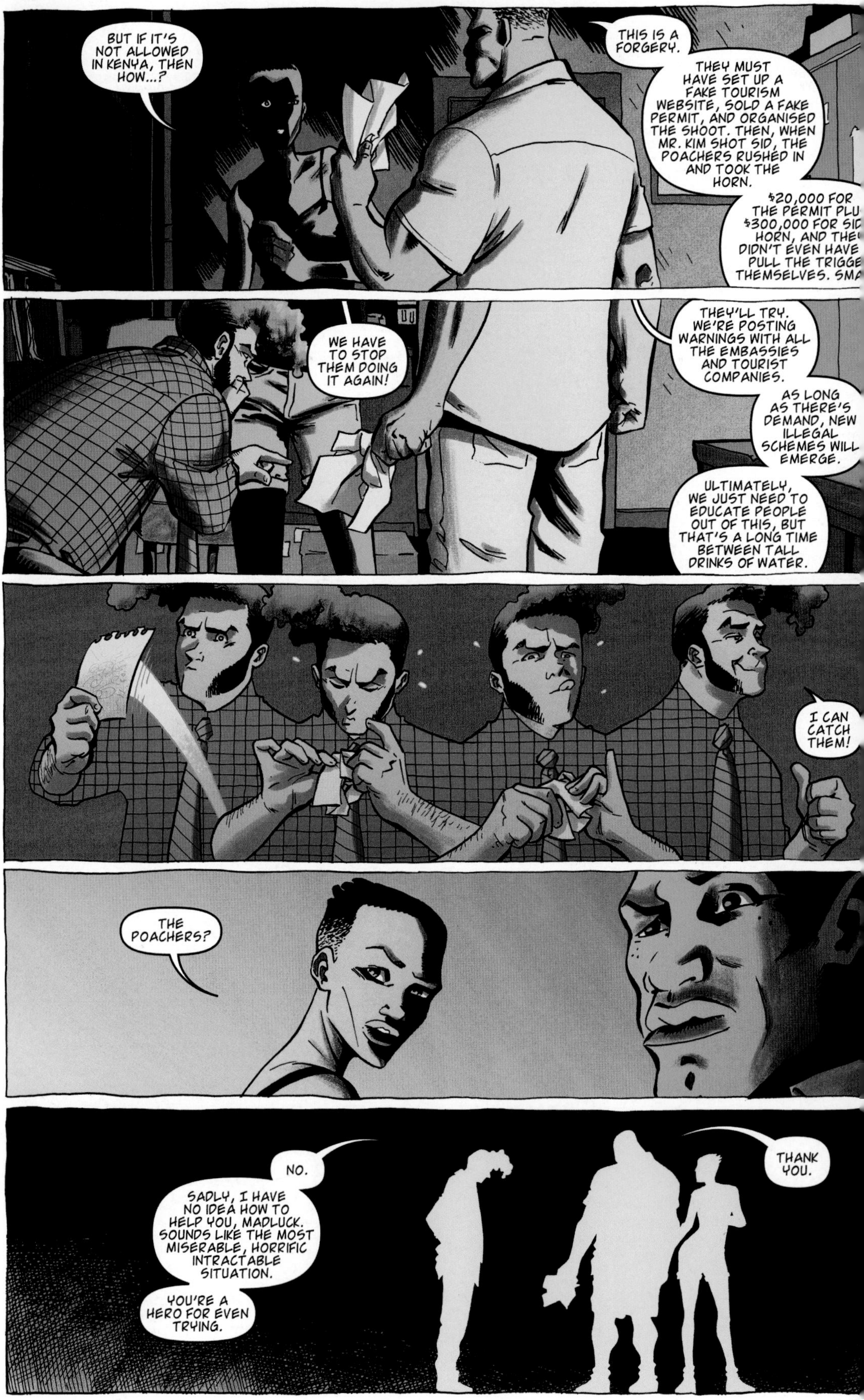

BUT IF IT'S NOT ALLOWED IN KENYA, THEN HOW...?
THIS IS A FORGERY.
THEY MUST HAVE SET UP A FAKE TOURISM WEBSITE, SOLD A FAKE PERMIT, AND ORGANISED THE SHOOT. THEN, WHEN MR. KIM SHOT SID, THE POACHERS RUSHED IN AND TOOK THE HORN.
$20,000 FOR THE PERMIT PLU $300,000 FOR SID HORN, AND THE DIDN'T EVEN HAVE PULL THE TRIGGE THEMSELVES. SMA
WE HAVE TO STOP THEM DOING IT AGAIN!
THEY'LL TRY. WE'RE POSTING WARNINGS WITH ALL THE EMBASSIES AND TOURIST COMPANIES.
AS LONG AS THERE'S DEMAND, NEW ILLEGAL SCHEMES WILL EMERGE.
ULTIMATELY, WE JUST NEED TO EDUCATE PEOPLE OUT OF THIS, BUT THAT'S A LONG TIME BETWEEN TALL DRINKS OF WATER.
I CAN CATCH THEM!
THE POACHERS?
NO.
SADLY, I HAVE NO IDEA HOW TO HELP YOU, MADLUCK. SOUNDS LIKE THE MOST MISERABLE, HORRIFIC INTRACTABLE SITUATION.
YOU'RE A HERO FOR EVEN TRYING.
THANK YOU.

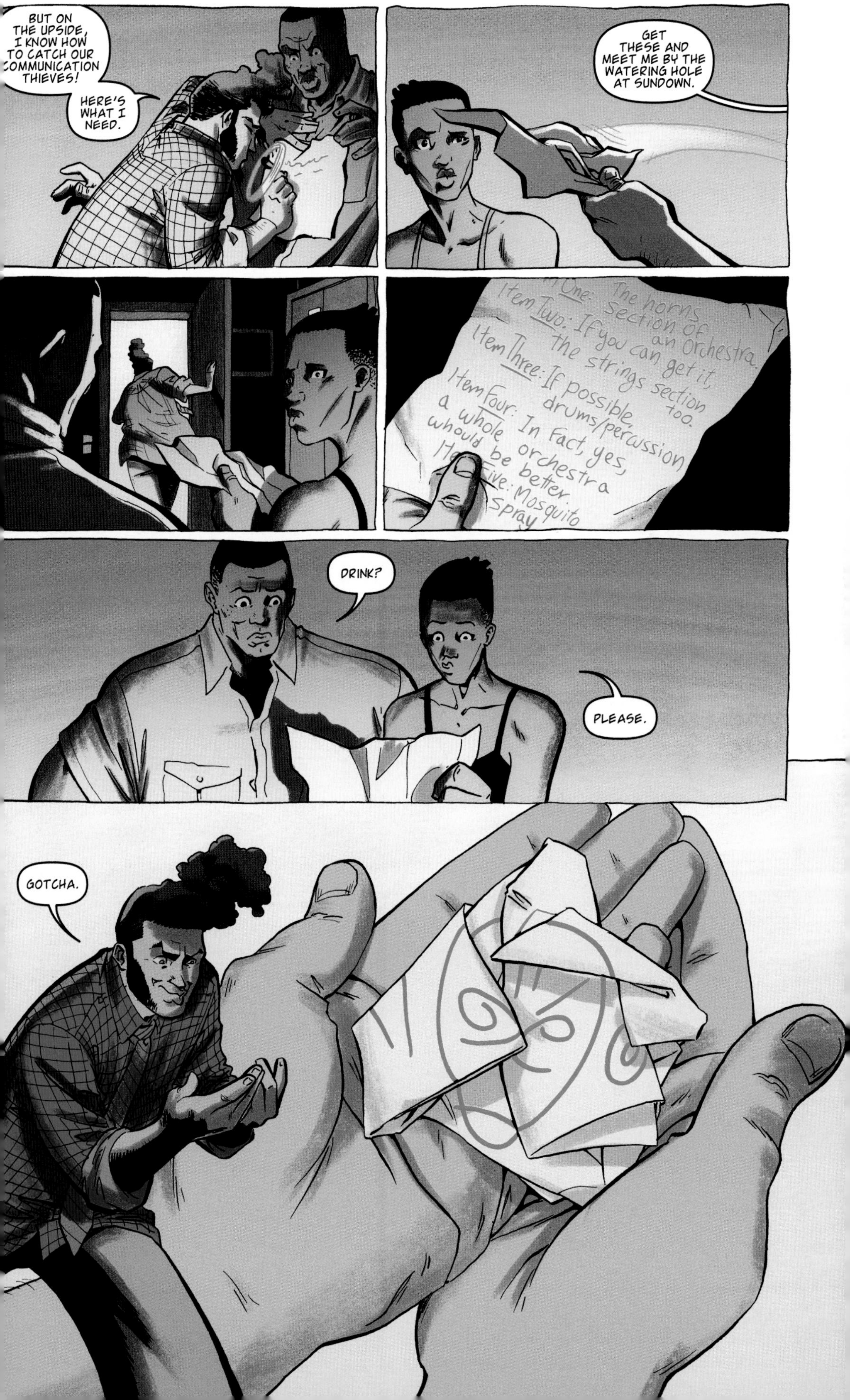
BUT ON THE UPSIDE, I KNOW HOW TO CATCH OUR COMMUNICATION THIEVES!
HERE'S WHAT I NEED.
GET THESE AND MEET ME BY THE WATERING HOLE AT SUNDOWN.
One: The horns section of an Orchestra.
Item Two: If you can get it, the strings section too.
Item Three: If possible, drums/percussion
Item Four: In Fact, yes, a whole orchestra whould be better.
Five: Mosquito spray
DRINK?
PLEASE.
GOTCHA.

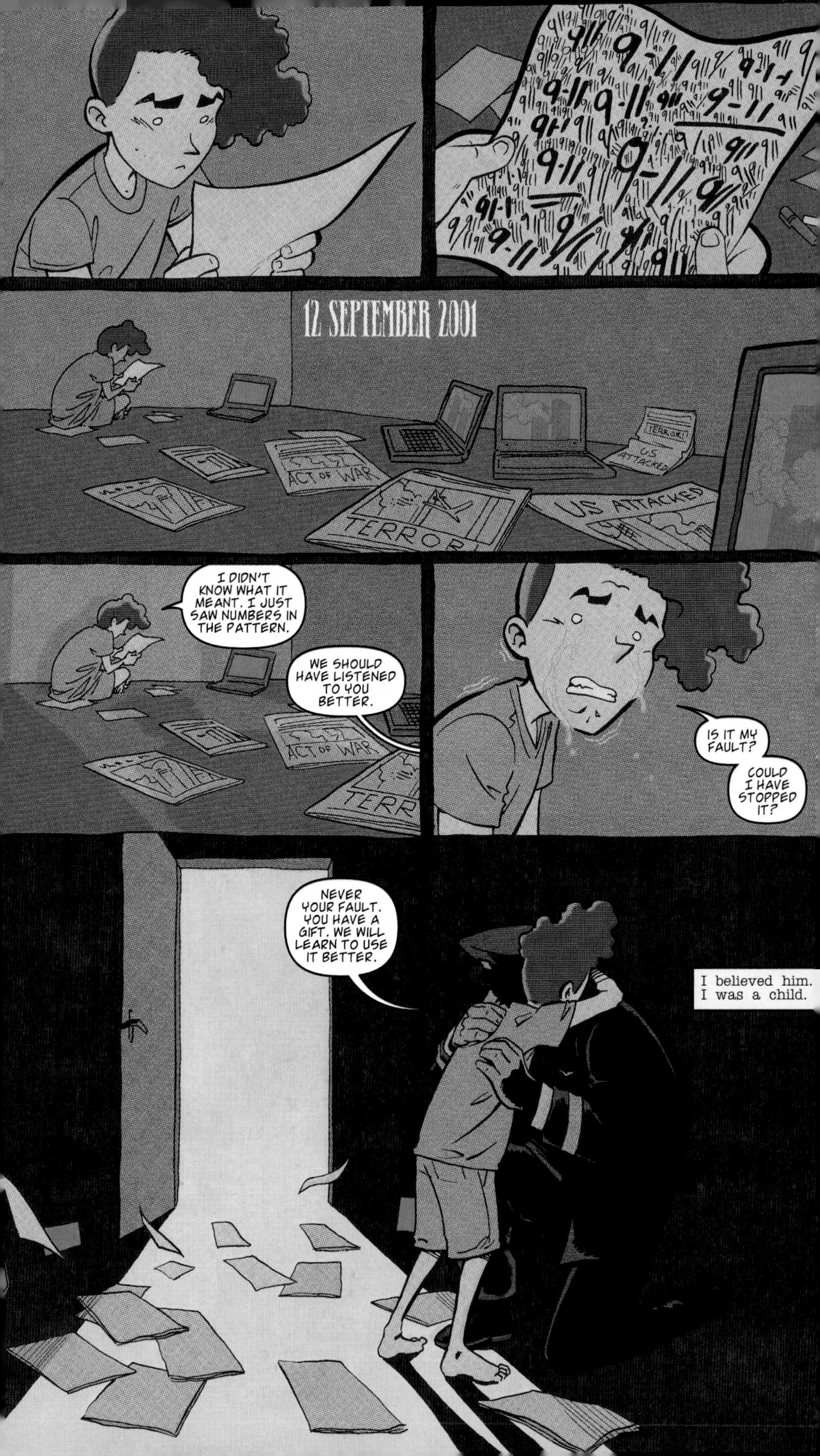
12 SEPTEMBER 2001
TERROR!
US ATTACKED
ACT OF WAR
TERROR
US ATTACKED
I DIDN'T KNOW WHAT IT MEANT. I JUST SAW NUMBERS IN THE PATTERN.
WE SHOULD HAVE LISTENED TO YOU BETTER.
IS IT MY FAULT?
COULD I HAVE STOPPED IT?
NEVER YOUR FAULT. YOU HAVE A GIFT. WE WILL LEARN TO USE IT BETTER.
I believed him. I was a child.

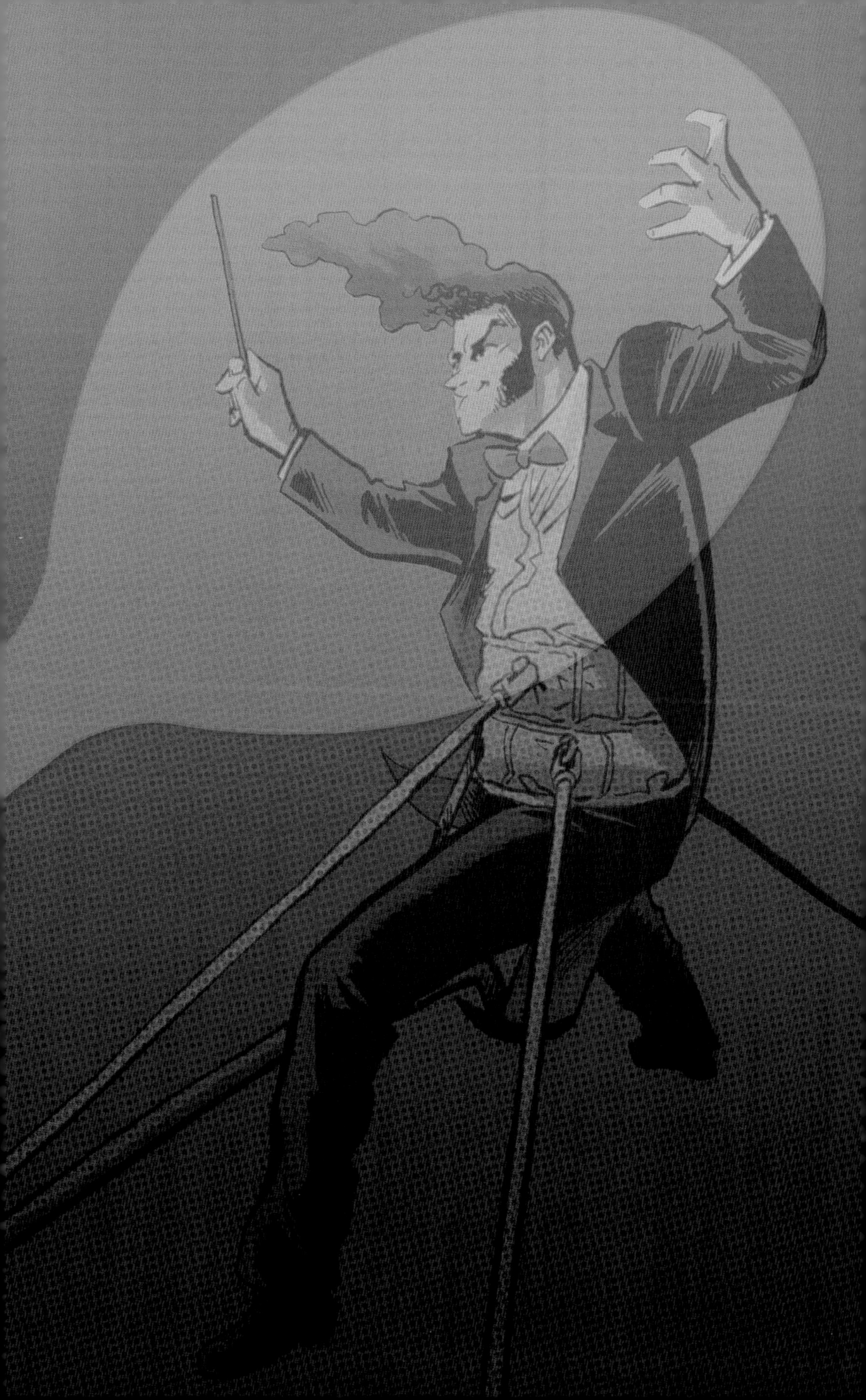

CHAPTER FOUR

Cover Art by **ILIAS KYRIAZIS**

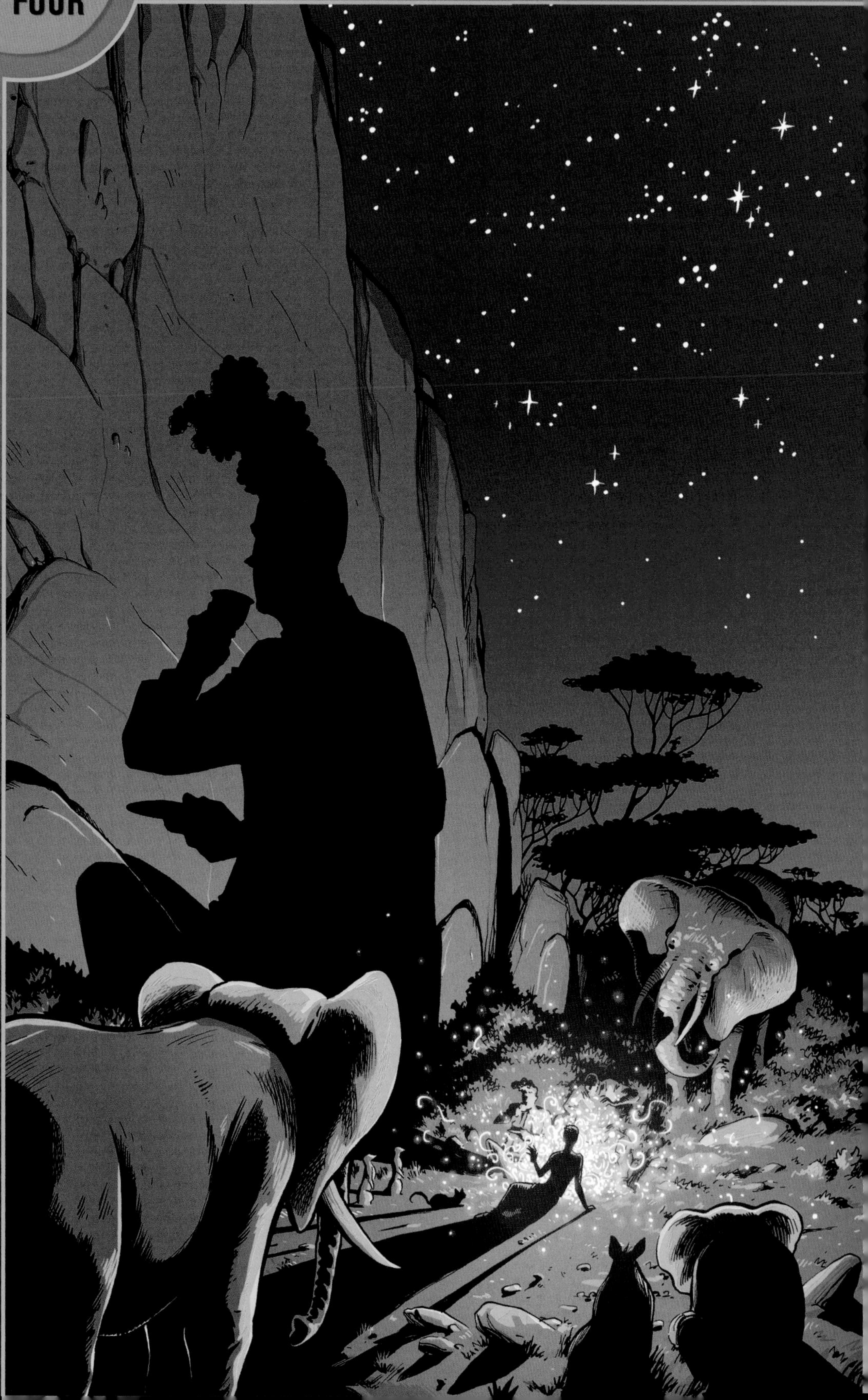

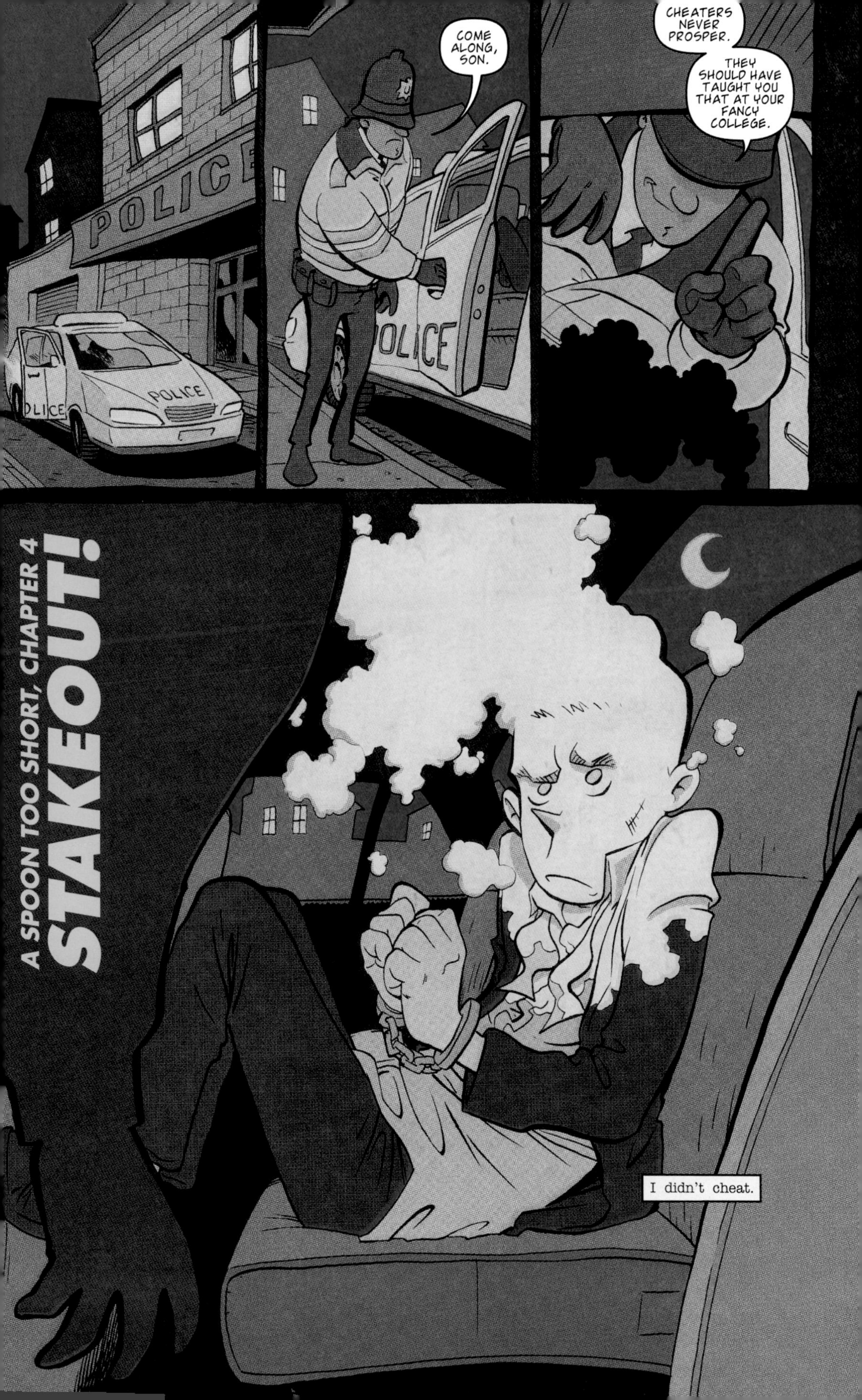
POLICE
COME ALONG, SON.
POLICE
CHEATERS NEVER PROSPER.
THEY SHOULD HAVE TAUGHT YOU THAT AT YOUR FANCY COLLEGE.
A SPOON TOO SHORT, CHAPTER 4
STAKEOUT!
I didn't cheat.

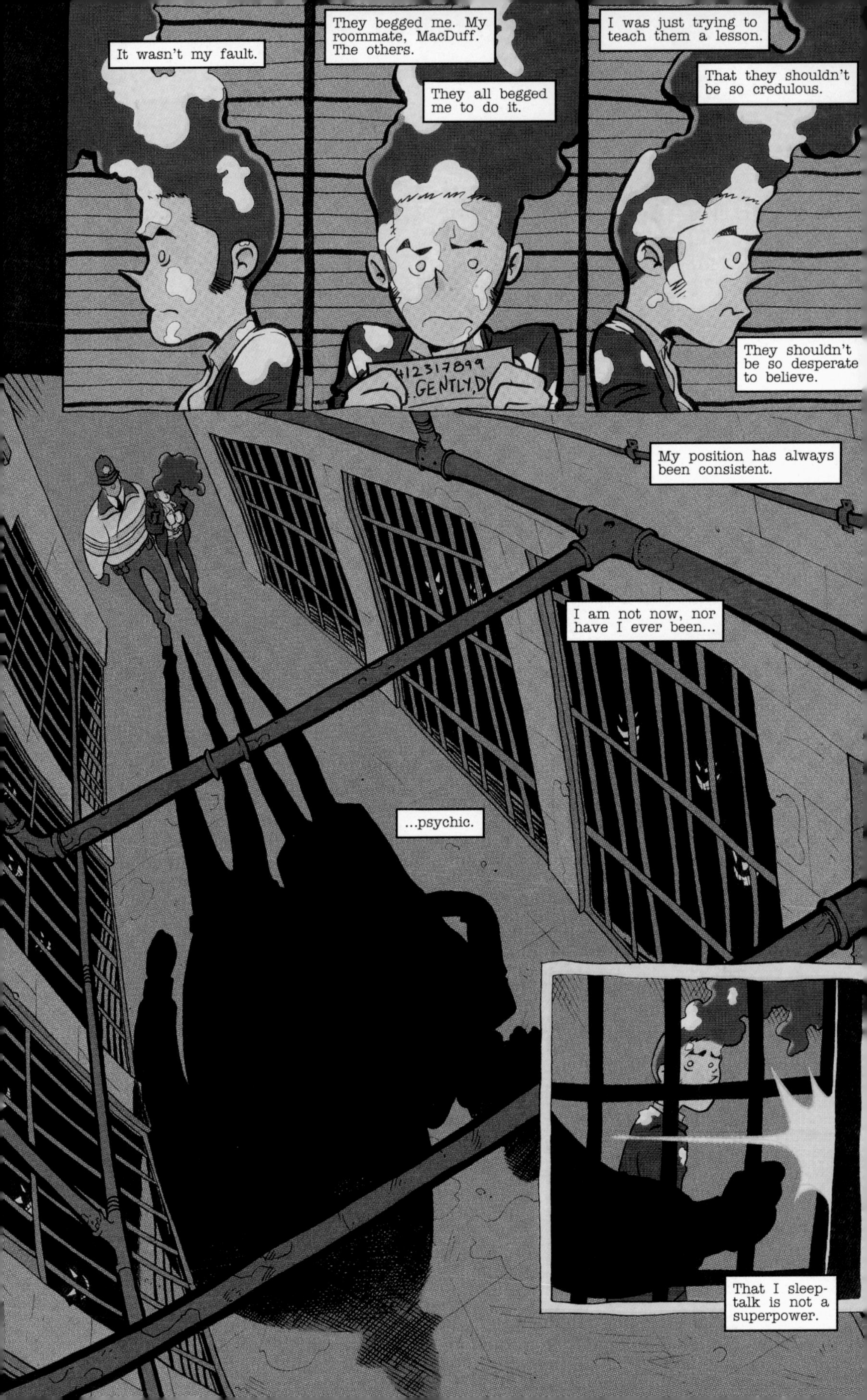
It wasn't my fault.
They begged me. My roommate, MacDuff. The others.
They all begged me to do it.
412317899 .GENTLY,D
I was just trying to teach them a lesson.
That they shouldn't be so credulous.
They shouldn't be so desperate to believe.
My position has always been consistent.
I am not now, nor have I ever been...
...psychic.
That I sleep-talk is not a superpower.

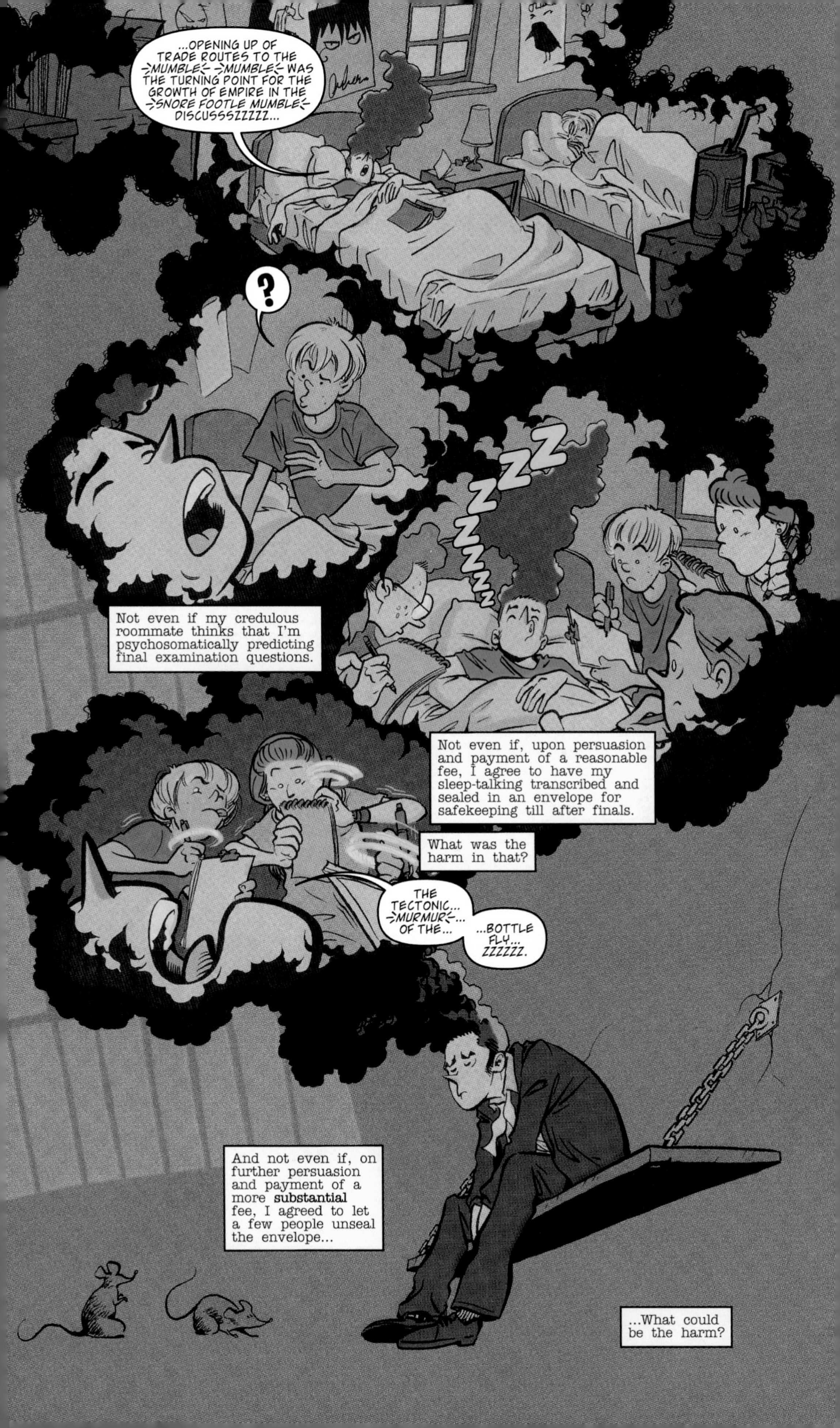

...OPENING UP OF TRADE ROUTES TO THE -MUMBLE- -MUMBLE- WAS THE TURNING POINT FOR THE GROWTH OF EMPIRE IN THE -SNORE FOOTLE MUMBLE- DISCUSSSSZZZZZ...
?
ZZZZZZZZ
Not even if my credulous roommate thinks that I'm psychosomatically predicting final examination questions.
Not even if, upon persuasion and payment of a reasonable fee, I agree to have my sleep-talking transcribed and sealed in an envelope for safekeeping till after finals.
What was the harm in that?
THE TECTONIC... -MURMUR-... OF THE...
...BOTTLE FLY... ZZZZZZ.
And not even if, on further persuasion and payment of a more **substantial** fee, I agreed to let a few people unseal the envelope...
...What could be the harm?

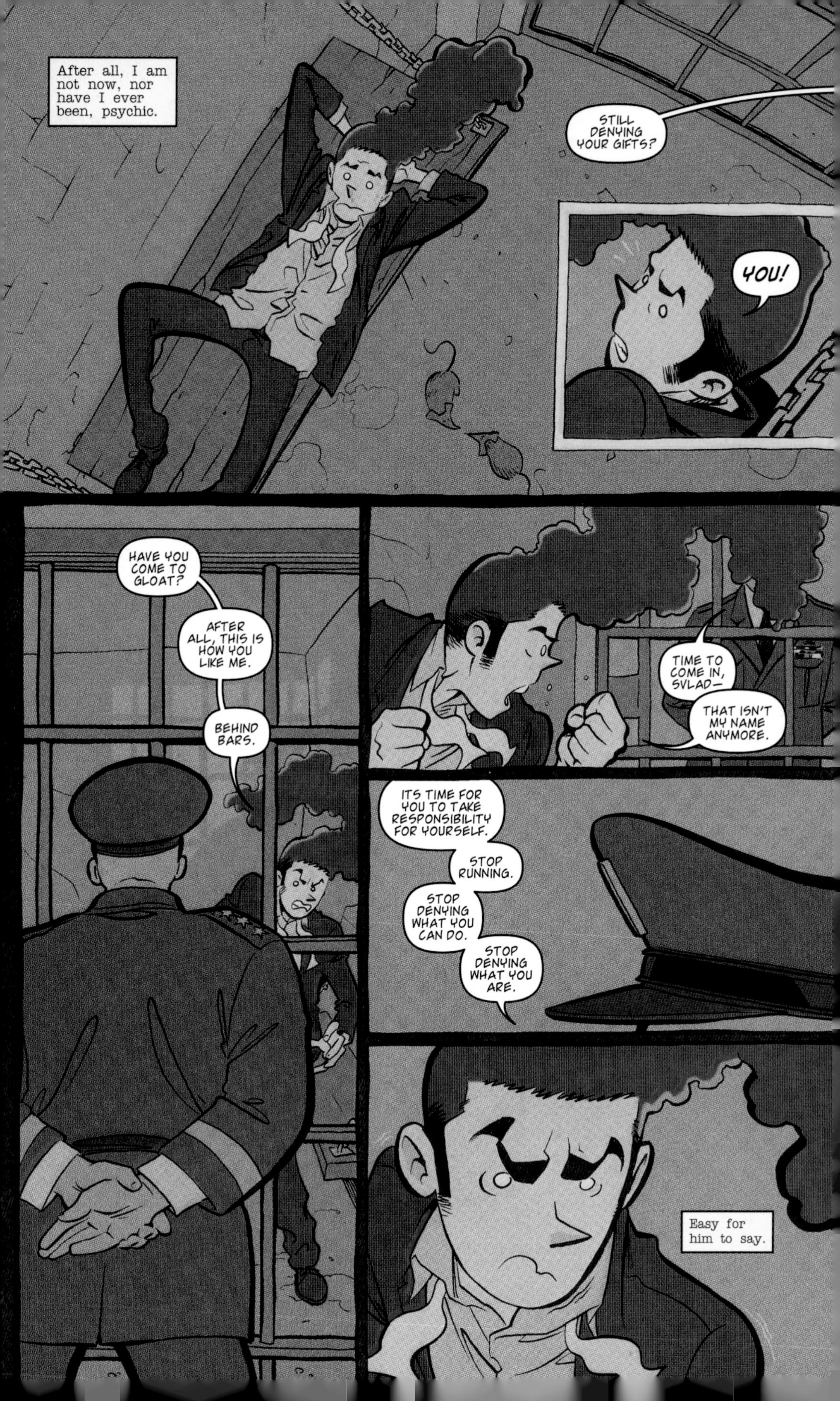
After all, I am not now, nor have I ever been, psychic.
STILL DENYING YOUR GIFTS?
YOU!
HAVE YOU COME TO GLOAT?
AFTER ALL, THIS IS HOW YOU LIKE ME.
BEHIND BARS.
TIME TO COME IN, SVLAD—
THAT ISN'T MY NAME ANYMORE.
ITS TIME FOR YOU TO TAKE RESPONSIBILITY FOR YOURSELF.
STOP RUNNING.
STOP DENYING WHAT YOU CAN DO.
STOP DENYING WHAT YOU ARE.
Easy for him to say.

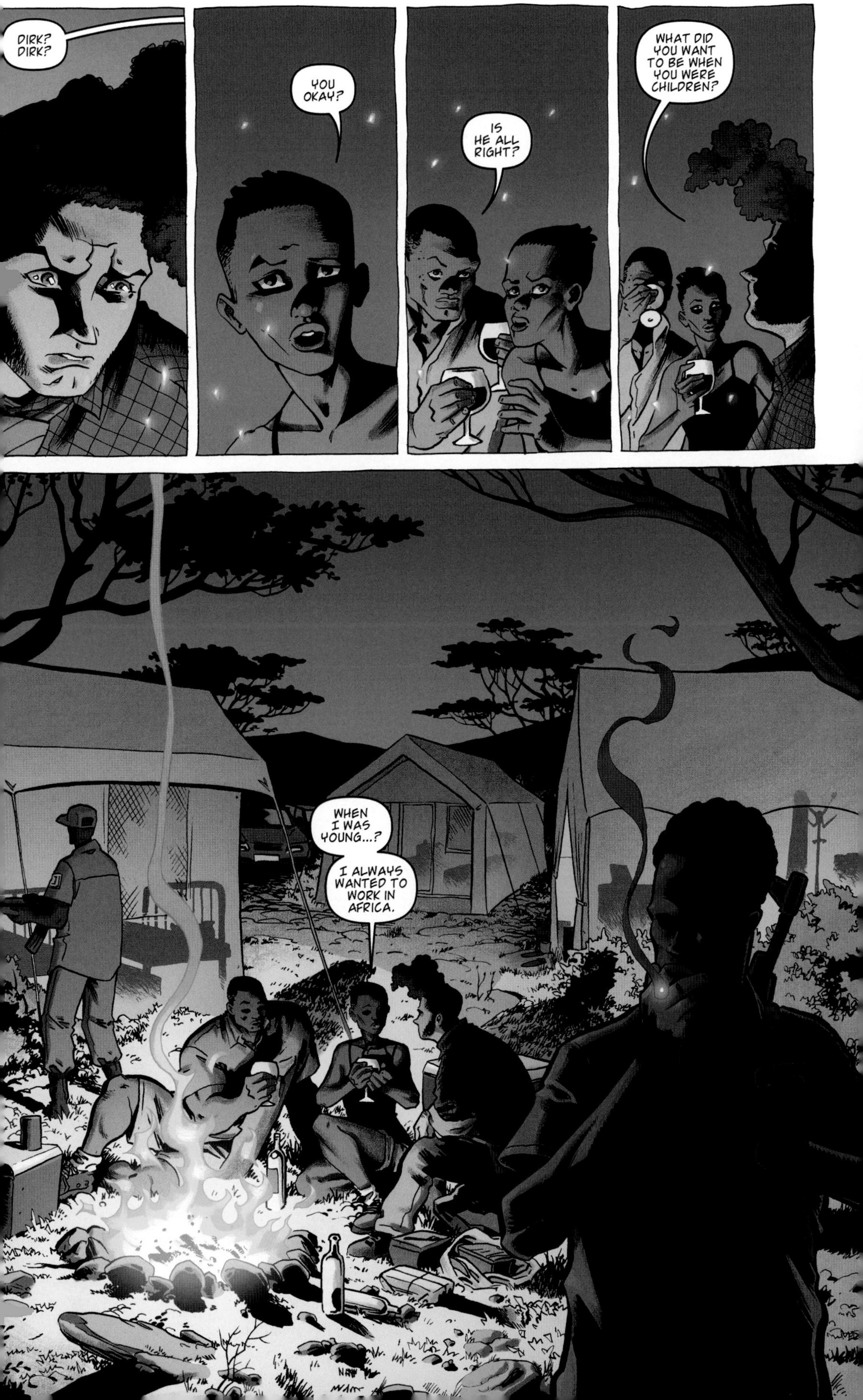
DIRK? DIRK?
YOU OKAY?
IS HE ALL RIGHT?
WHAT DID YOU WANT TO BE WHEN YOU WERE CHILDREN?
WHEN I WAS YOUNG...?
I ALWAYS WANTED TO WORK IN AFRICA.

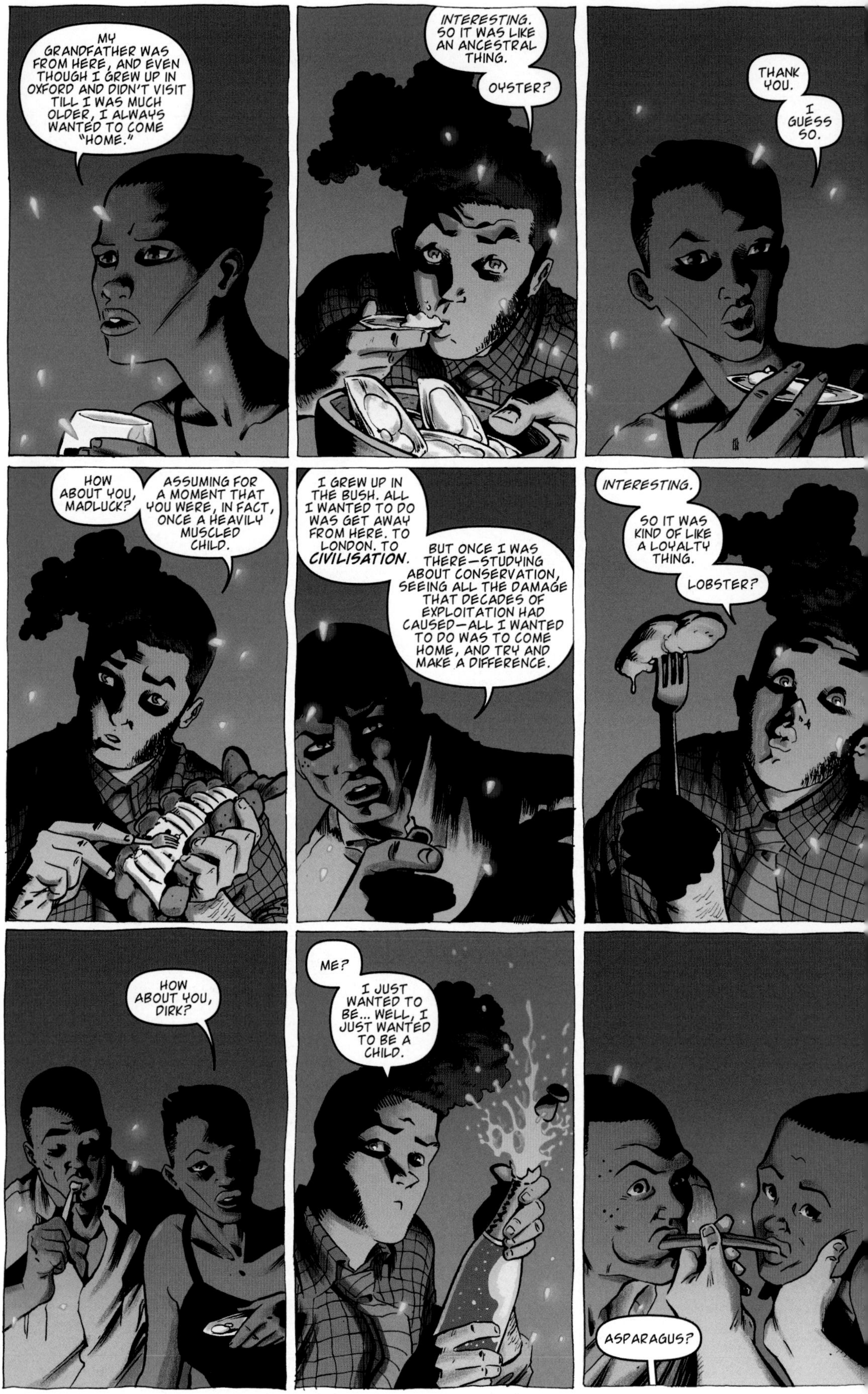
MY GRANDFATHER WAS FROM HERE, AND EVEN THOUGH I GREW UP IN OXFORD AND DIDN'T VISIT TILL I WAS MUCH OLDER, I ALWAYS WANTED TO COME "HOME."
INTERESTING. SO IT WAS LIKE AN ANCESTRAL THING.
OYSTER?
THANK YOU.
I GUESS SO.
HOW ABOUT YOU, MADLUCK?
ASSUMING FOR A MOMENT THAT YOU WERE, IN FACT, ONCE A HEAVILY MUSCLED CHILD.
I GREW UP IN THE BUSH. ALL I WANTED TO DO WAS GET AWAY FROM HERE. TO LONDON. TO CIVILISATION.
BUT ONCE I WAS THERE—STUDYING ABOUT CONSERVATION, SEEING ALL THE DAMAGE THAT DECADES OF EXPLOITATION HAD CAUSED—ALL I WANTED TO DO WAS TO COME HOME, AND TRY AND MAKE A DIFFERENCE.
INTERESTING.
SO IT WAS KIND OF LIKE A LOYALTY THING.
LOBSTER?
HOW ABOUT YOU, DIRK?
ME?
I JUST WANTED TO BE... WELL, I JUST WANTED TO BE A CHILD.
ASPARAGUS?

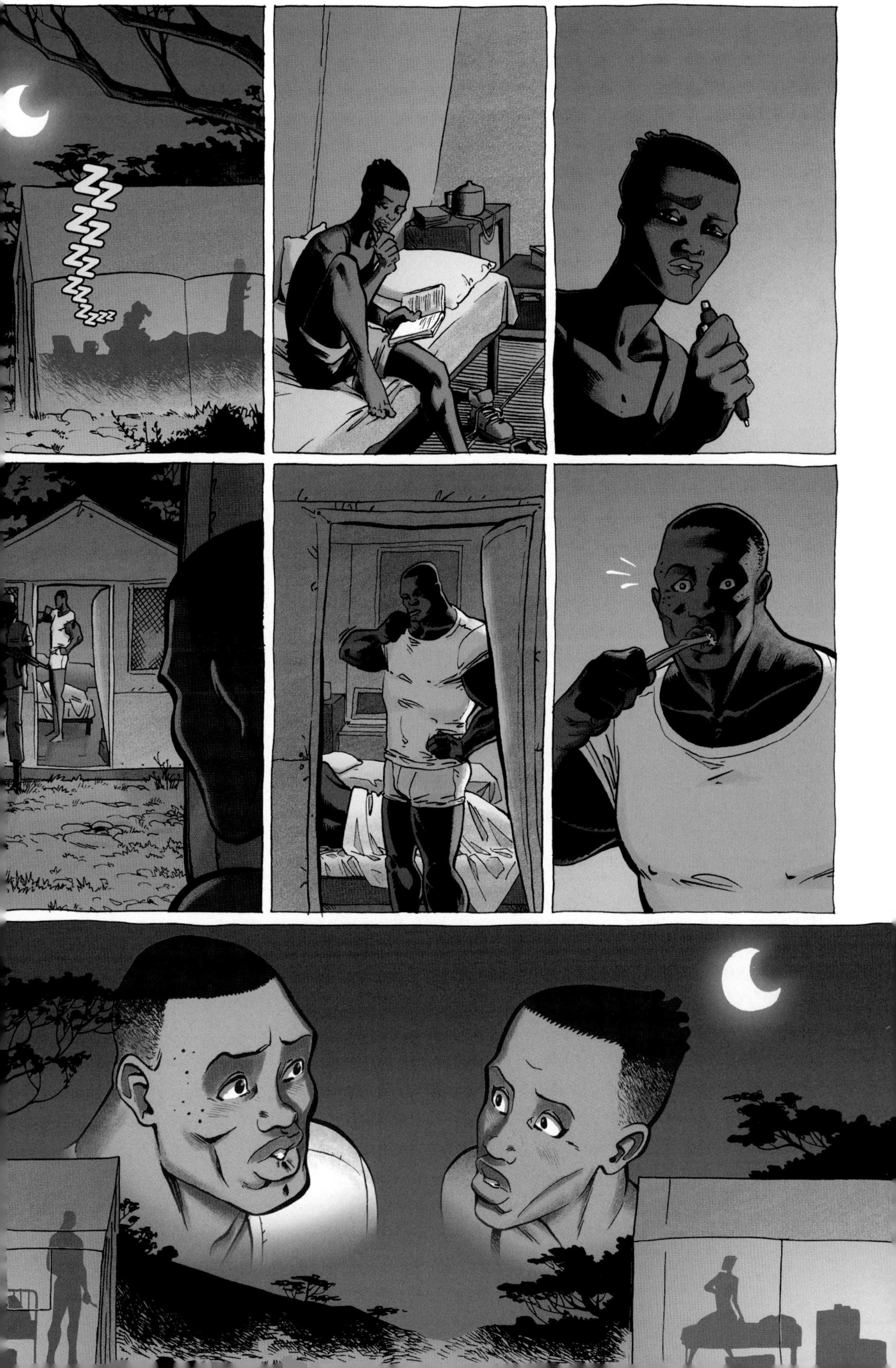
ZZZZZZZZZzzz

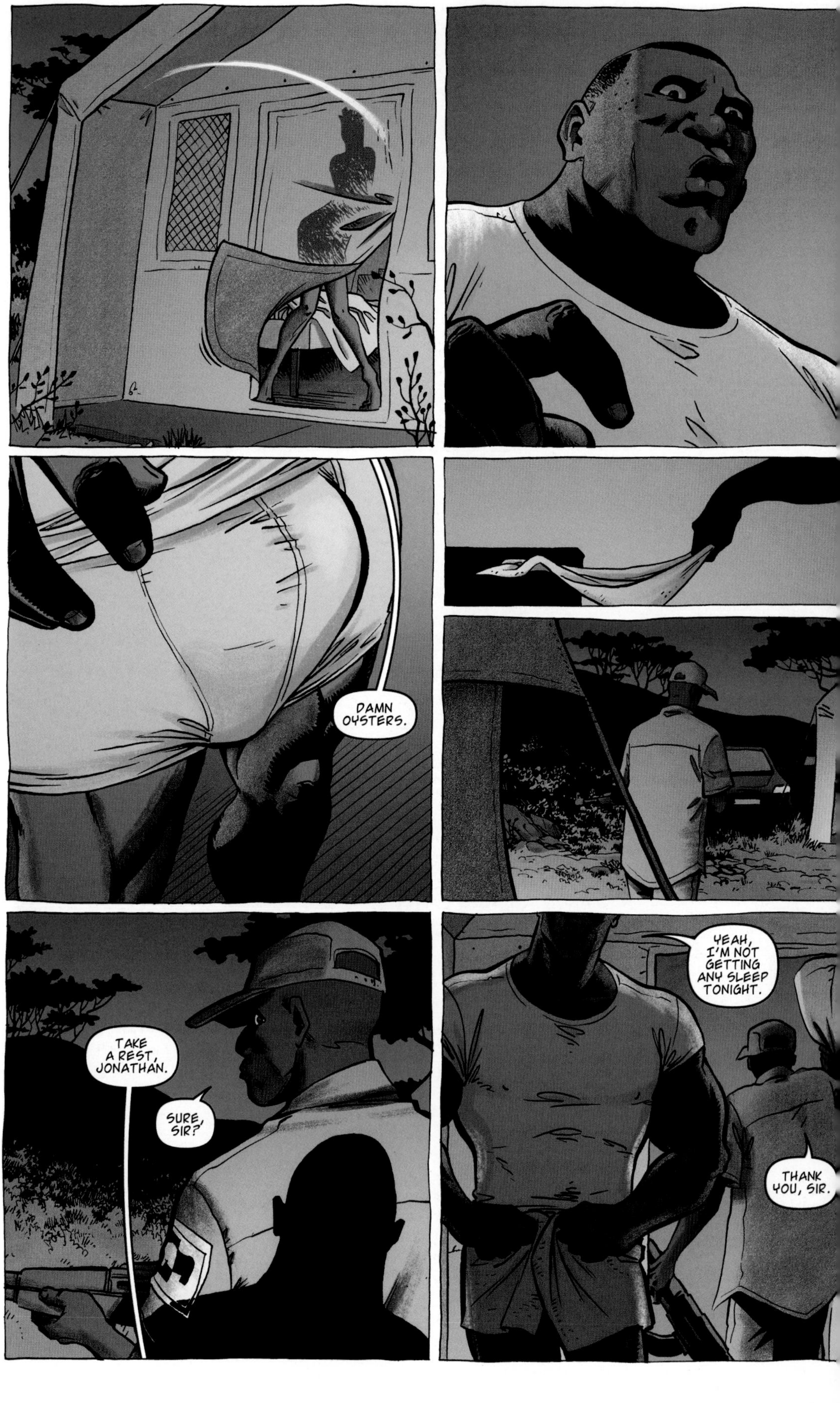
DAMN OYSTERS.
TAKE A REST, JONATHAN.
SURE, SIR?
YEAH, I'M NOT GETTING ANY SLEEP TONIGHT.
THANK YOU, SIR.

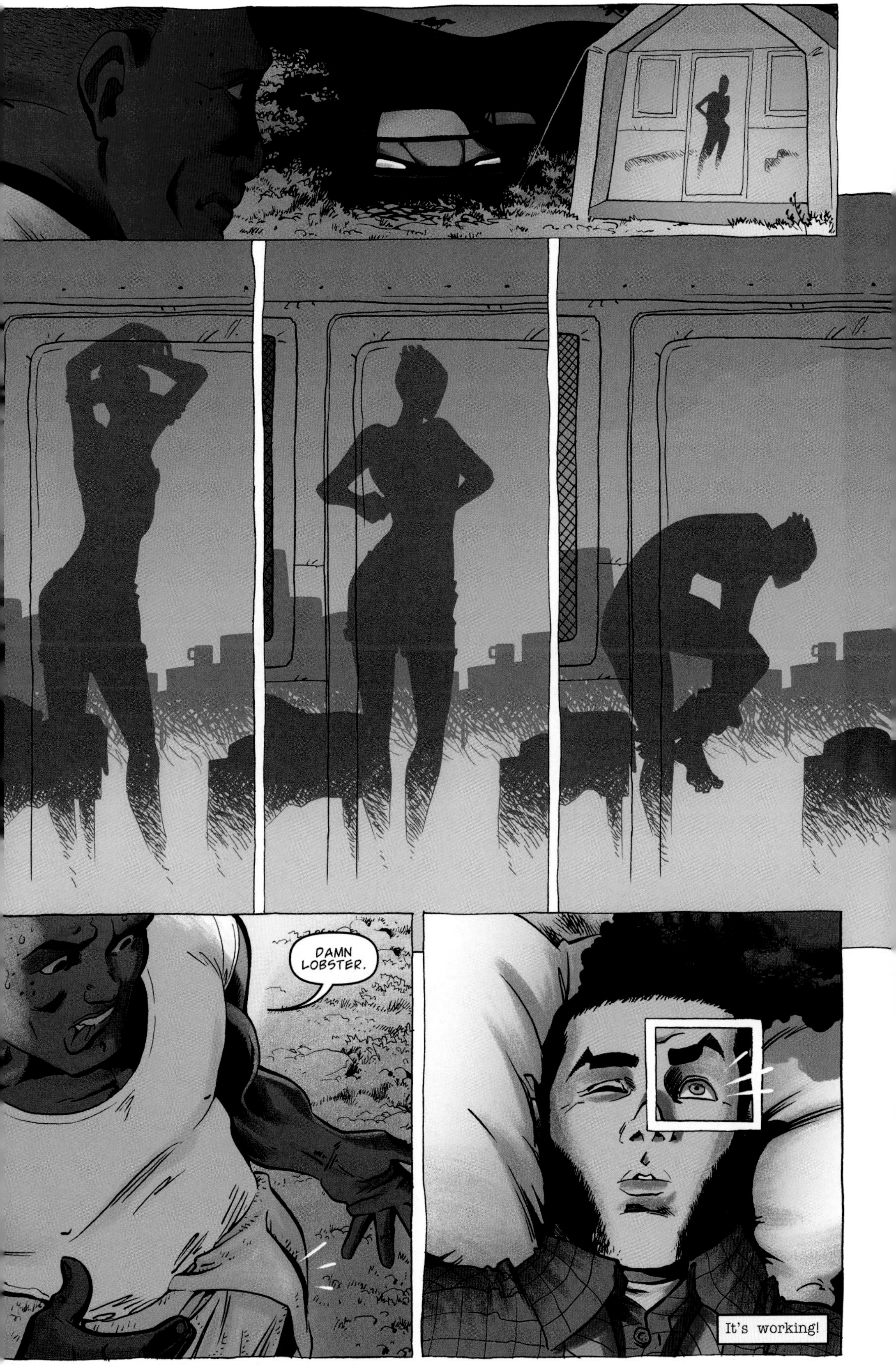
DAMN LOBSTER.
It's working!

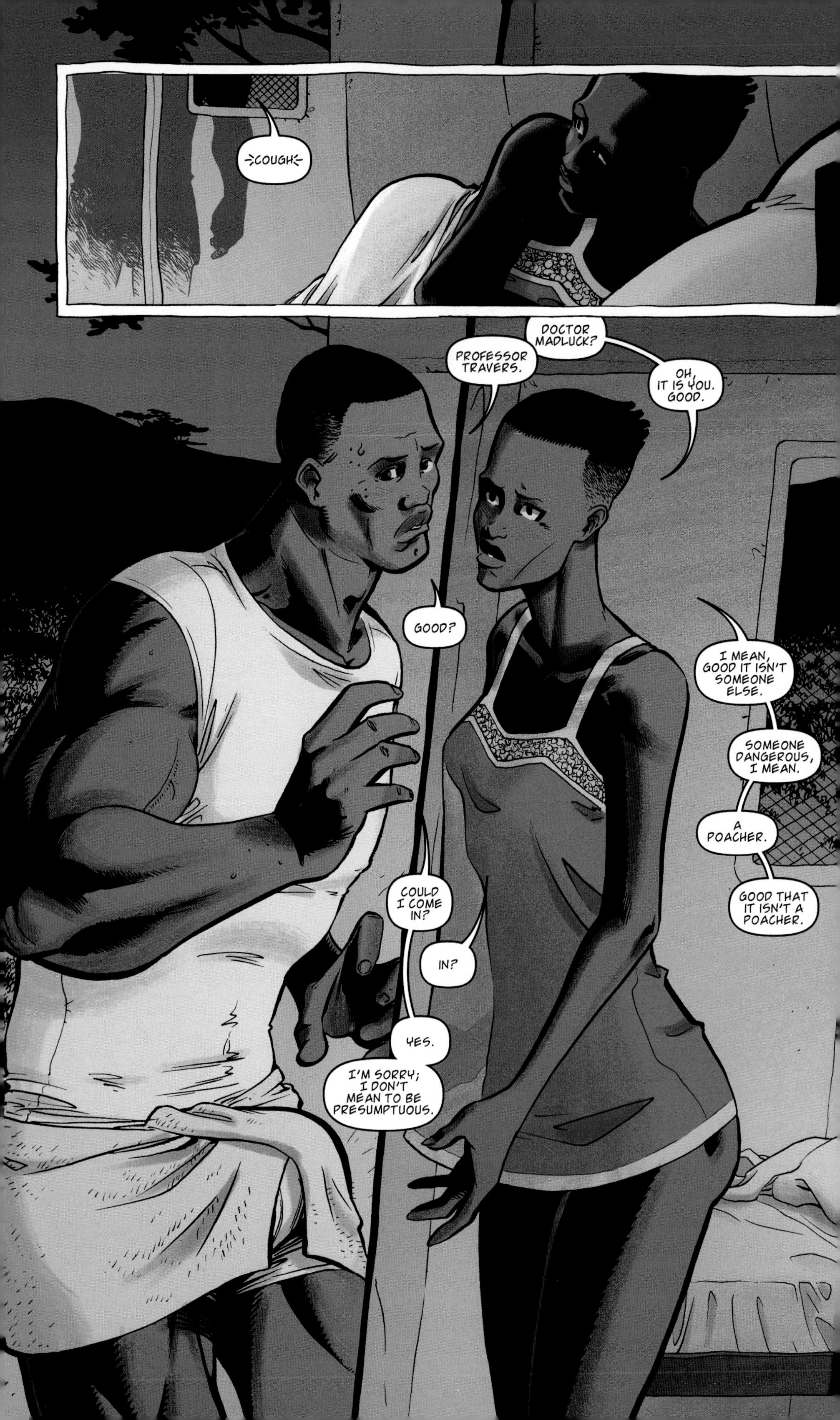
COUGH
DOCTOR MADLUCK?
PROFESSOR TRAVERS.
OH, IT IS YOU. GOOD.
GOOD?
I MEAN, GOOD IT ISN'T SOMEONE ELSE.
SOMEONE DANGEROUS, I MEAN.
A POACHER.
GOOD THAT IT ISN'T A POACHER.
COULD I COME IN?
IN?
YES.
I'M SORRY; I DON'T MEAN TO BE PRESUMPTUOUS.

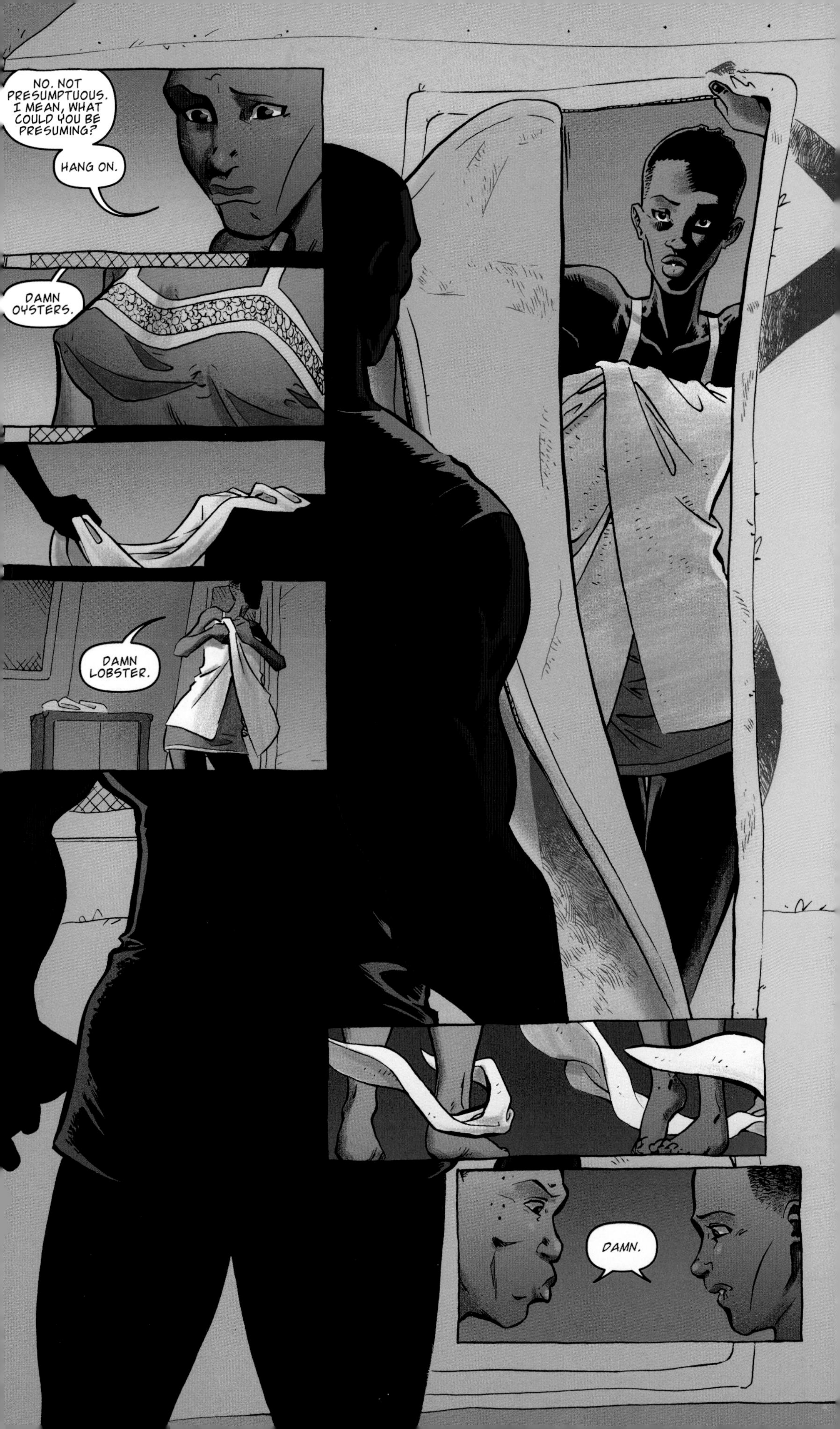
NO. NOT PRESUMPTUOUS. I MEAN, WHAT COULD YOU BE PRESUMING?
HANG ON.
DAMN OYSTERS.
DAMN LOBSTER.
DAMN.

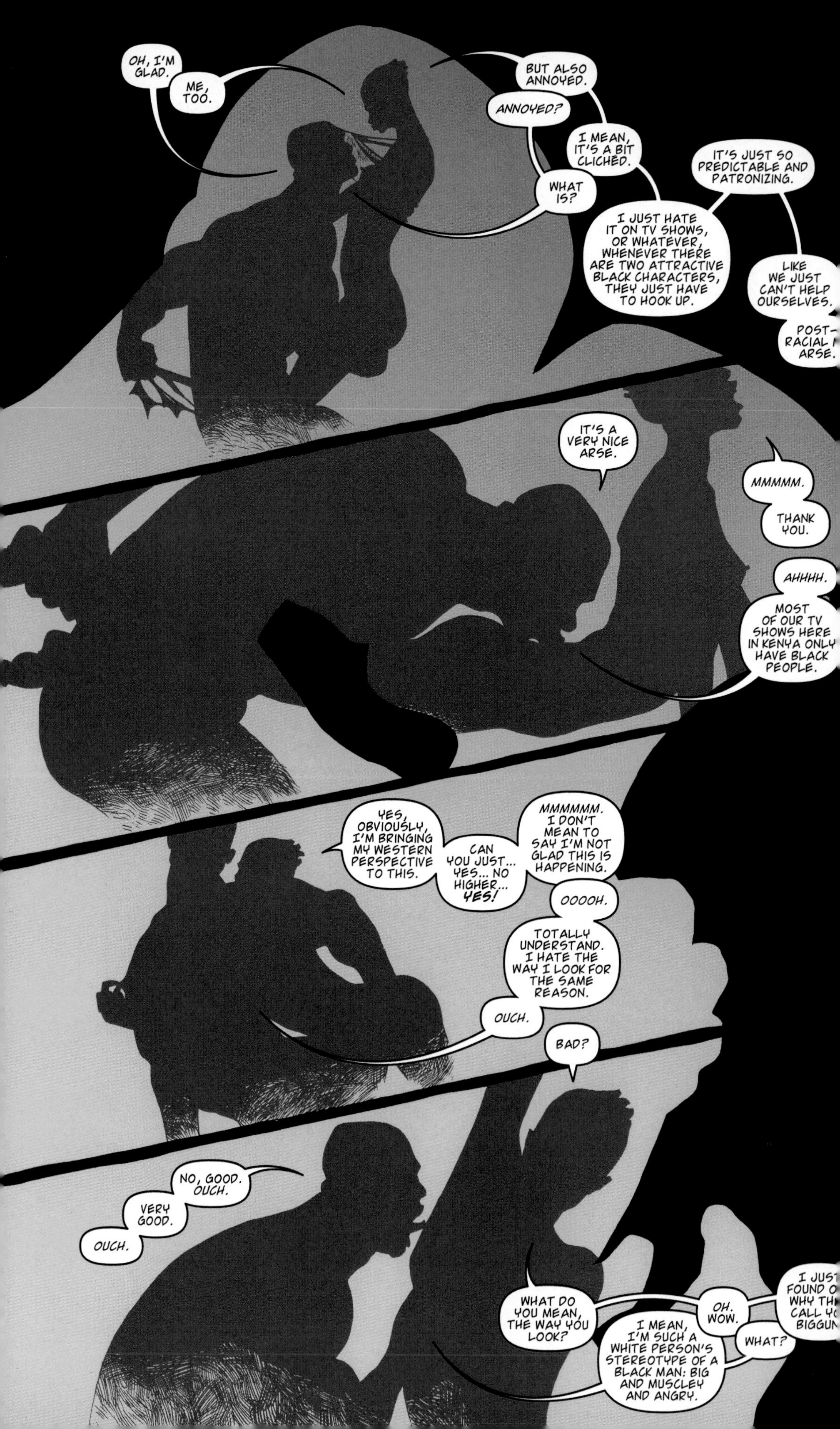
OH, I'M GLAD.
ME, TOO.
BUT ALSO ANNOYED.
ANNOYED?
I MEAN, IT'S A BIT CLICHED.
WHAT IS?
I JUST HATE IT ON TV SHOWS, OR WHATEVER, WHENEVER THERE ARE TWO ATTRACTIVE BLACK CHARACTERS, THEY JUST HAVE TO HOOK UP.
IT'S JUST SO PREDICTABLE AND PATRONIZING.
LIKE WE JUST CAN'T HELP OURSELVES.
IT'S A VERY NICE ARSE.
MMMMM.
THANK YOU.
AHHHH.
MOST OF OUR TV SHOWS HERE IN KENYA ONLY HAVE BLACK PEOPLE.
YES, OBVIOUSLY, I'M BRINGING MY WESTERN PERSPECTIVE TO THIS.
MMMMMM. I DON'T MEAN TO SAY I'M NOT GLAD THIS IS HAPPENING.
CAN YOU JUST... YES... NO HIGHER... YES!
OOOOH.
TOTALLY UNDERSTAND. I HATE THE WAY I LOOK FOR THE SAME REASON.
OUCH.
BAD?
NO, GOOD. OUCH.
VERY GOOD.
OUCH.
WHAT DO YOU MEAN, THE WAY YOU LOOK?
I MEAN, I'M SUCH A WHITE PERSON'S STEREOTYPE OF A BLACK MAN: BIG AND MUSCLEY AND ANGRY.
OH. WOW.
WHAT?

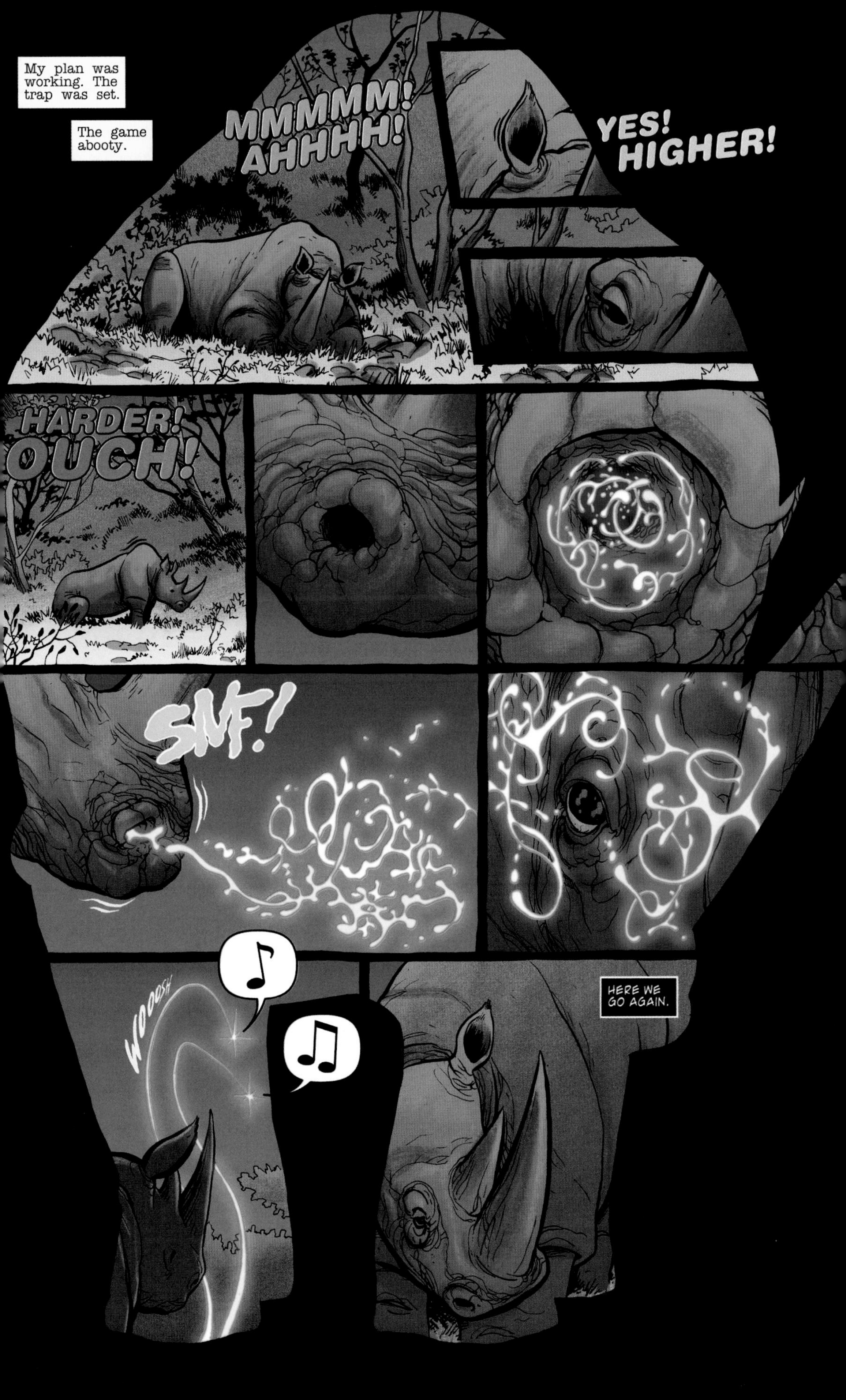

My plan was working. The trap was set.
The game abooty.
MMMMM! AHHHH!
YES! HIGHER!
HARDER! OUCH!
SNF!
WOOOSH
HERE WE GO AGAIN.

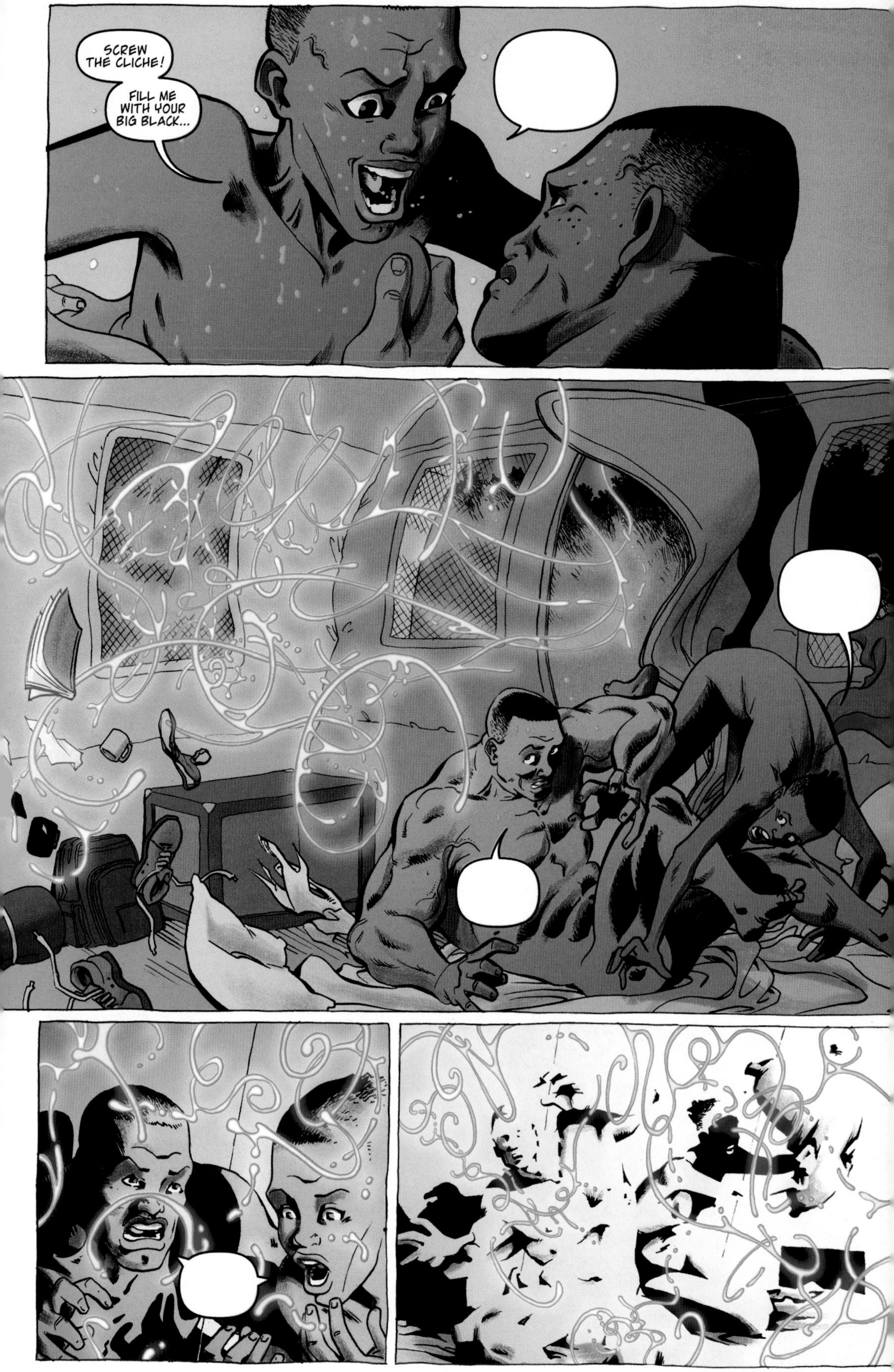
SCREW THE CLICHE!
FILL ME WITH YOUR BIG BLACK...

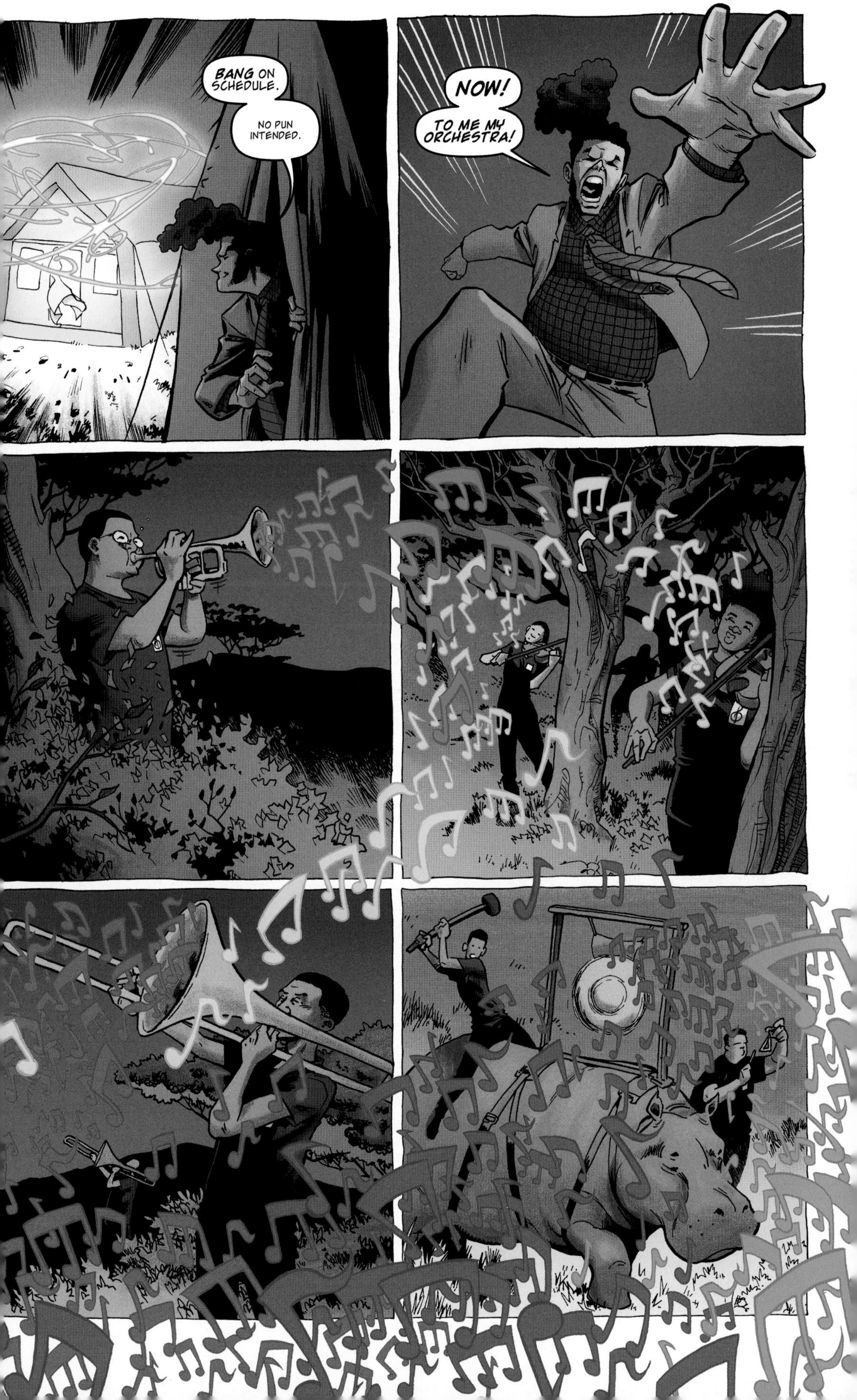
BANG ON SCHEDULE.
NO PUN INTENDED.
NOW!
TO ME MY ORCHESTRA!

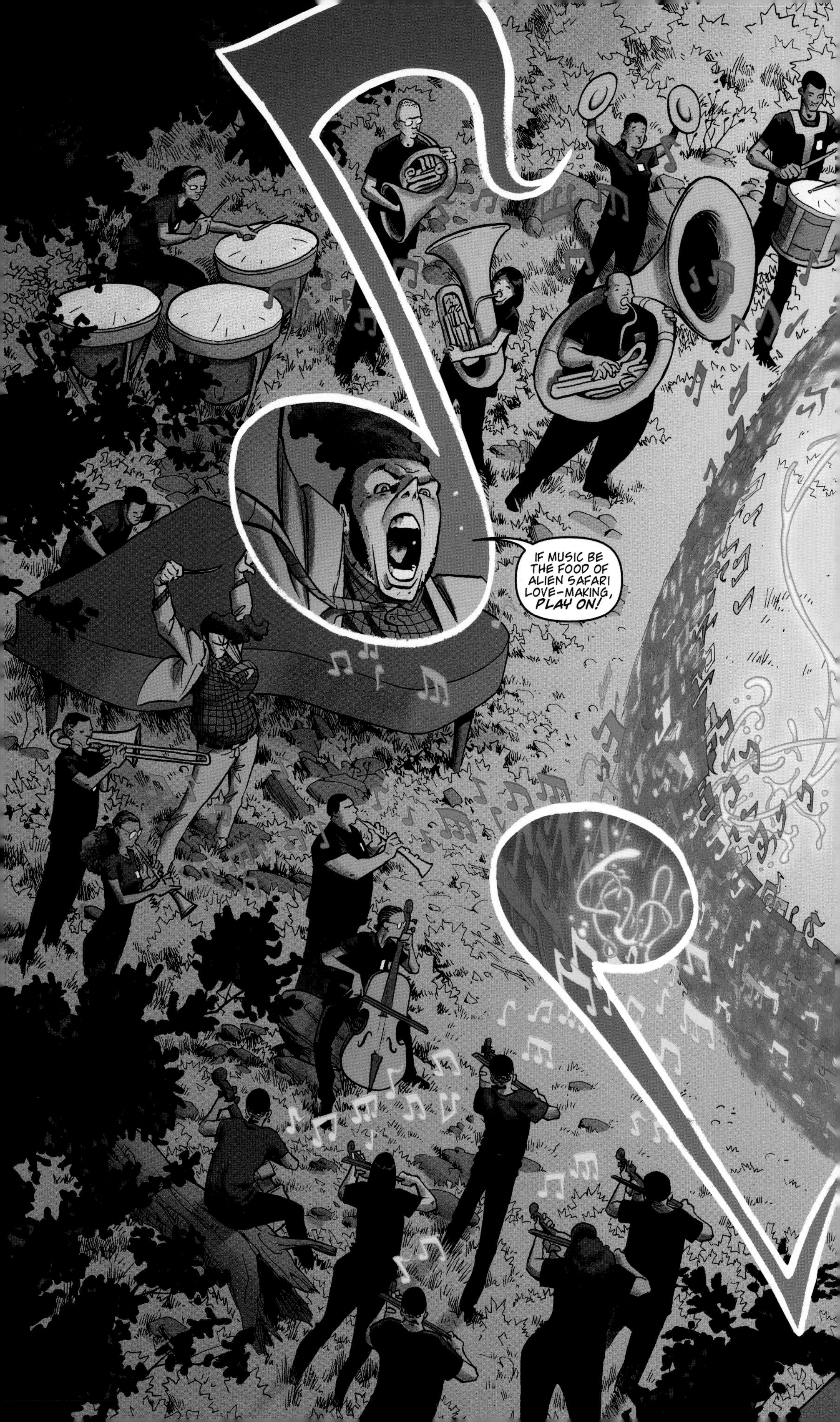
IF MUSIC BE THE FOOD OF ALIEN SAFARI LOVE-MAKING, PLAY ON!

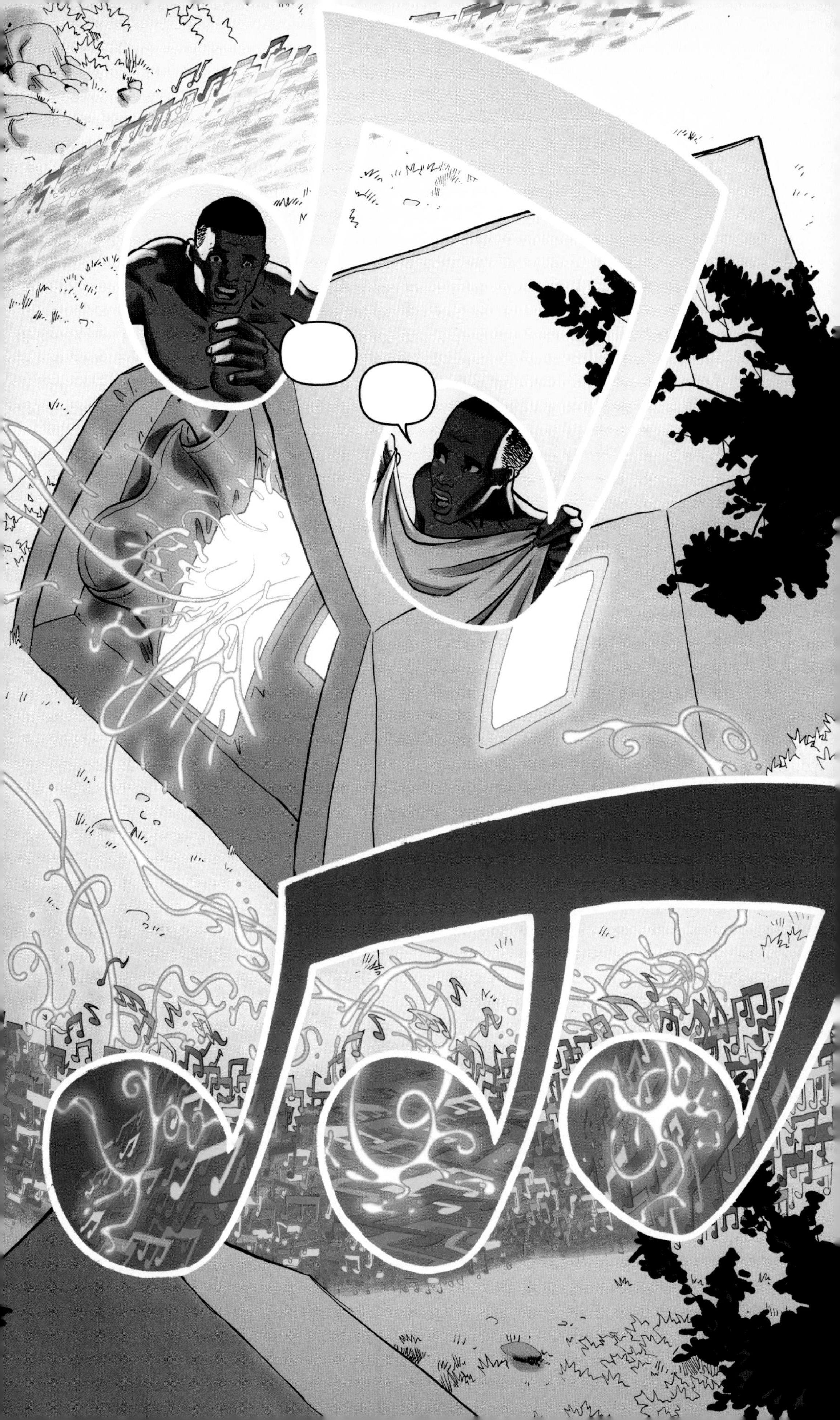

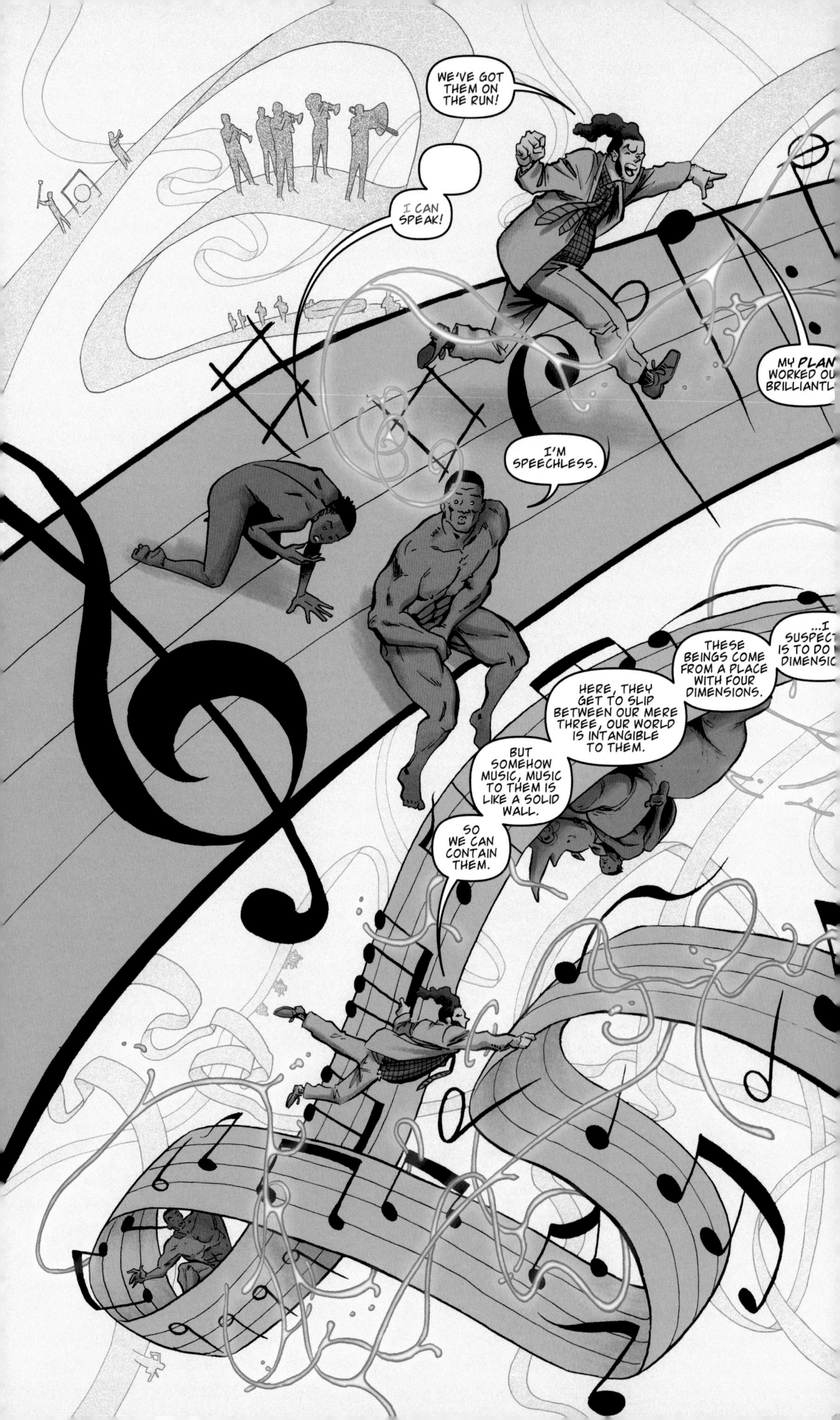
WE'VE GOT THEM ON THE RUN!
I CAN SPEAK!
MY PLAN WORKED OU BRILLIANTL
I'M SPEECHLESS.
...I SUSPECT IS TO DO DIMENSIO
THESE BEINGS COME FROM A PLACE WITH FOUR DIMENSIONS.
HERE, THEY GET TO SLIP BETWEEN OUR MERE THREE, OUR WORLD IS INTANGIBLE TO THEM.
BUT SOMEHOW MUSIC, MUSIC TO THEM IS LIKE A SOLID WALL.
SO WE CAN CONTAIN THEM.

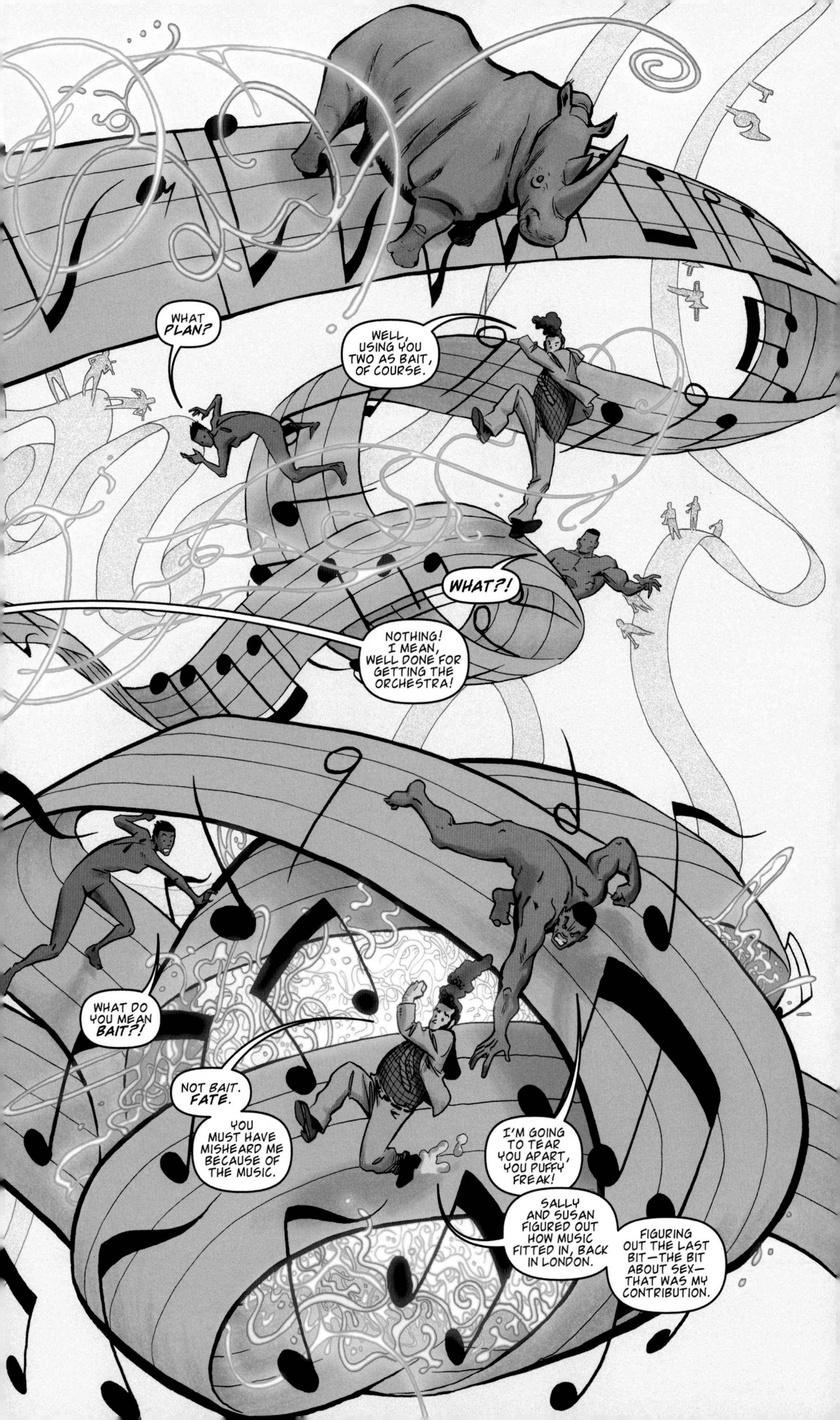
WHAT PLAN?
WELL, USING YOU TWO AS BAIT, OF COURSE.
WHAT?!
NOTHING! I MEAN, WELL DONE FOR GETTING THE ORCHESTRA!
WHAT DO YOU MEAN BAIT?!
NOT BAIT. FATE.
YOU MUST HAVE MISHEARD ME BECAUSE OF THE MUSIC.
I'M GOING TO TEAR YOU APART, YOU PUFFY FREAK!
SALLY AND SUSAN FIGURED OUT HOW MUSIC FITTED IN, BACK IN LONDON.
FIGURING OUT THE LAST BIT—THE BIT ABOUT SEX—THAT WAS MY CONTRIBUTION.

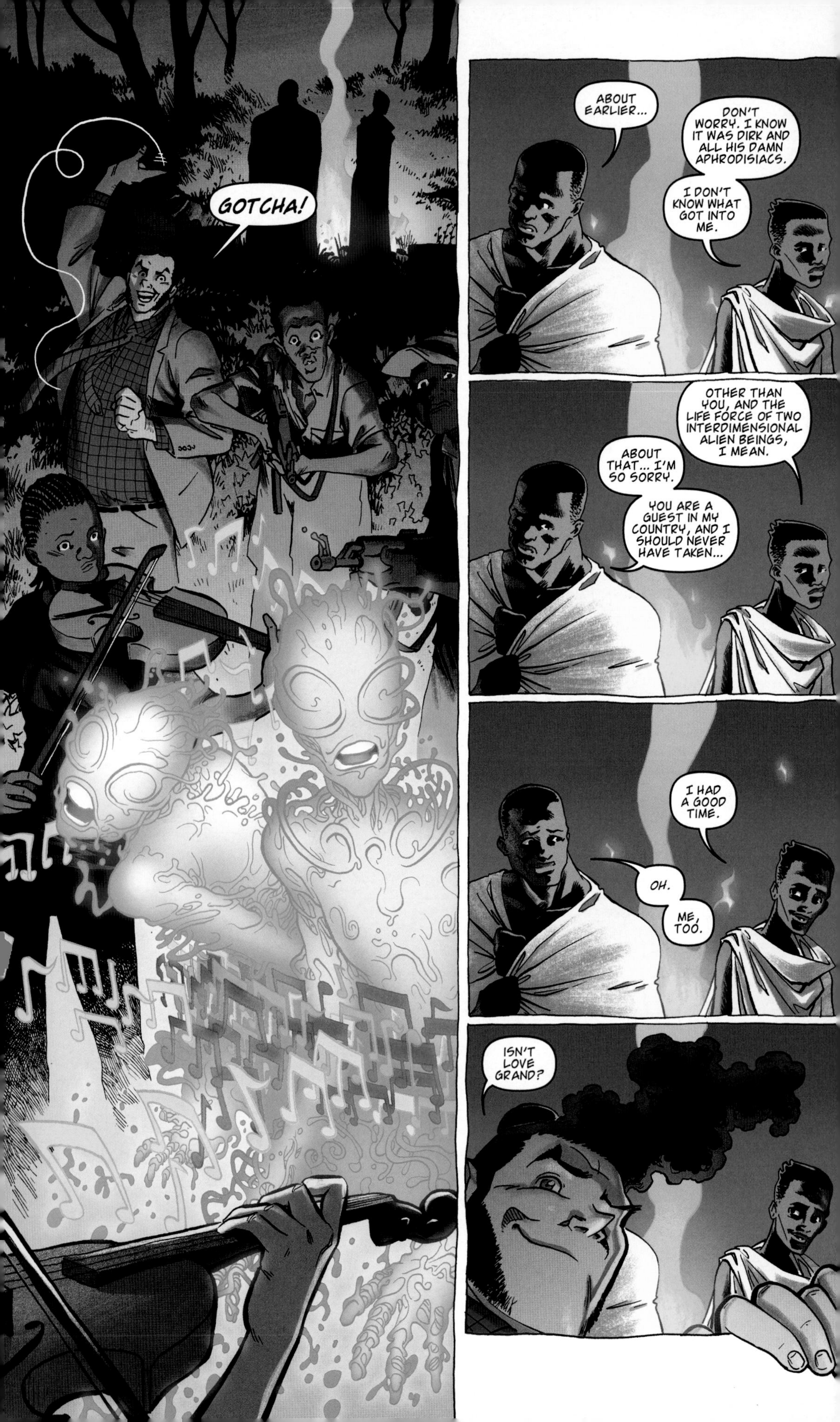
GOTCHA!
ABOUT EARLIER...
DON'T WORRY. I KNOW IT WAS DIRK AND ALL HIS DAMN APHRODISIACS.
I DON'T KNOW WHAT GOT INTO ME.
OTHER THAN YOU, AND THE LIFE FORCE OF TWO INTERDIMENSIONAL ALIEN BEINGS, I MEAN.
ABOUT THAT... I'M SO SORRY.
YOU ARE A GUEST IN MY COUNTRY, AND I SHOULD NEVER HAVE TAKEN...
I HAD A GOOD TIME.
OH.
ME, TOO.
ISN'T LOVE GRAND?

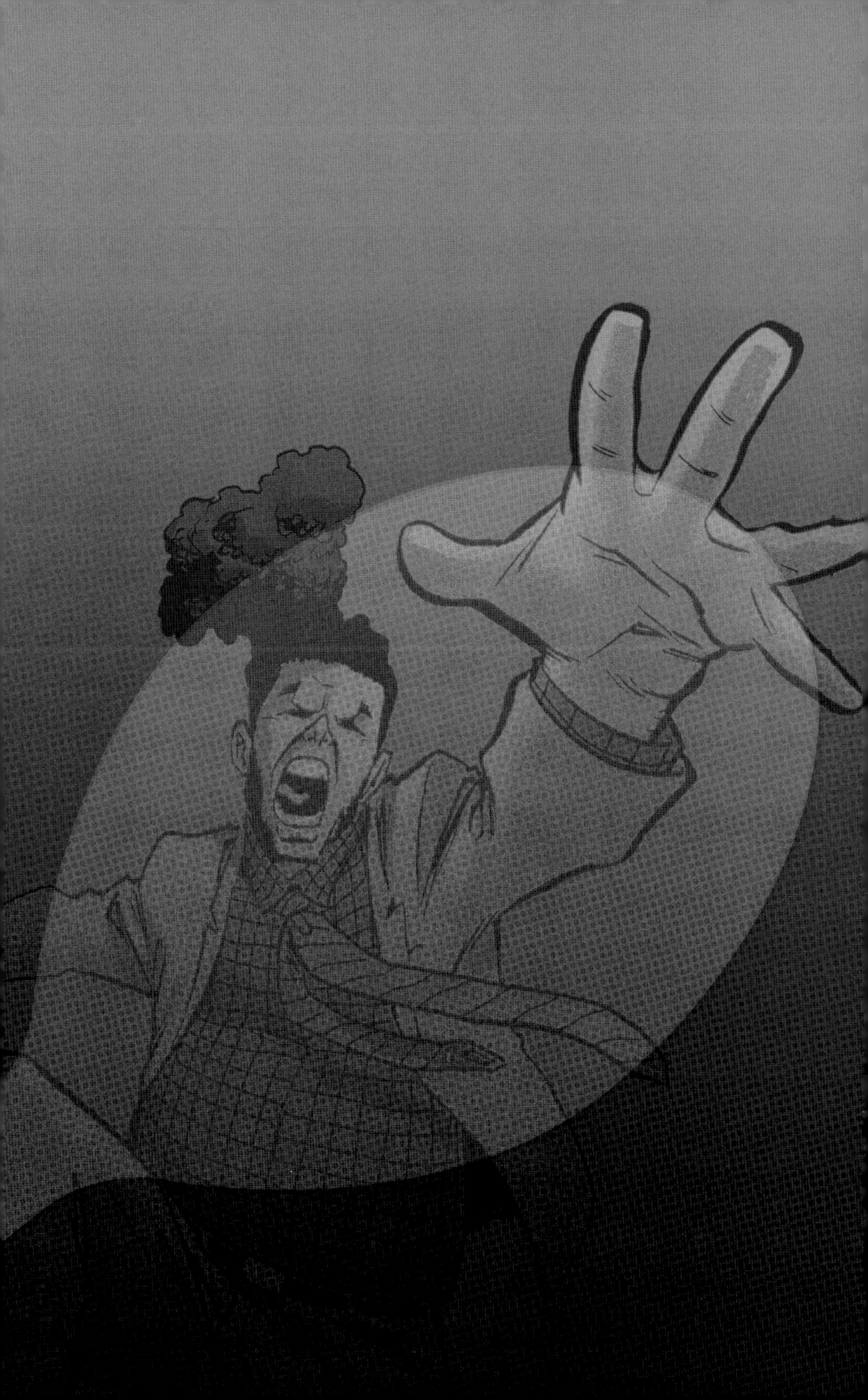

CHAPTER FIVE

Cover Art by **ILIAS KYRIAZI**

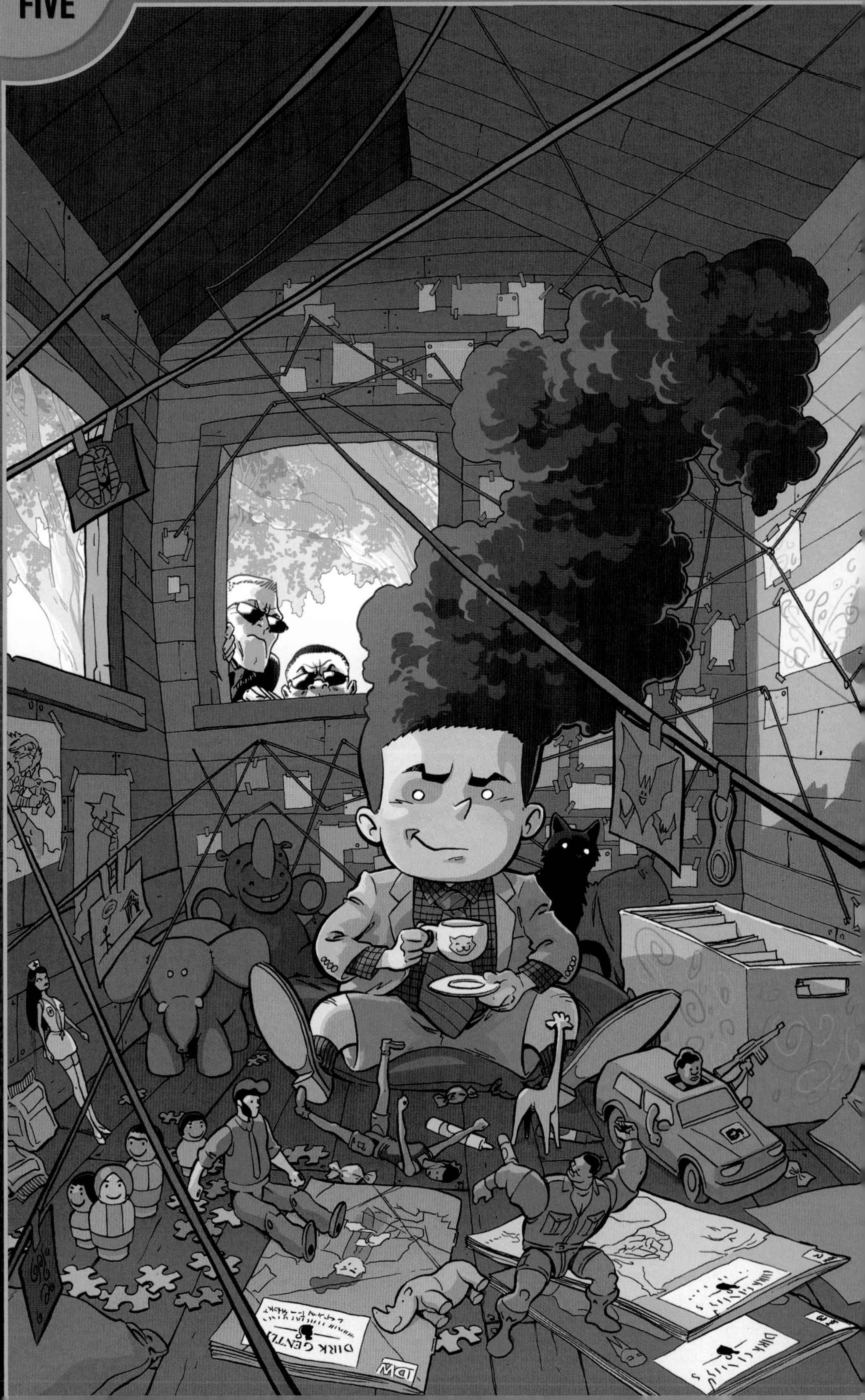

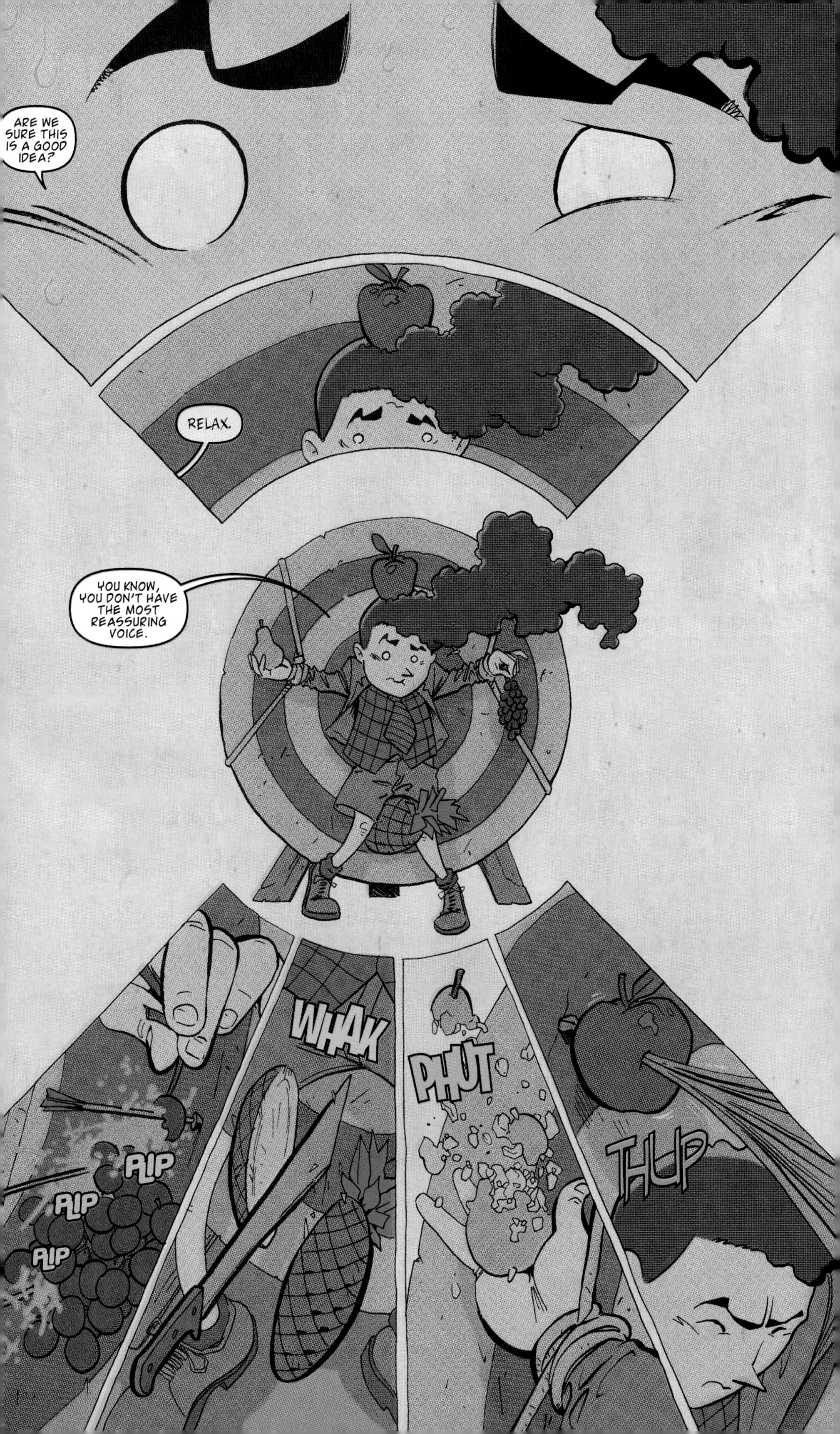
ARE WE SURE THIS IS A GOOD IDEA?
RELAX.
YOU KNOW, YOU DON'T HAVE THE MOST REASSURING VOICE.
PLIP
PLIP
PLIP
WHAK
PHUT
THUP

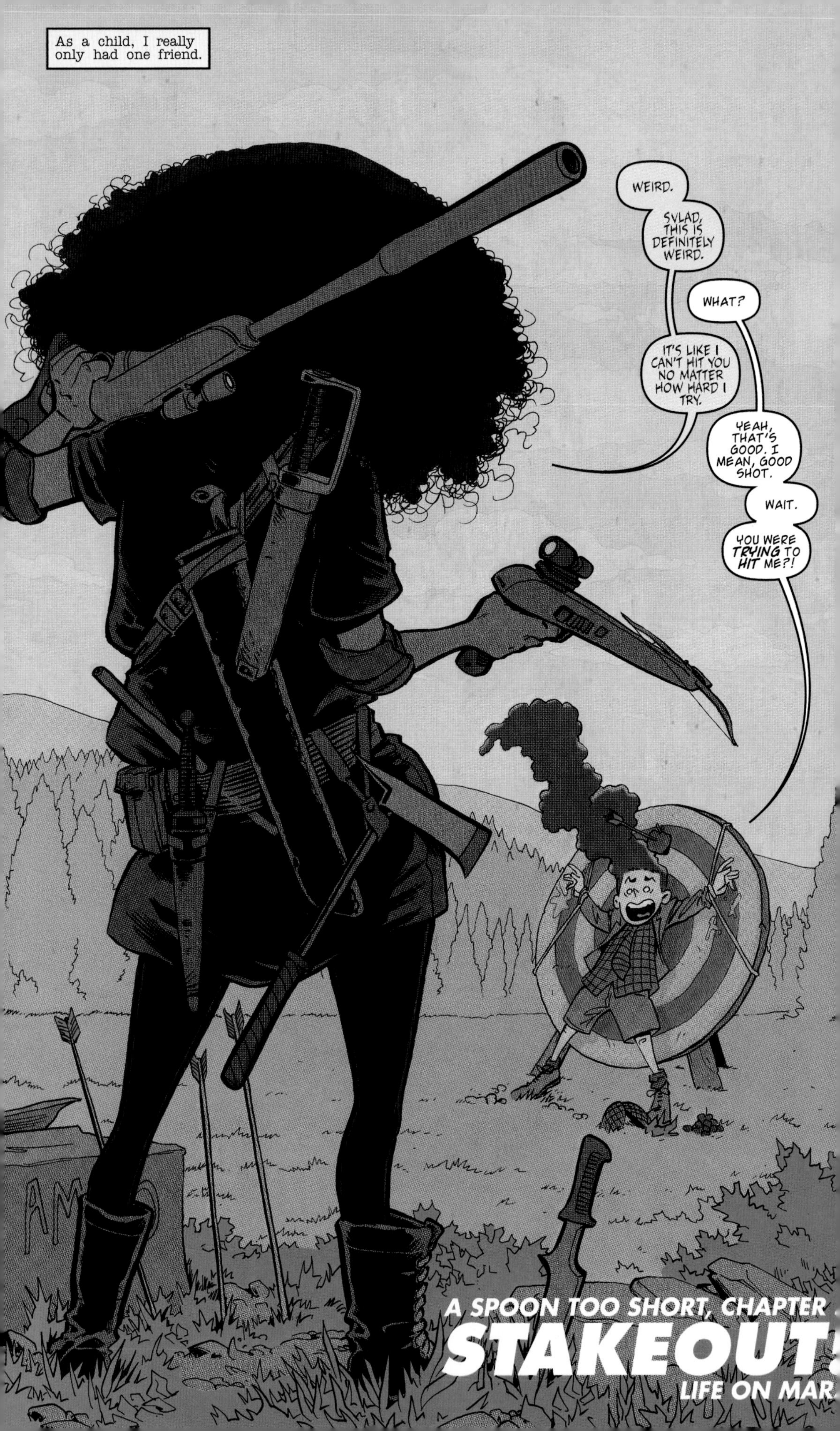
As a child, I really only had one friend.
WEIRD.
SVLAD, THIS IS DEFINITELY WEIRD.
WHAT?
IT'S LIKE I CAN'T HIT YOU NO MATTER HOW HARD I TRY.
YEAH, THAT'S GOOD. I MEAN, GOOD SHOT.
WAIT.
YOU WERE TRYING TO HIT ME?!
A SPOON TOO SHORT, CHAPTER
STAKEOUT
LIFE ON MAR

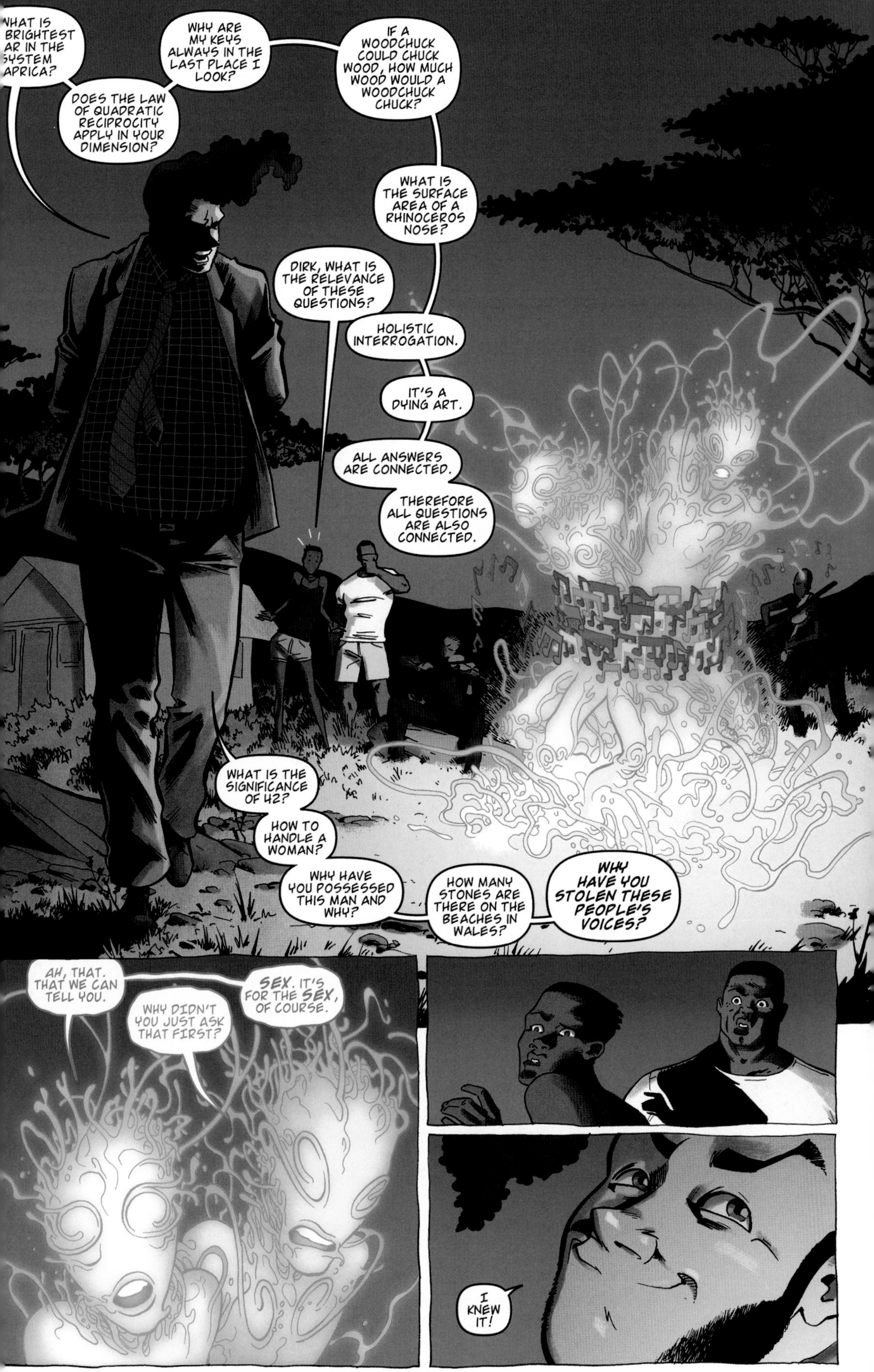
WHAT IS BRIGHTEST AR IN THE SYSTEM APRICA?
DOES THE LAW OF QUADRATIC RECIPROCITY APPLY IN YOUR DIMENSION?
WHY ARE MY KEYS ALWAYS IN THE LAST PLACE I LOOK?
IF A WOODCHUCK COULD CHUCK WOOD, HOW MUCH WOOD WOULD A WOODCHUCK CHUCK?
WHAT IS THE SURFACE AREA OF A RHINOCEROS NOSE?
DIRK, WHAT IS THE RELEVANCE OF THESE QUESTIONS?
HOLISTIC INTERROGATION.
IT'S A DYING ART.
ALL ANSWERS ARE CONNECTED.
THEREFORE ALL QUESTIONS ARE ALSO CONNECTED.
WHAT IS THE SIGNIFICANCE OF 42?
HOW TO HANDLE A WOMAN?
WHY HAVE YOU POSSESSED THIS MAN AND WHY?
HOW MANY STONES ARE THERE ON THE BEACHES IN WALES?
WHY HAVE YOU STOLEN THESE PEOPLE'S VOICES?
AH, THAT. THAT WE CAN TELL YOU.
WHY DIDN'T YOU JUST ASK THAT FIRST?
SEX. IT'S FOR THE SEX, OF COURSE.
I KNEW IT!

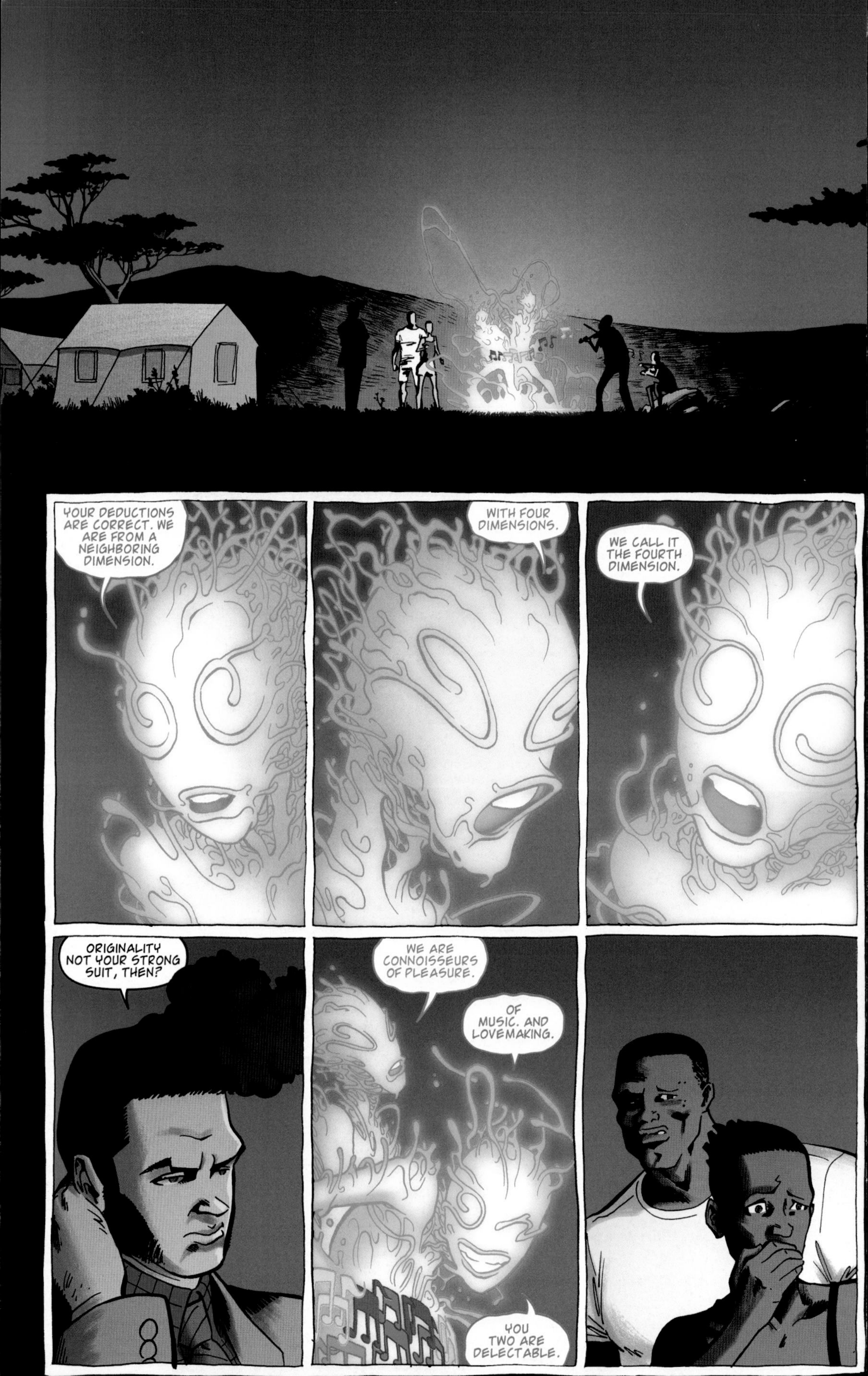
YOUR DEDUCTIONS ARE CORRECT. WE ARE FROM A NEIGHBORING DIMENSION.
WITH FOUR DIMENSIONS.
WE CALL IT THE FOURTH DIMENSION.
ORIGINALITY NOT YOUR STRONG SUIT, THEN?
WE ARE CONNOISSEURS OF PLEASURE.
OF MUSIC. AND LOVEMAKING.
YOU TWO ARE DELECTABLE.

WHEN WE FOUND A PATH INTO YOUR DIMENSION...

WE WERE IMMEDIATELY DRAWN BY THE CARNAL OPPORTUNITIES OFFERED BY YOUR DELIGHTFUL RACE.

SO WARM. SO SQUIRMY. SO FULL OF SOUNDS AND SQUEALS.

ABOUT THAT...

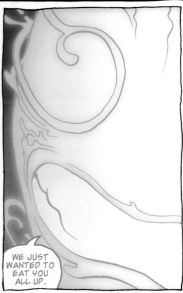

WE JUST WANTED TO EAT YOU ALL UP.

SUCK THE MARROW FROM YOUR BONES.

BUT NOT IN A CANNIBAL-LY TYPE OF WAY.

NO. JUST AS A KIND OF... ORAL STIMULANT...

YOU SUCKED OUT OUR VOICES, OUR ABILITY TO COMMUNICATE...

...AS AN APHRODISIAC?

YES! SOLVED IT!

FOR REALS THIS TIME.

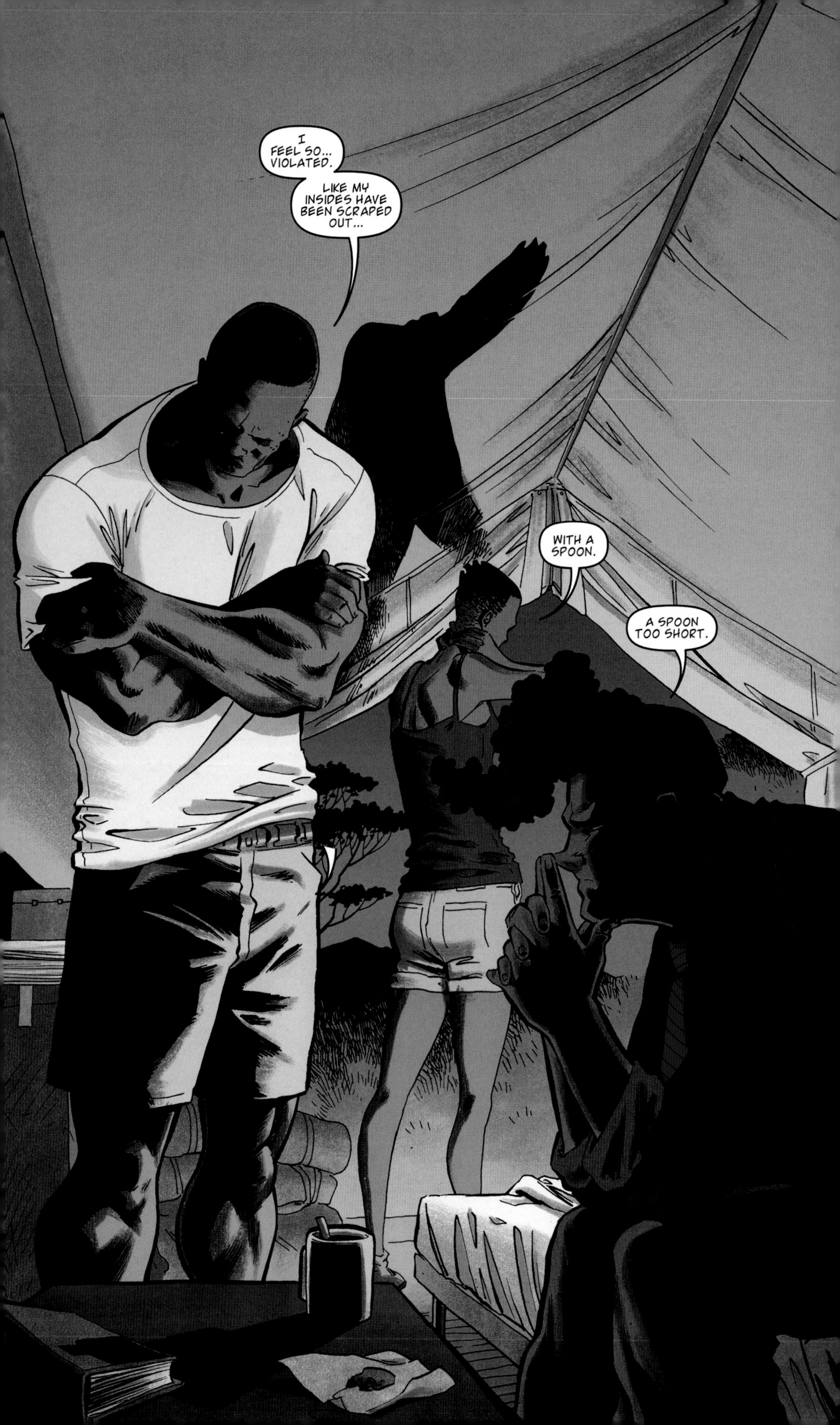
I FEEL SO... VIOLATED.
LIKE MY INSIDES HAVE BEEN SCRAPED OUT...
WITH A SPOON.
A SPOON TOO SHORT.

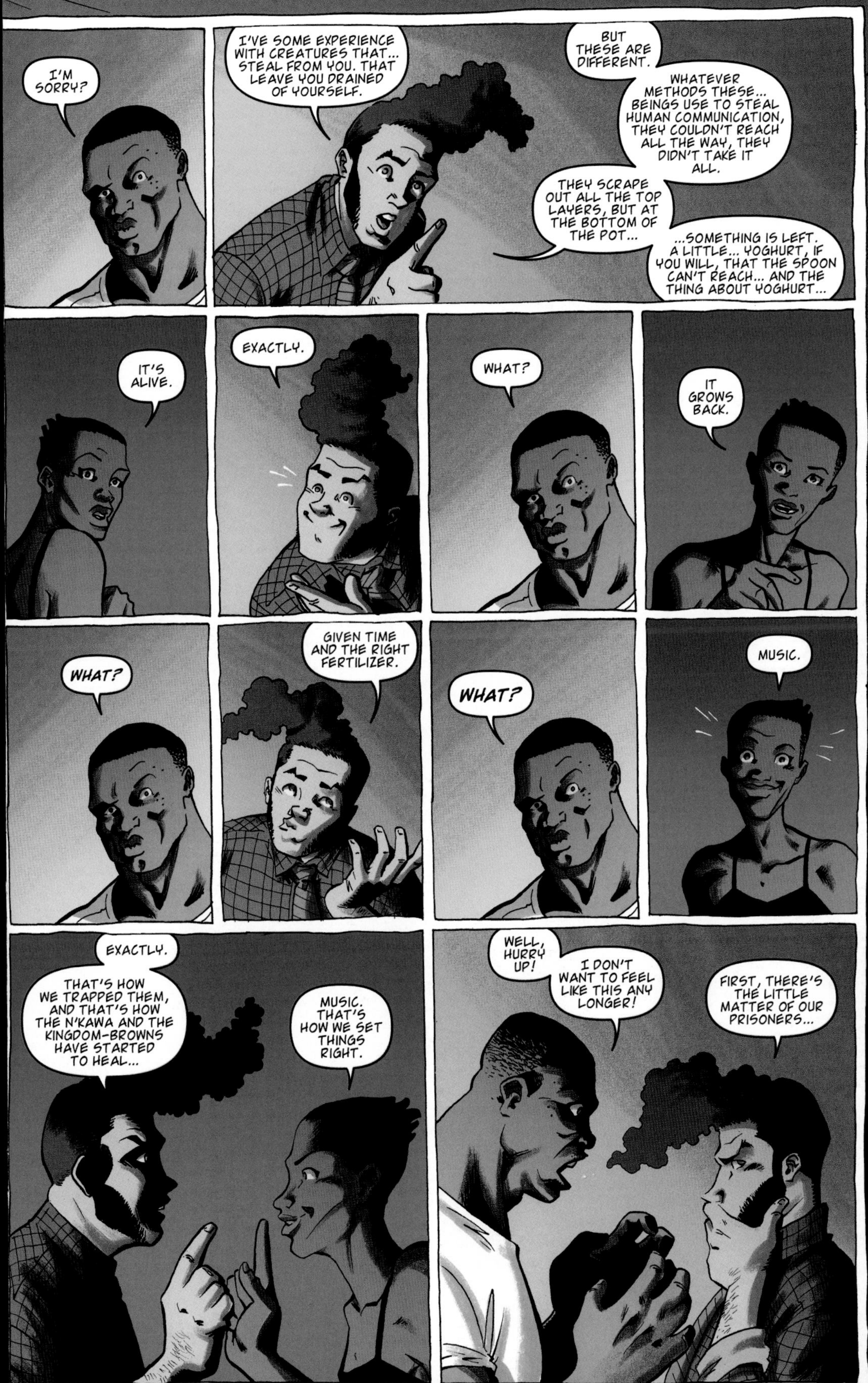
I'M SORRY?
I'VE SOME EXPERIENCE WITH CREATURES THAT... STEAL FROM YOU. THAT LEAVE YOU DRAINED OF YOURSELF.
BUT THESE ARE DIFFERENT.
WHATEVER METHODS THESE... BEINGS USE TO STEAL HUMAN COMMUNICATION, THEY COULDN'T REACH ALL THE WAY, THEY DIDN'T TAKE IT ALL.
THEY SCRAPE OUT ALL THE TOP LAYERS, BUT AT THE BOTTOM OF THE POT...
...SOMETHING IS LEFT. A LITTLE... YOGHURT, IF YOU WILL, THAT THE SPOON CAN'T REACH... AND THE THING ABOUT YOGHURT...
IT'S ALIVE.
EXACTLY.
WHAT?
IT GROWS BACK.
WHAT?
GIVEN TIME AND THE RIGHT FERTILIZER.
WHAT?
MUSIC.
EXACTLY.
THAT'S HOW WE TRAPPED THEM, AND THAT'S HOW THE N'KAWA AND THE KINGDOM-BROWNS HAVE STARTED TO HEAL...
MUSIC. THAT'S HOW WE SET THINGS RIGHT.
WELL, HURRY UP!
I DON'T WANT TO FEEL LIKE THIS ANY LONGER!
FIRST, THERE'S THE LITTLE MATTER OF OUR PRISONERS...

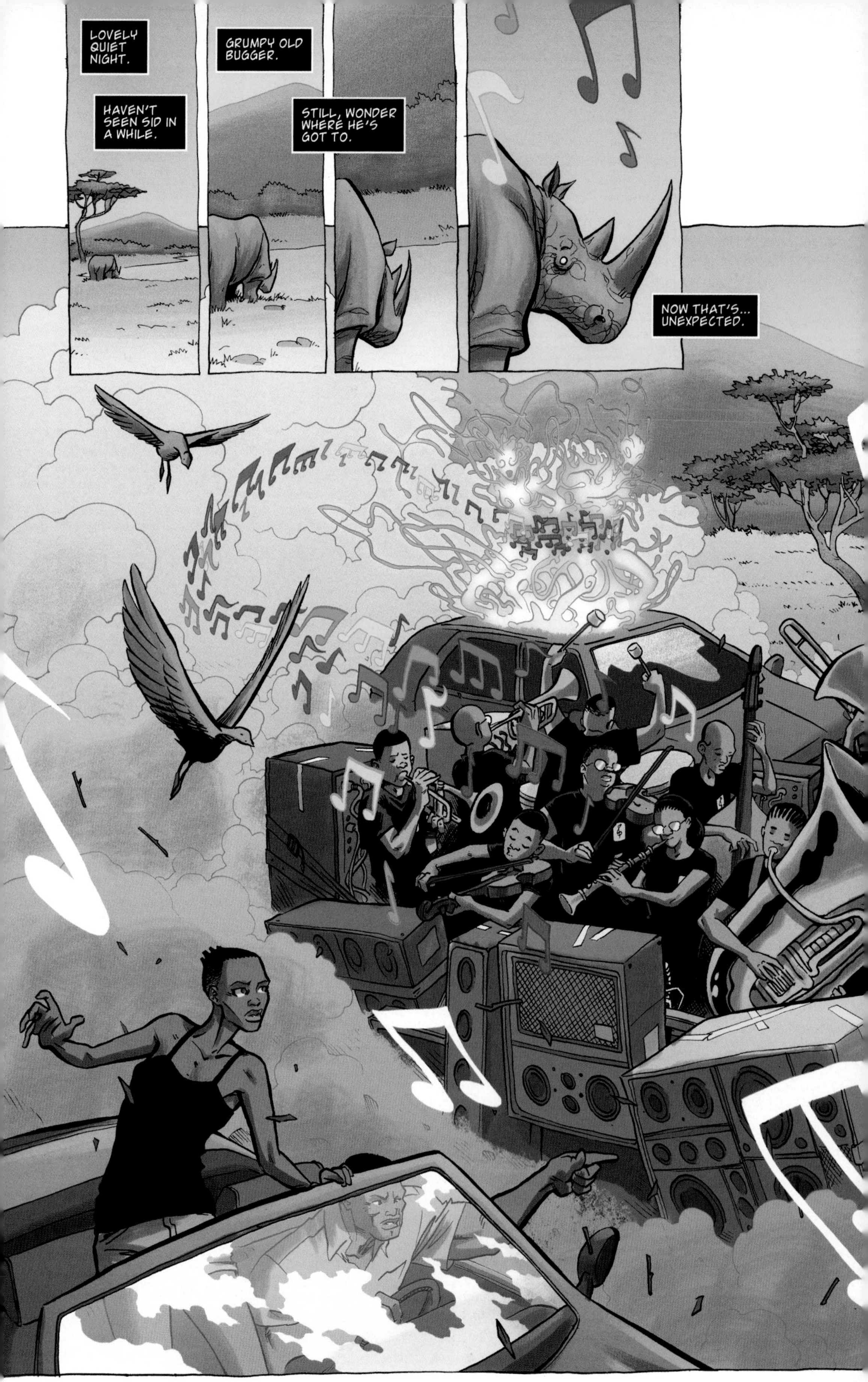

LOVELY QUIET NIGHT.
HAVEN'T SEEN SID IN A WHILE.
GRUMPY OLD BUGGER.
STILL, WONDER WHERE HE'S GOT TO.
NOW THAT'S... UNEXPECTED.

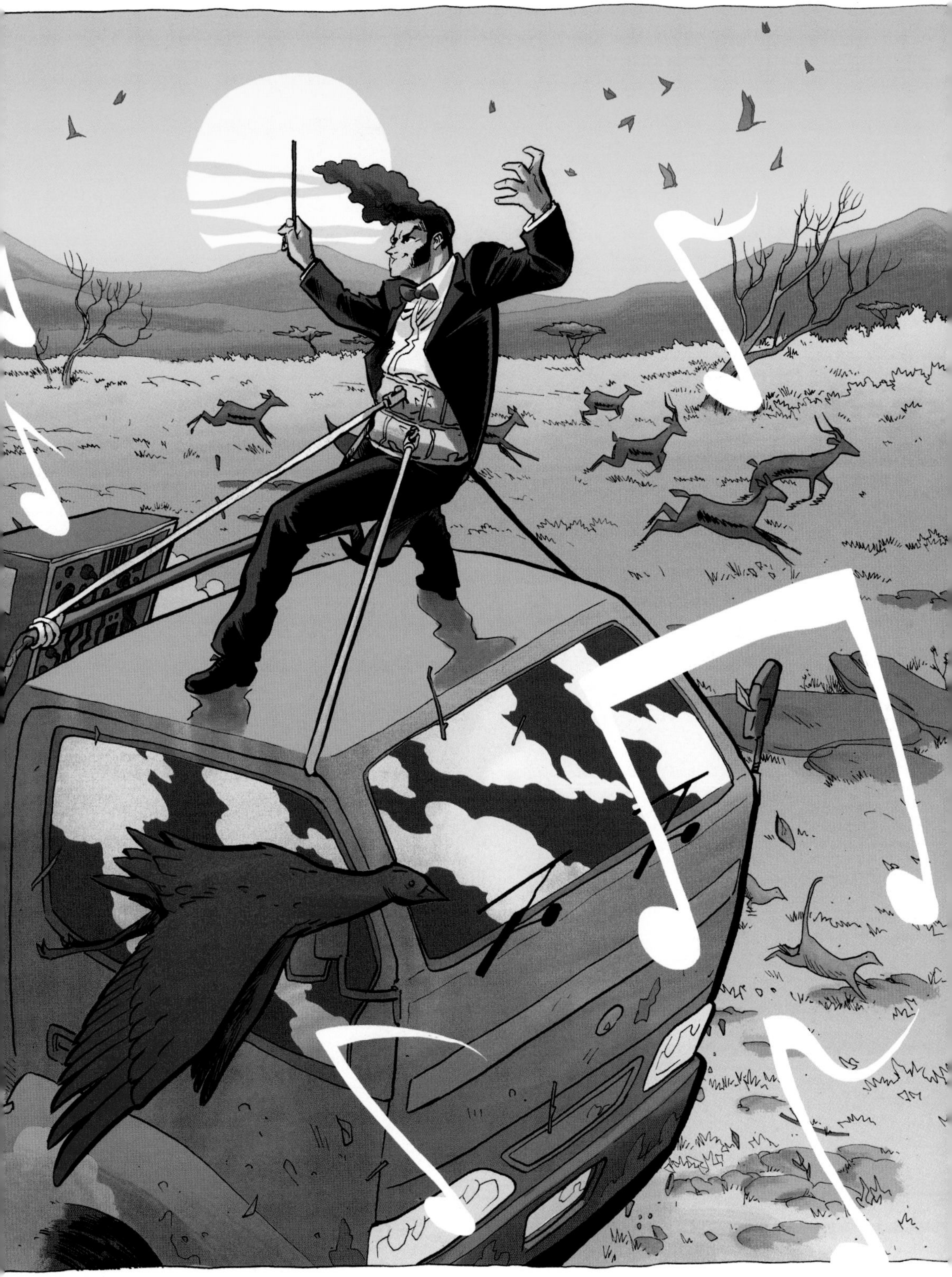

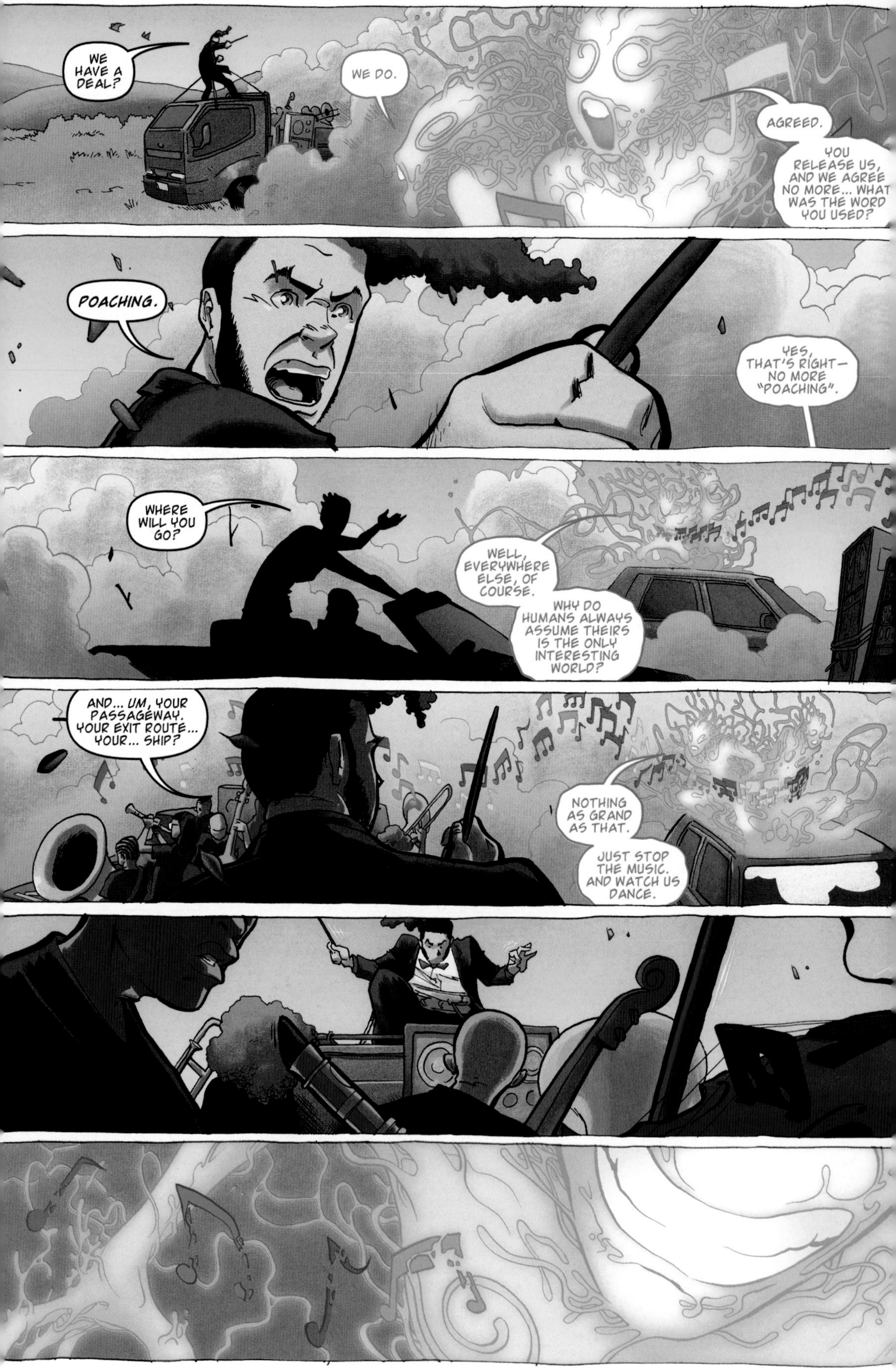
WE HAVE A DEAL?
WE DO.
AGREED.
YOU RELEASE US, AND WE AGREE NO MORE... WHAT WAS THE WORD YOU USED?
POACHING.
YES, THAT'S RIGHT— NO MORE "POACHING".
WHERE WILL YOU GO?
WELL, EVERYWHERE ELSE, OF COURSE.
WHY DO HUMANS ALWAYS ASSUME THEIRS IS THE ONLY INTERESTING WORLD?
AND... UM, YOUR PASSAGEWAY. YOUR EXIT ROUTE... YOUR... SHIP?
NOTHING AS GRAND AS THAT.
JUST STOP THE MUSIC. AND WATCH US DANCE.

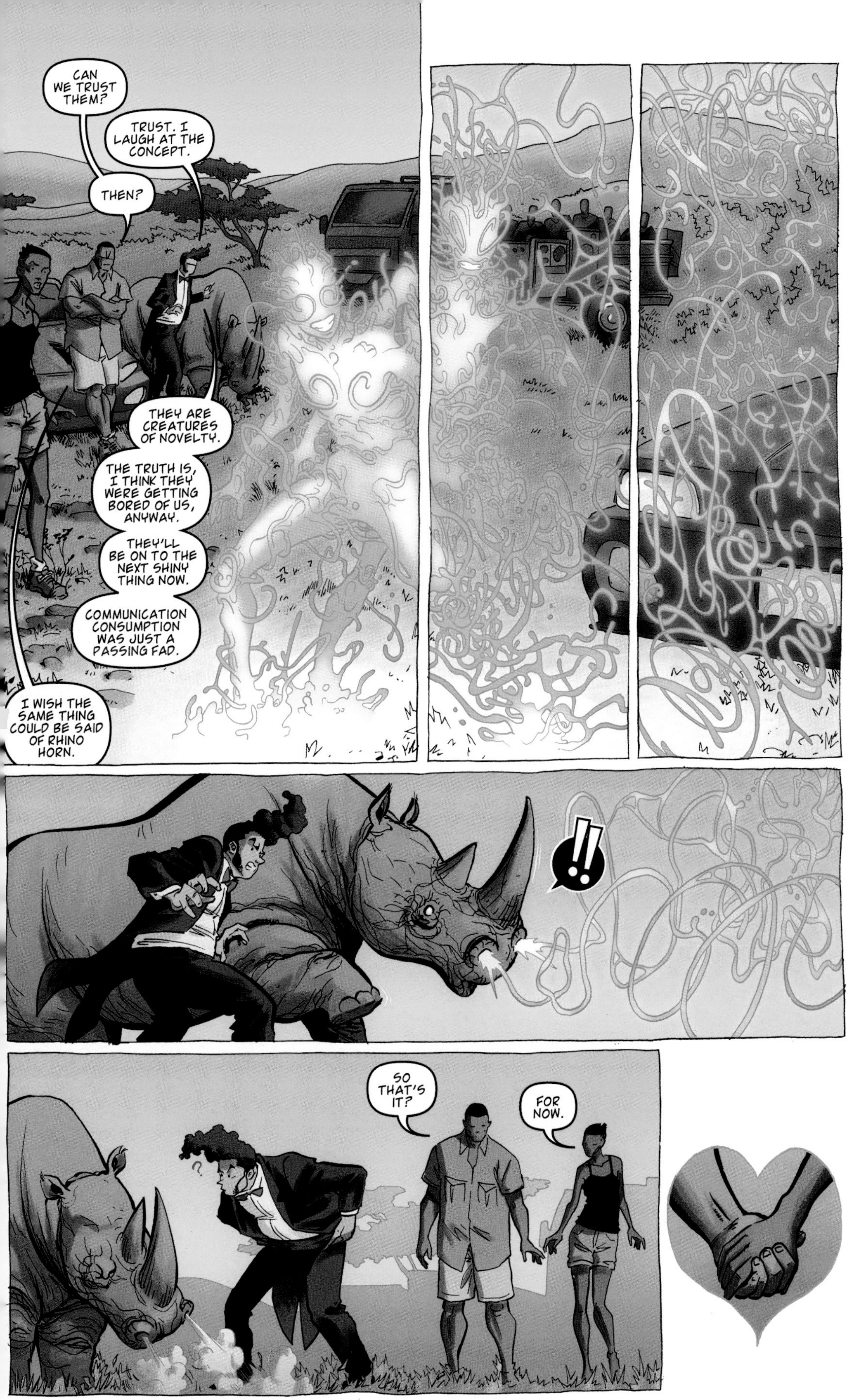
CAN WE TRUST THEM?
TRUST. I LAUGH AT THE CONCEPT.
THEN?
THEY ARE CREATURES OF NOVELTY.
THE TRUTH IS, I THINK THEY WERE GETTING BORED OF US, ANYWAY.
THEY'LL BE ON TO THE NEXT SHINY THING NOW.
COMMUNICATION CONSUMPTION WAS JUST A PASSING FAD.
I WISH THE SAME THING COULD BE SAID OF RHINO HORN.
!!
SO THAT'S IT?
FOR NOW.

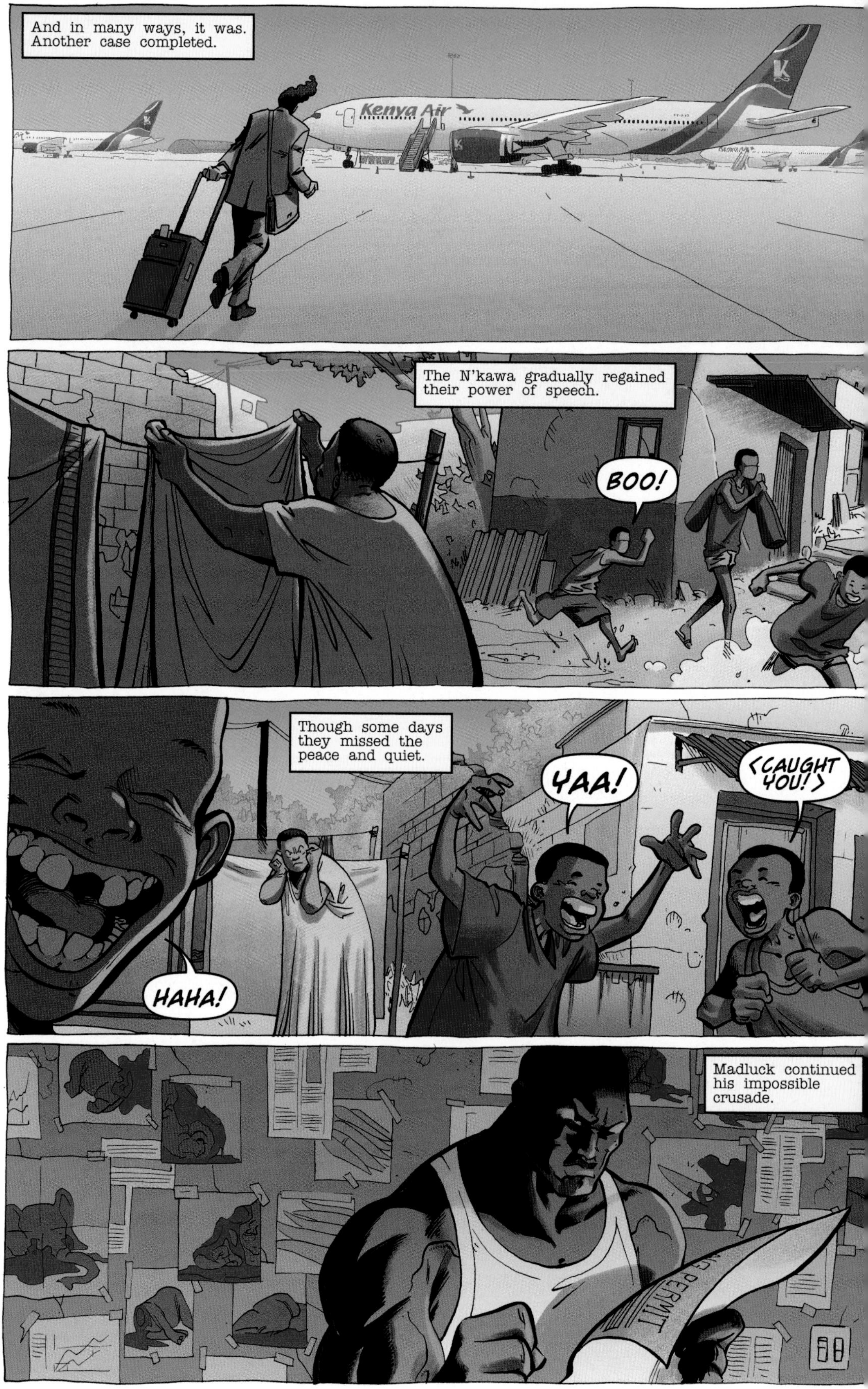
And in many ways, it was. Another case completed.
Kenya Air
The N'kawa gradually regained their power of speech.
BOO!
Though some days they missed the peace and quiet.
YAA!
<CAUGHT YOU!>
HAHA!
Madluck continued his impossible crusade.
PERMIT

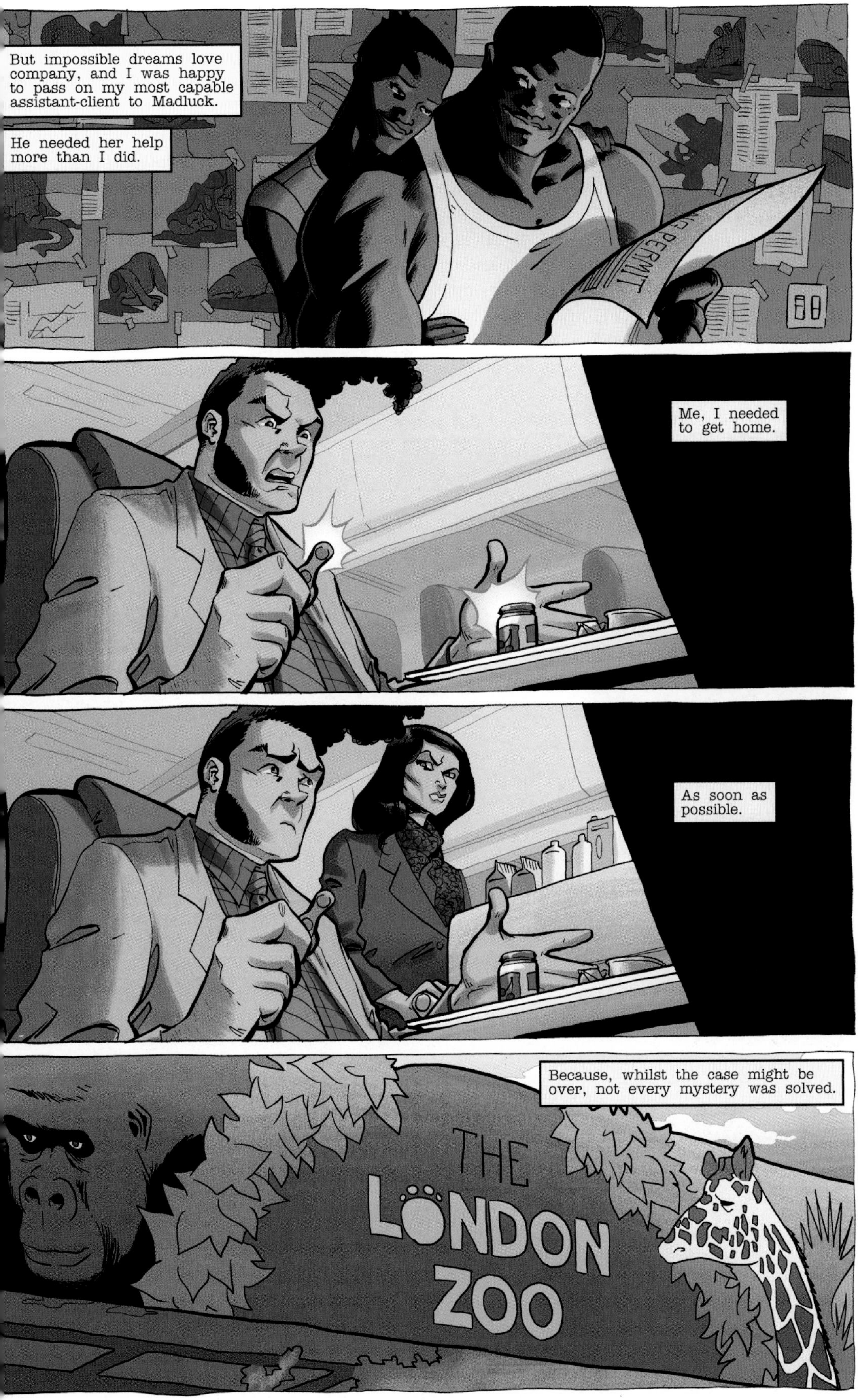
But impossible dreams love company, and I was happy to pass on my most capable assistant-client to Madluck.
He needed her help more than I did.
Me, I needed to get home.
As soon as possible.
Because, whilst the case might be over, not every mystery was solved.
THE LONDON ZOO

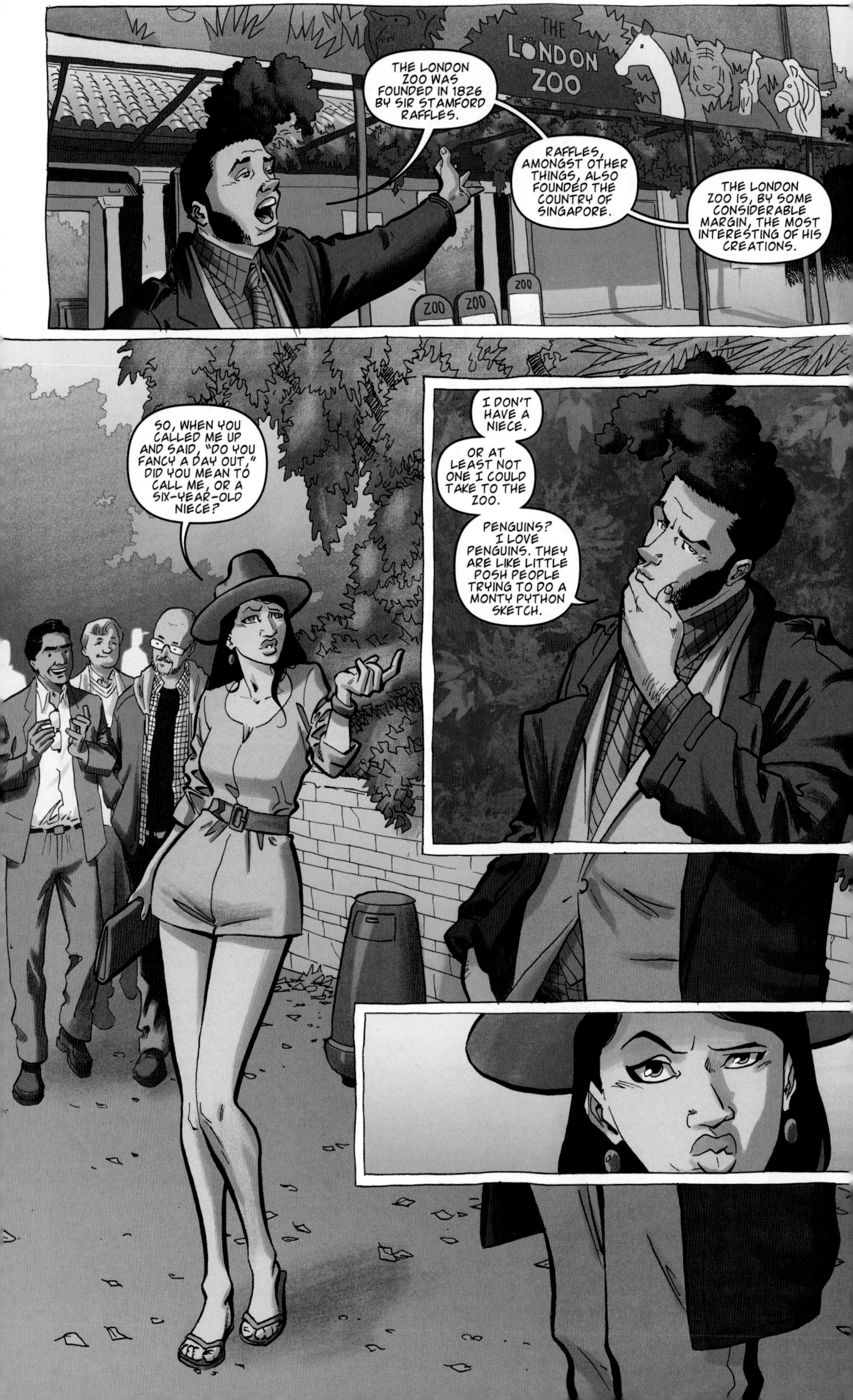
THE LONDON ZOO
THE LONDON ZOO WAS FOUNDED IN 1826 BY SIR STAMFORD RAFFLES.
RAFFLES, AMONGST OTHER THINGS, ALSO FOUNDED THE COUNTRY OF SINGAPORE.
THE LONDON ZOO IS, BY SOME CONSIDERABLE MARGIN, THE MOST INTERESTING OF HIS CREATIONS.
ZOO
ZOO
ZOO
SO, WHEN YOU CALLED ME UP AND SAID, "DO YOU FANCY A DAY OUT," DID YOU MEAN TO CALL ME, OR A SIX-YEAR-OLD NIECE?
I DON'T HAVE A NIECE.
OR AT LEAST NOT ONE I COULD TAKE TO THE ZOO.
PENGUINS? I LOVE PENGUINS. THEY ARE LIKE LITTLE POSH PEOPLE TRYING TO DO A MONTY PYTHON SKETCH.

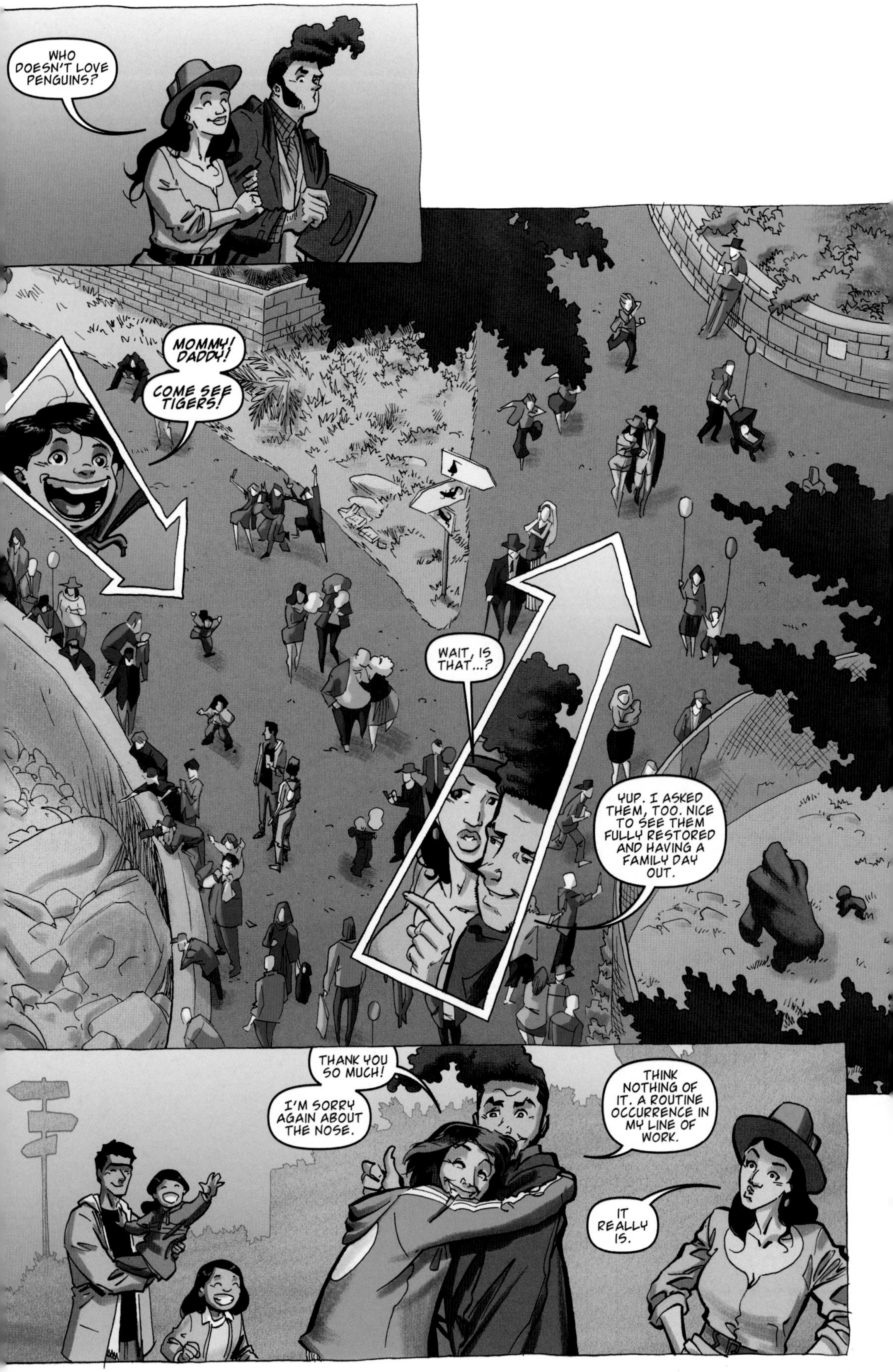
WHO DOESN'T LOVE PENGUINS?
MOMMY! DADDY!
COME SEE TIGERS!
WAIT, IS THAT...?
YUP. I ASKED THEM, TOO. NICE TO SEE THEM FULLY RESTORED AND HAVING A FAMILY DAY OUT.
THANK YOU SO MUCH!
I'M SORRY AGAIN ABOUT THE NOSE.
THINK NOTHING OF IT. A ROUTINE OCCURRENCE IN MY LINE OF WORK.
IT REALLY IS.

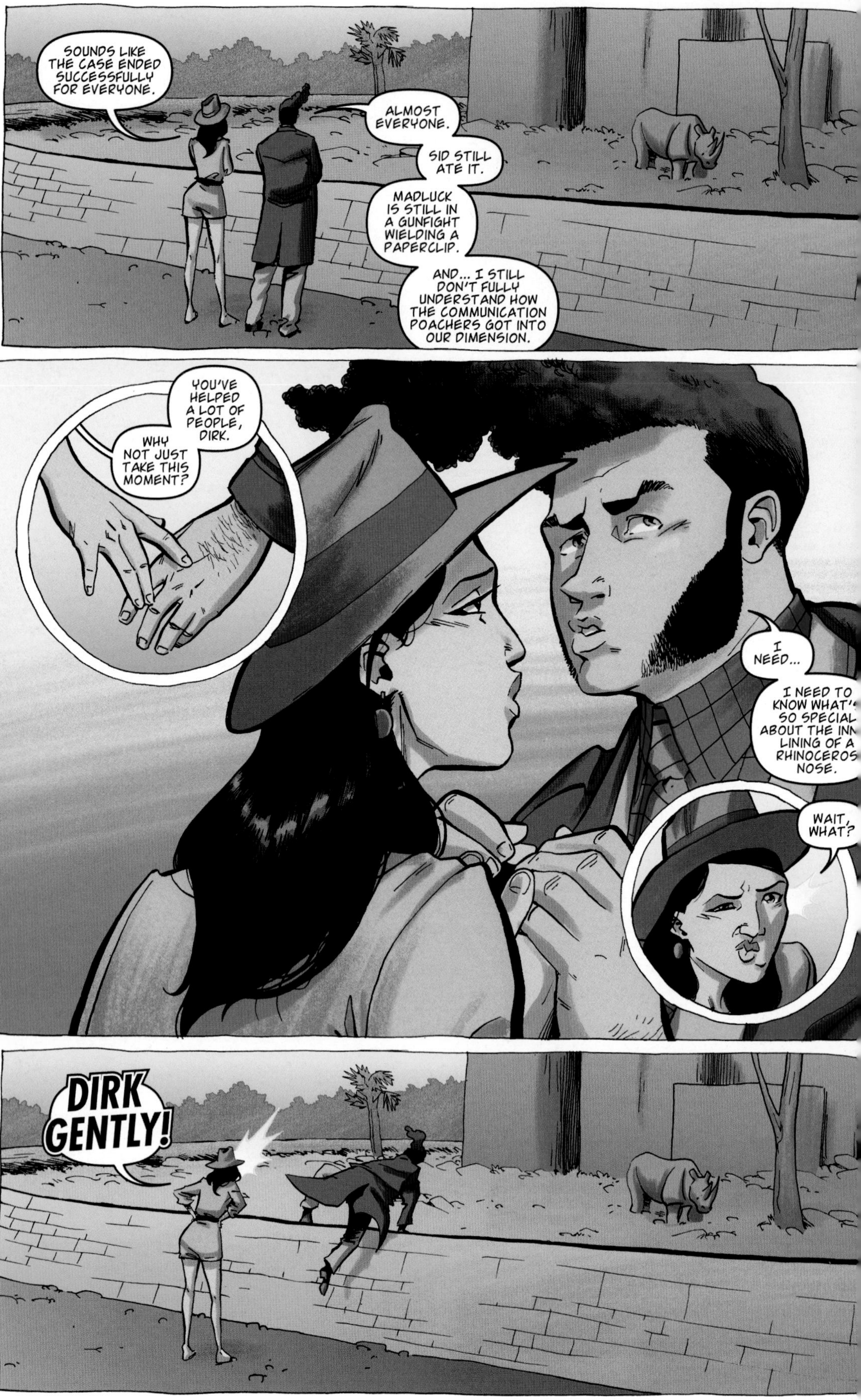
SOUNDS LIKE THE CASE ENDED SUCCESSFULLY FOR EVERYONE.
ALMOST EVERYONE.
SID STILL ATE IT.
MADLUCK IS STILL IN A GUNFIGHT WIELDING A PAPERCLIP.
AND... I STILL DON'T FULLY UNDERSTAND HOW THE COMMUNICATION POACHERS GOT INTO OUR DIMENSION.
YOU'VE HELPED A LOT OF PEOPLE, DIRK.
WHY NOT JUST TAKE THIS MOMENT?
I NEED...
I NEED TO KNOW WHAT'S SO SPECIAL ABOUT THE INNER LINING OF A RHINOCEROS NOSE.
WAIT, WHAT?
DIRK GENTLY!

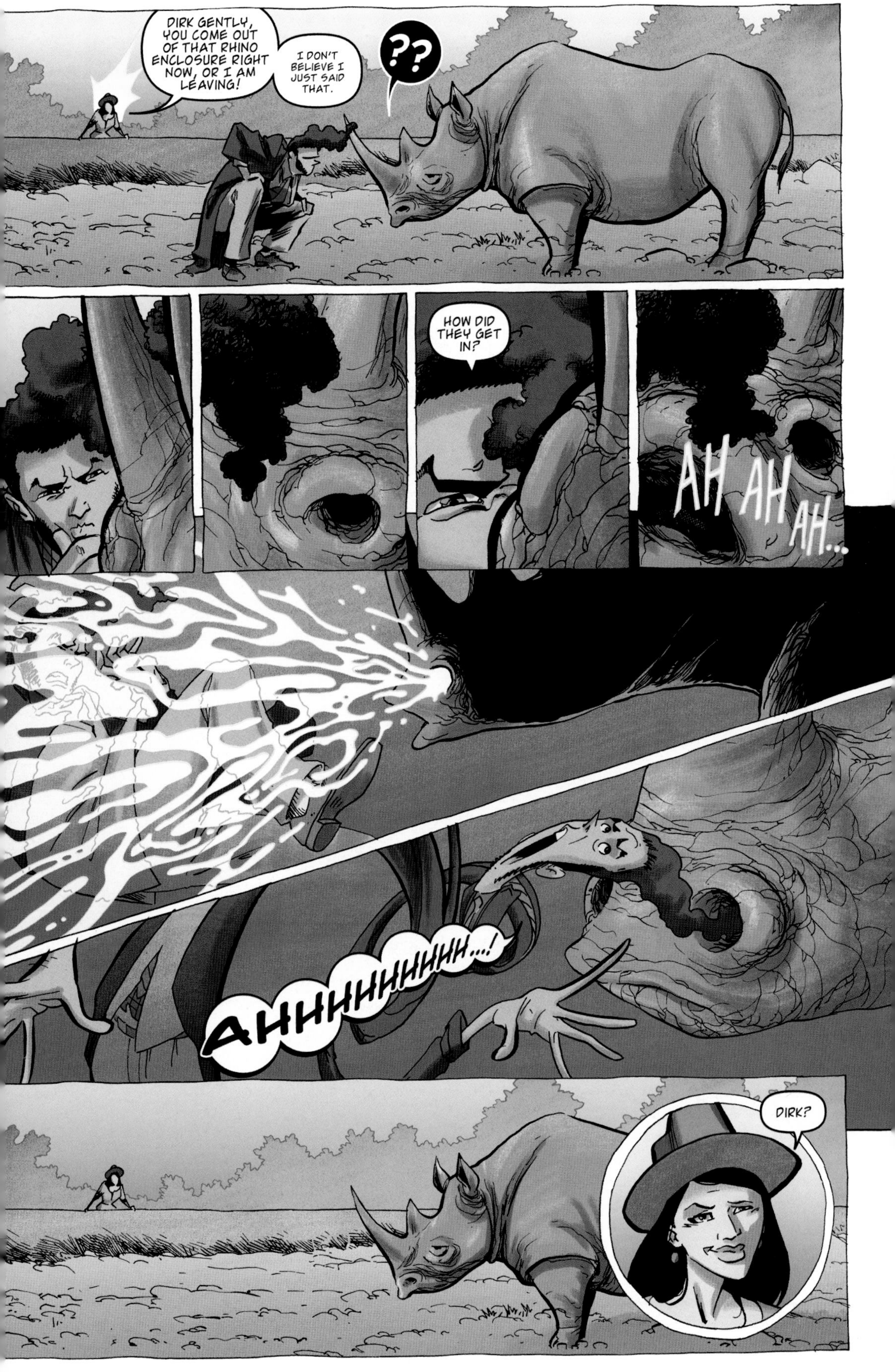
DIRK GENTLY, YOU COME OUT OF THAT RHINO ENCLOSURE RIGHT NOW, OR I AM LEAVING!
I DON'T BELIEVE I JUST SAID THAT.
??
HOW DID THEY GET IN?
AH AH AH...
AHHHHHHHHHH...!
DIRK?

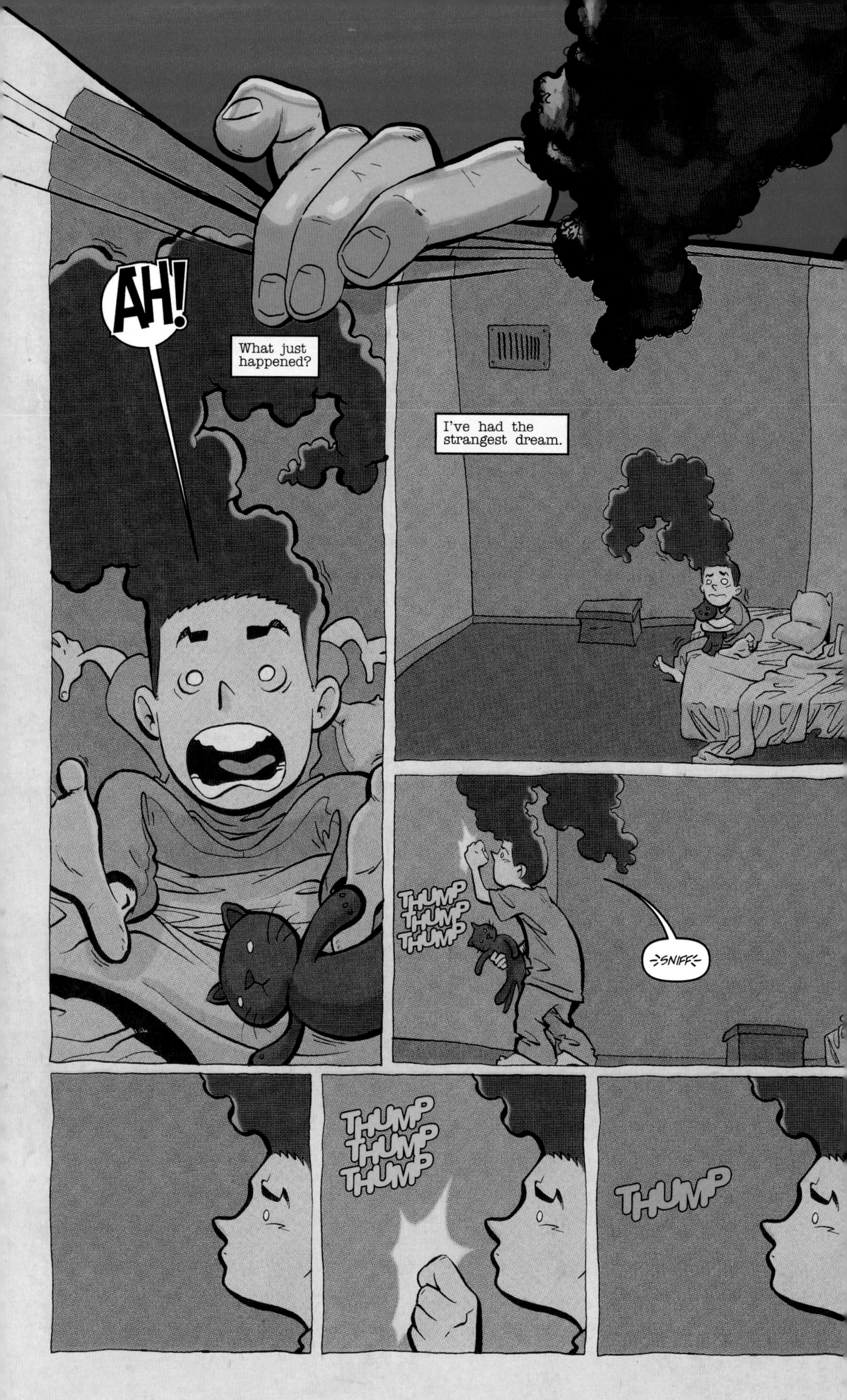
AH!
What just happened?
I've had the strangest dream.
THUMP THUMP THUMP
SNIFF
THUMP THUMP THUMP
THUMP

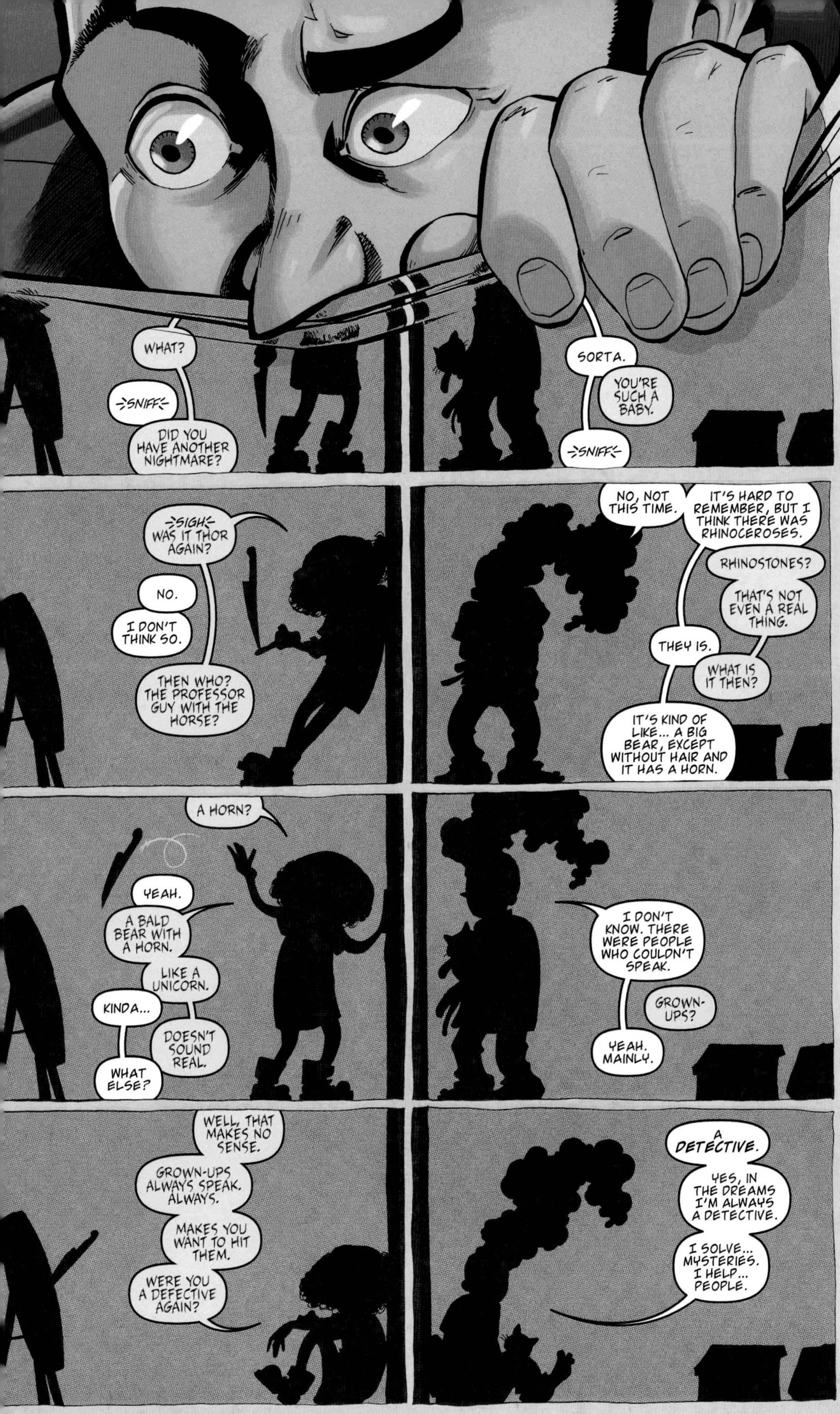
WHAT?
-SNIFF-
DID YOU HAVE ANOTHER NIGHTMARE?
SORTA.
YOU'RE SUCH A BABY.
-SNIFF-
-SIGH- WAS IT THOR AGAIN?
NO.
I DON'T THINK SO.
THEN WHO? THE PROFESSOR GUY WITH THE HORSE?
NO, NOT THIS TIME.
IT'S HARD TO REMEMBER, BUT I THINK THERE WAS RHINOCEROSES.
RHINOSTONES?
THAT'S NOT EVEN A REAL THING.
THEY IS.
WHAT IS IT THEN?
IT'S KIND OF LIKE... A BIG BEAR, EXCEPT WITHOUT HAIR AND IT HAS A HORN.
A HORN?
YEAH.
A BALD BEAR WITH A HORN.
LIKE A UNICORN.
KINDA...
DOESN'T SOUND REAL.
WHAT ELSE?
I DON'T KNOW. THERE WERE PEOPLE WHO COULDN'T SPEAK.
GROWN-UPS?
YEAH. MAINLY.
WELL, THAT MAKES NO SENSE.
GROWN-UPS ALWAYS SPEAK. ALWAYS.
MAKES YOU WANT TO HIT THEM.
WERE YOU A DEFECTIVE AGAIN?
A *DETECTIVE*.
YES, IN THE DREAMS I'M ALWAYS A DETECTIVE.
I SOLVE... MYSTERIES. I HELP... PEOPLE.

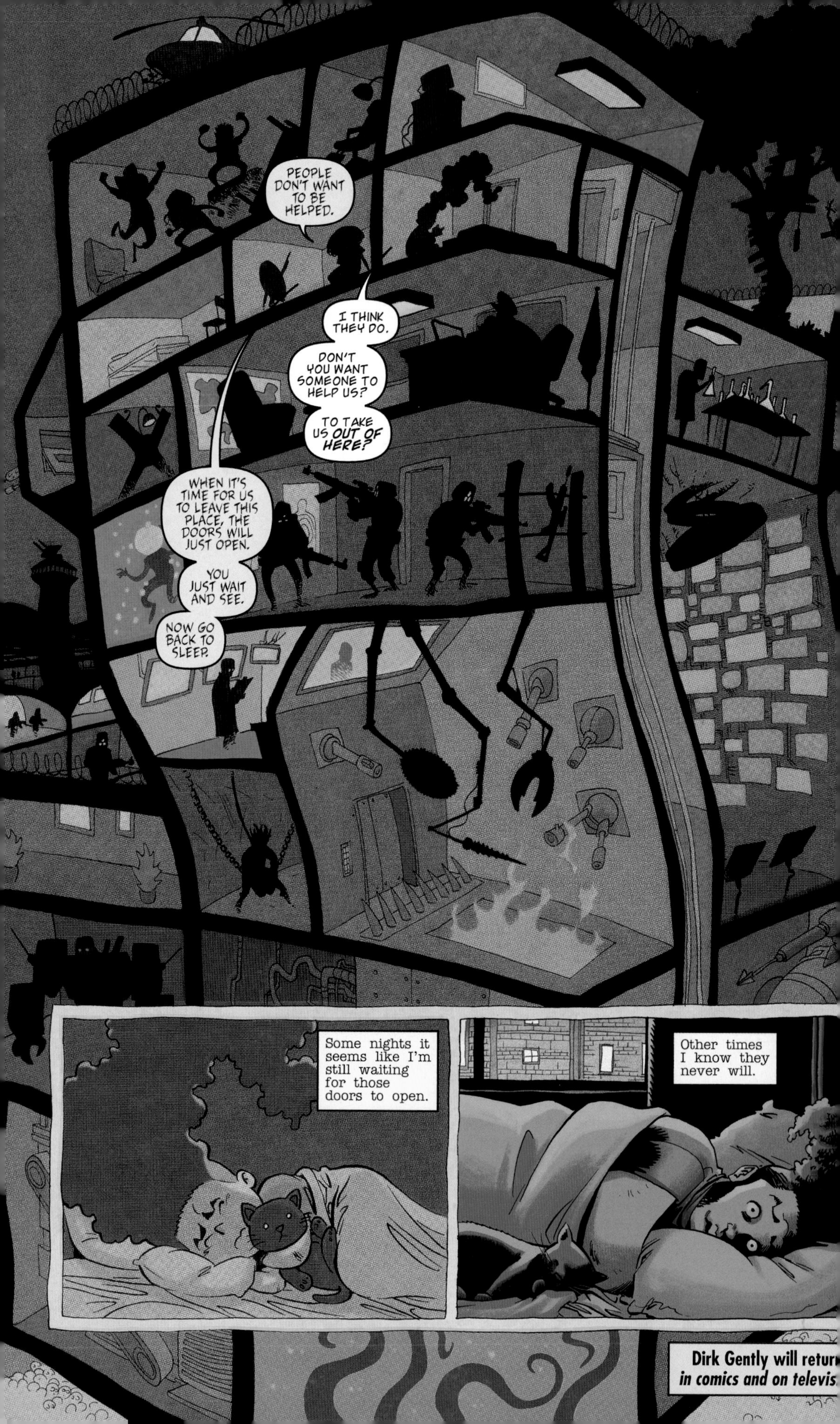
PEOPLE DON'T WANT TO BE HELPED.
I THINK THEY DO.
DON'T YOU WANT SOMEONE TO HELP US?
TO TAKE US OUT OF HERE?
WHEN IT'S TIME FOR US TO LEAVE THIS PLACE, THE DOORS WILL JUST OPEN.
YOU JUST WAIT AND SEE.
NOW GO BACK TO SLEEP.
Some nights it seems like I'm still waiting for those doors to open.
Other times I know they never will.
Dirk Gently will retur
in comics and on televis

SAVE THE RHINO

www.savetherhino.org

If you've read Douglas Adams's book, *Last Chance to See*, you'll know that Douglas had more than a soft spot for rhinos. His account of standing on a termite mound deep in the Garamba National Park, in a remote area of the Democratic Republic of Congo, staring at another termite hill through binoculars, in the hope that it would morph into a Northern white rhino, is both funny and horribly prescient. Today there are just three Northern whites left in the world: the subspecies is doomed to extinction.

Douglas became a Founder Patron of Save the Rhino International, a UK-registered charity. He was an active supporter, joining us for part of a walk-in rhino costume of course-from Mombasa on the Kenyan coast to the summit of Mt. Kilimanjaro. The route took Douglas and companions through Tsavo West National Park, an area that had lost virtually all of its black rhinos during the previous poaching crisis of the 1970s, 80s, and early 90s.

Today we're facing another poaching crisis, 20 years after the last one. Douglas is no longer with us-he died just before I joined Save the Rhino in 2001-and we wish he were here. But we're thrilled that his famous detective, Dirk Gently, is having new adventures, and that *A Spoon Too Short* focuses on the rhino crisis.

Figures released by the International Union for the Conservation of Nature in early March 2016 show that poaching is hitting hard, with nearly 6,000 rhinos killed in Africa since 2008. South Africa alone is losing three animals per day.

It doesn't need a skilled detective to work out what the problem is. Rhinos are being killed for their horn, for consumers in East Asia, predominantly in Vietnam and China. The most significant demand comes from wealthy businessmen, who are keen to show off how wealthy they are by buying whole rhino horns as a status symbol. Another group of buyers does so for medicinal reasons, buying powdered horn that they ingest to cure fevers. The criminal networks profiting from the illegal wildlife trade have also created propaganda promoting new uses for horn: as a cure for cancer or to be taken like cocaine-snorted up human noses rather than sitting on the nose of a charismatic mega-herbivore somewhere in the African savannah.

Douglas was an optimist, and so are rhino conservationists. We are convinced that we can solve this problem. It's going to need time, and money, and a holistic approach.

Save the Rhino has five interconnected strategies for ensuring that all five species of rhino thrive in the wild in Africa and Asia for future generations: supporting law enforcement efforts to protect key populations; building networks with other organizations to coordinate activities; ensuring that local communities are the first to benefit from wildlife-related opportunities; working on behavior-change campaigns to reduce the demand for illegal rhino horn; and raising global awareness of the issues involved. Our international partners bring further expertise: investigating smuggling routes; monitoring arrests, prosecutions and convictions; putting pressure on governments to prioritize tackling wildlife crime; training rangers how to use tracker and sniffer dogs; and so on.

We're delighted that Dirk Gently's Holistic Detective Agency investigated rhino poaching in *A Spoon Too Short*, helping us to reach new audiences to garner support for rhino conservation efforts. Douglas's Estate has agreed that a share of royalties from the Dirk Gently play and from these comics will come to Save the Rhino International to help our work on the ground. We are extremely grateful to the Estate and to Arvind Ethan David for leading the charge to save rhinos.

[redacted]

Cover Art by **ROBERT HACK**   Colors by **STEPHEN DOWNER**

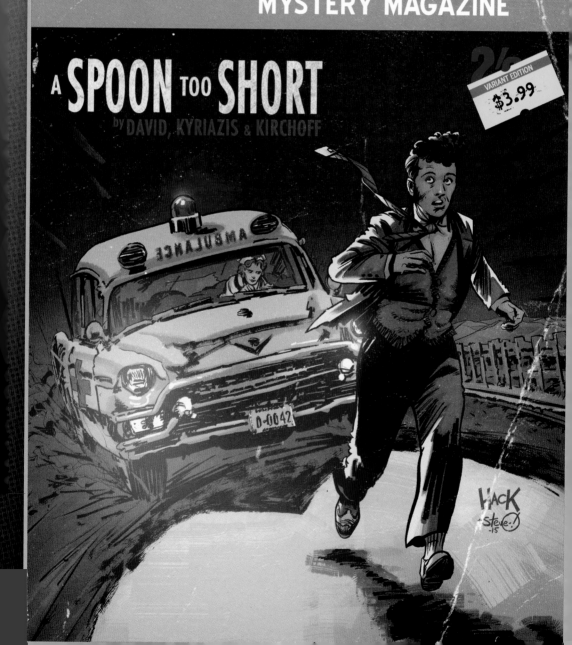

~A DOUGLAS ADAMS PUBLICATION~

IDW
ISSUE No1

HOLISTIC DETECTIVE

MYSTERY MAGAZINE

DIRK
GENTLY

A SPOON TOO SHORT

by DAVID, KYRIAZIS & KIRCHOFF

VARIANT EDITION
$3.99

AMBULANCE

D-0042

HACK
steve!
-15

Cover Art by **ROBERT HACK** Colors by **STEPHEN DOWNER**

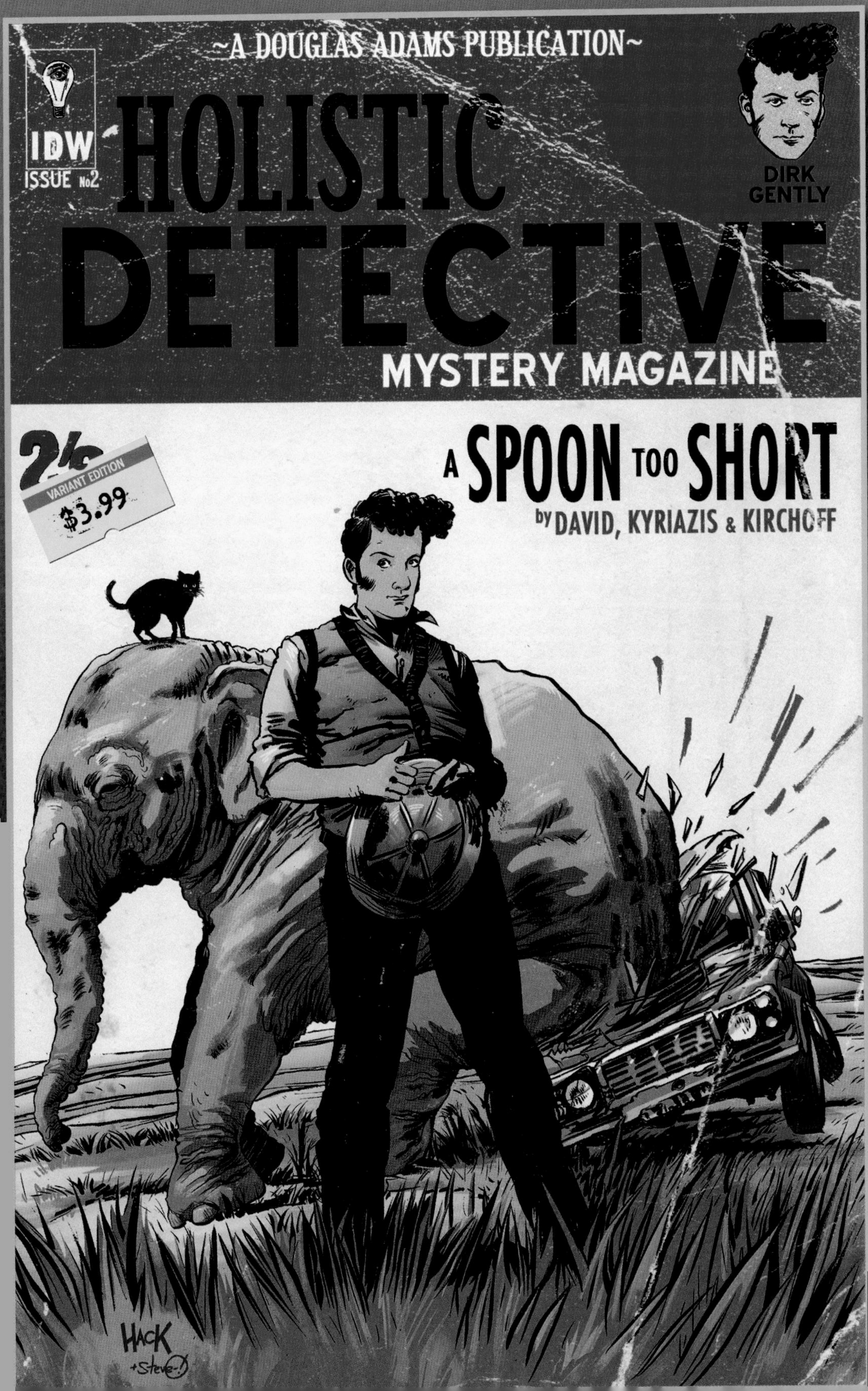
~A DOUGLAS ADAMS PUBLICATION~
IDW
ISSUE No2
HOLISTIC
DETECTIVE
MYSTERY MAGAZINE
DIRK GENTLY
A SPOON TOO SHORT
by DAVID, KYRIAZIS & KIRCHOFF
VARIANT EDITION
$3.99
HACK
+Steve

Cover Art by **ROBERT HACK** Colors by **STEPHEN DOWNER**

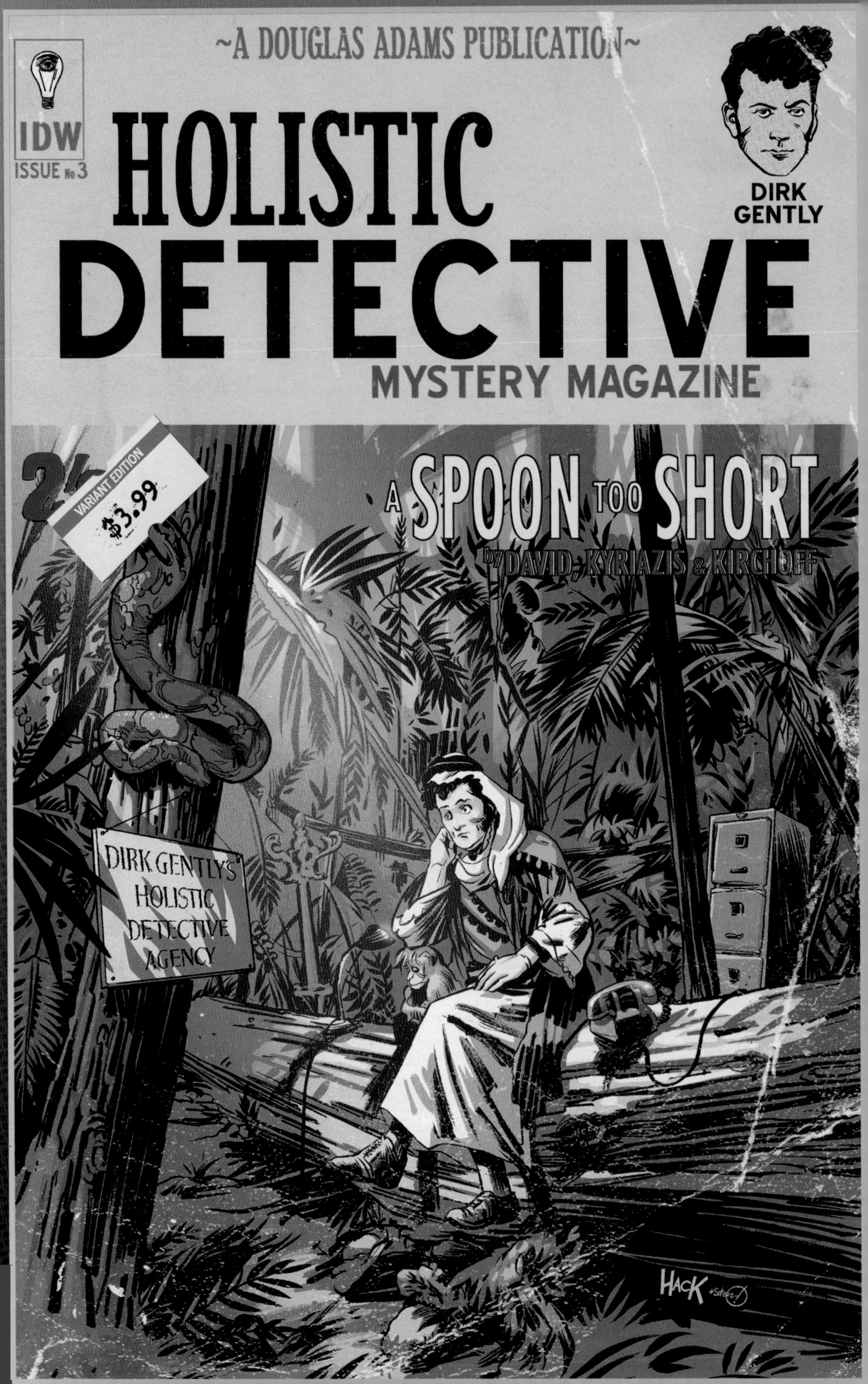

~A DOUGLAS ADAMS PUBLICATION~
IDW
ISSUE No 3
HOLISTIC
DETECTIVE
MYSTERY MAGAZINE
DIRK GENTLY
VARIANT EDITION
$3.99
A SPOON TOO SHORT
by DAVID, KYRIAZIS & KIRCHOFF
DIRK GENTLY'S HOLISTIC DETECTIVE AGENCY
HACK

Cover Art by **ROBERT HACK** Colors by **STEPHEN DOWNER**

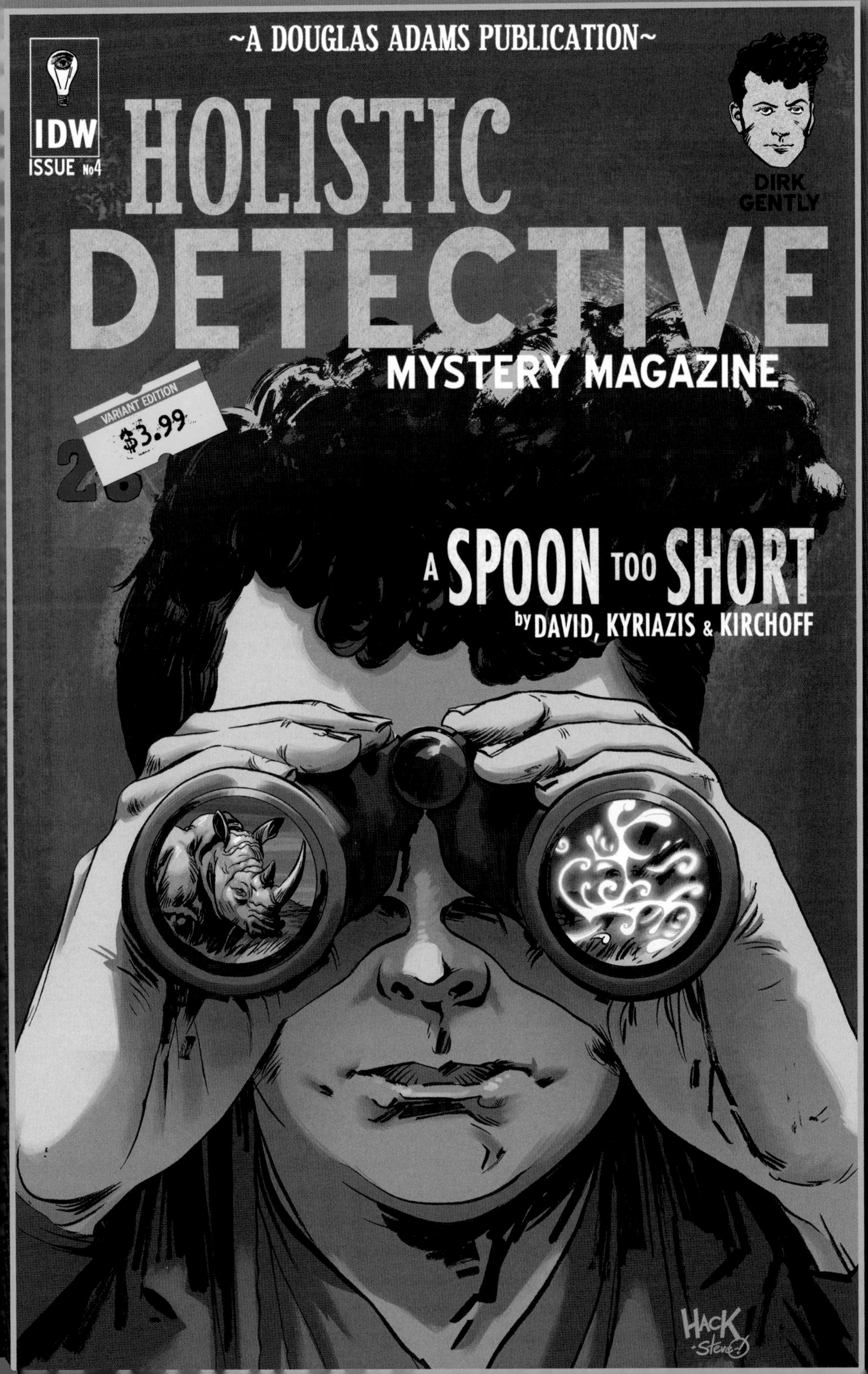
~A DOUGLAS ADAMS PUBLICATION~
IDW
ISSUE No4
HOLISTIC
DETECTIVE
MYSTERY MAGAZINE
DIRK GENTLY
VARIANT EDITION
$3.99
A SPOON TOO SHORT
by DAVID, KYRIAZIS & KIRCHOFF
HACK

Cover Art by **ROBERT HACK** Colors by **STEPHEN DOWNER**

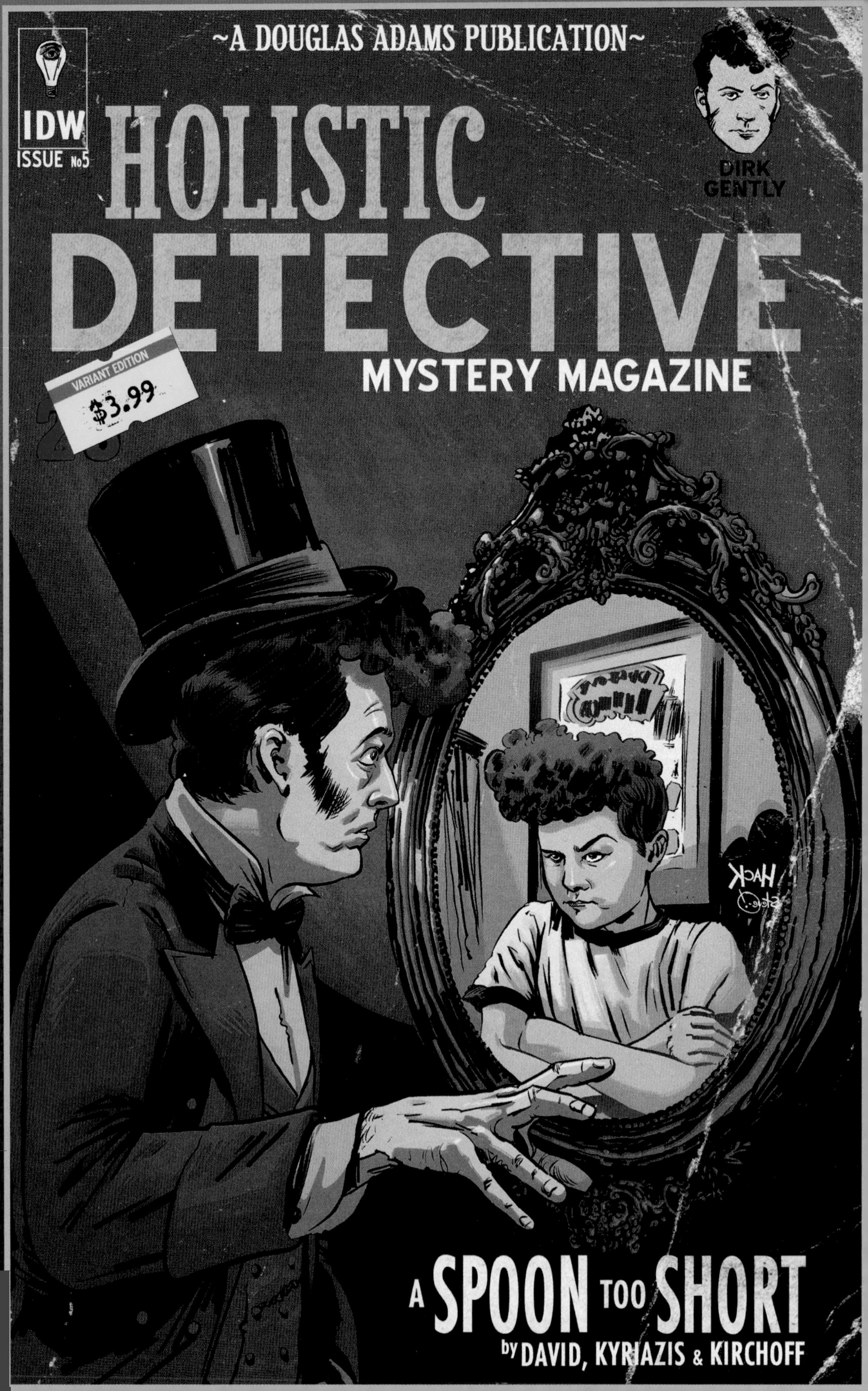
~A DOUGLAS ADAMS PUBLICATION~
IDW
ISSUE No5
HOLISTIC
DETECTIVE
MYSTERY MAGAZINE
DIRK GENTLY
VARIANT EDITION
$3.99
HACK
A SPOON TOO SHORT
by DAVID, KYRIAZIS & KIRCHOFF

Cover Art by **BRIAN MILLER**

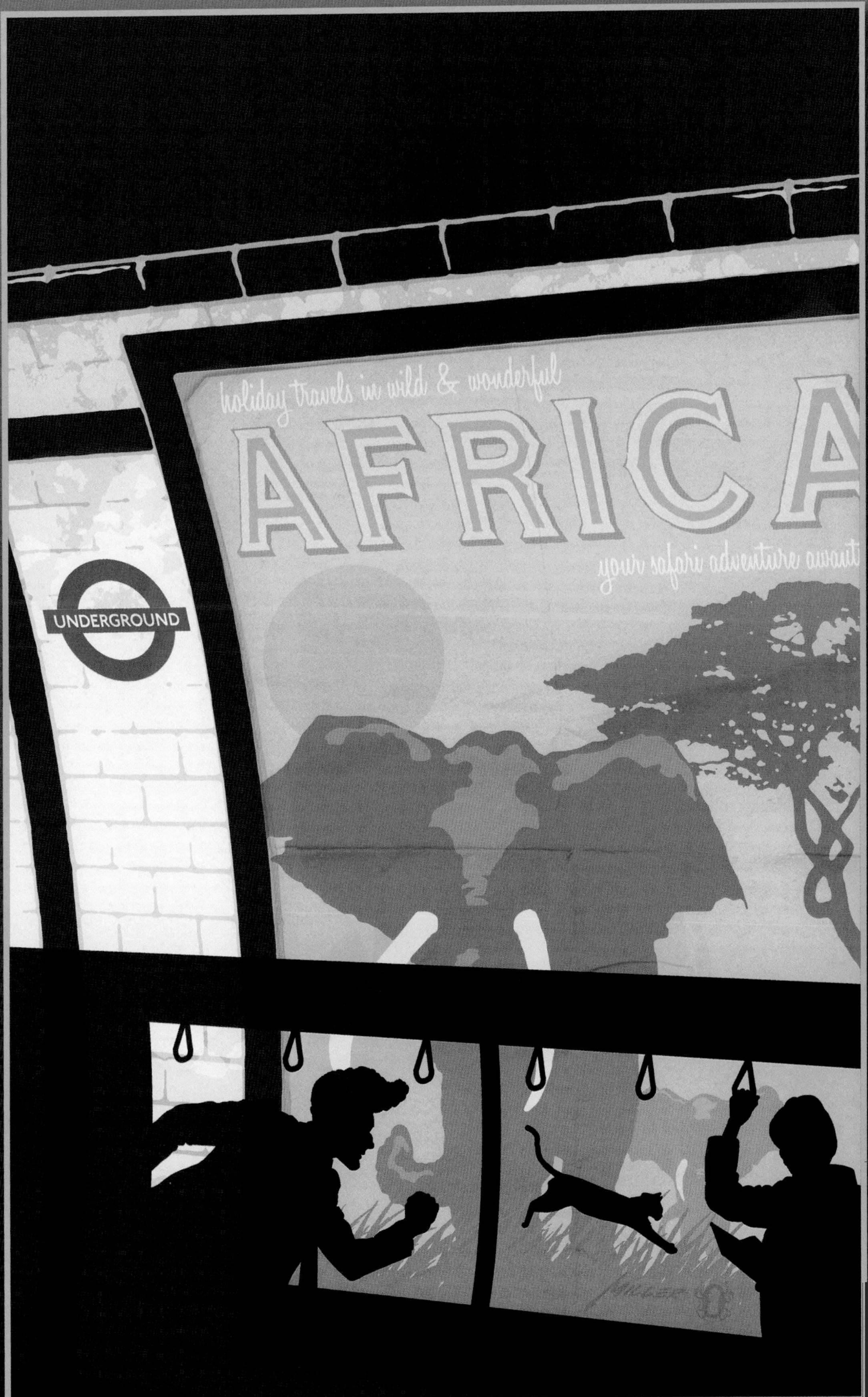
holiday travels in wild & wonderful
AFRICA
your safari adventure await
UNDERGROUND

Cover Art by **BRIAN MILLER**

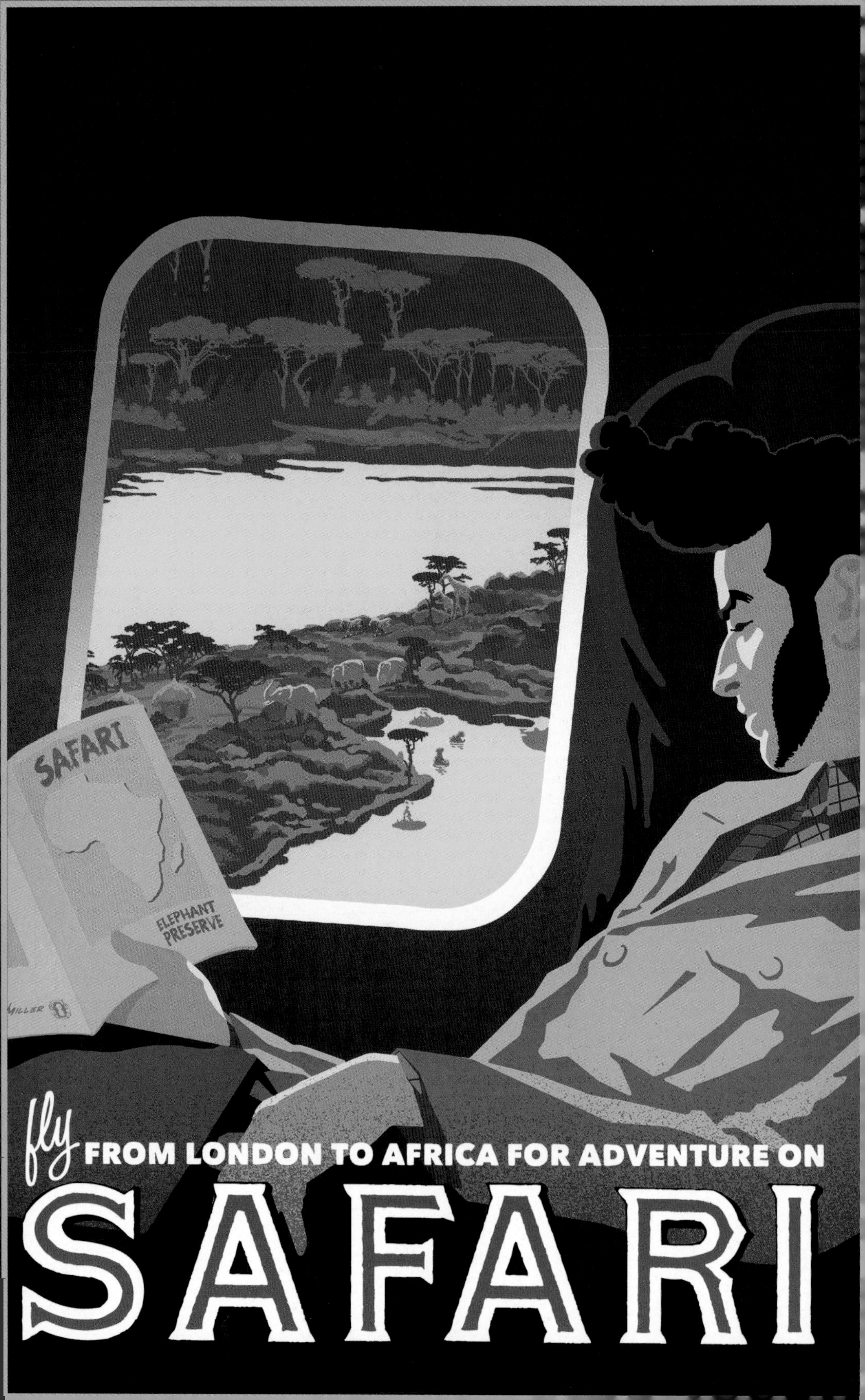

SAFARI
ELEPHANT PRESERVE
MILLER
fly FROM LONDON TO AFRICA FOR ADVENTURE ON
SAFARI

Cover Art by **BRIAN MILLER**

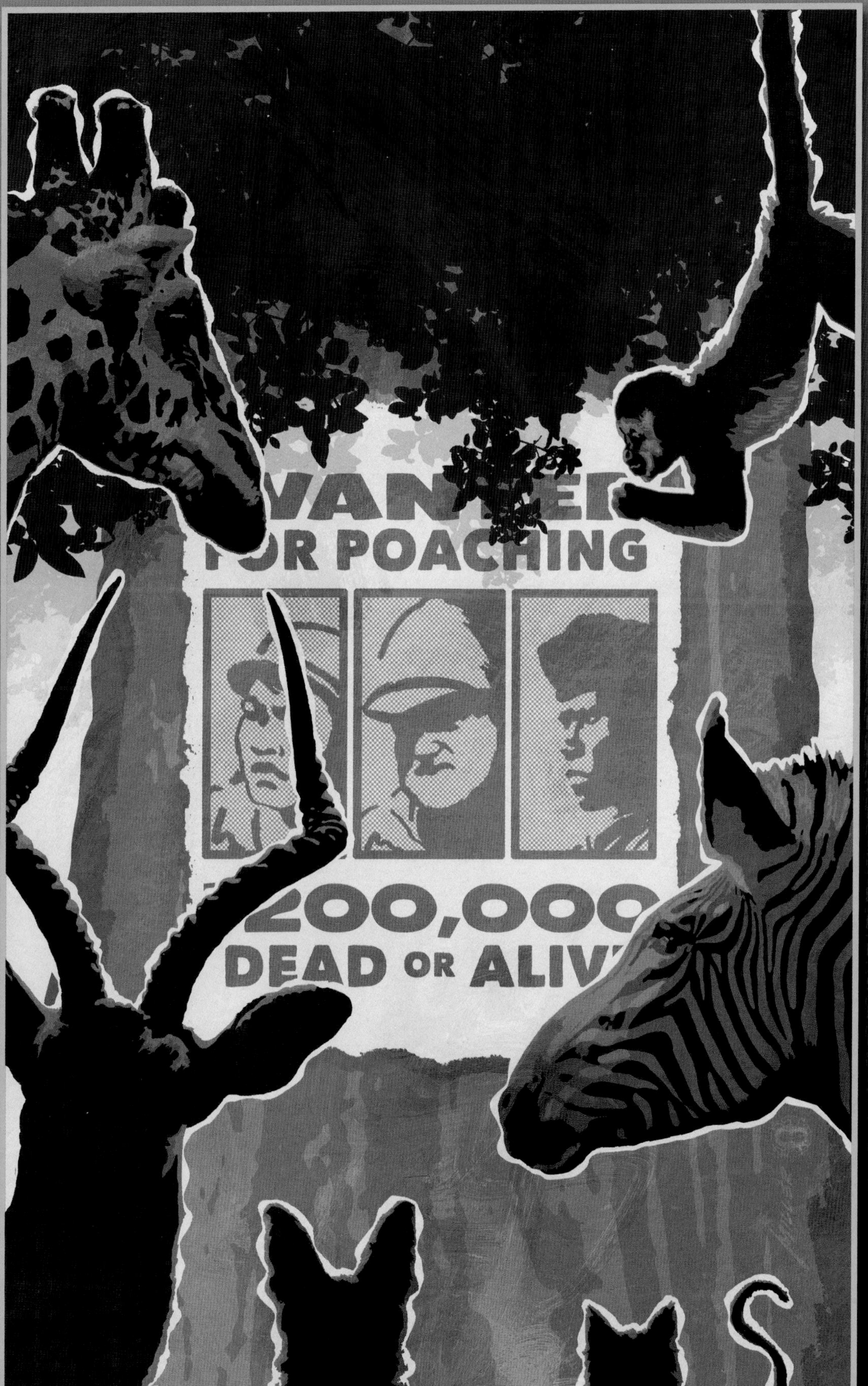

WANTED
FOR POACHING
200,000
DEAD OR ALIVE

Cover Art by **BRIAN MILLER**

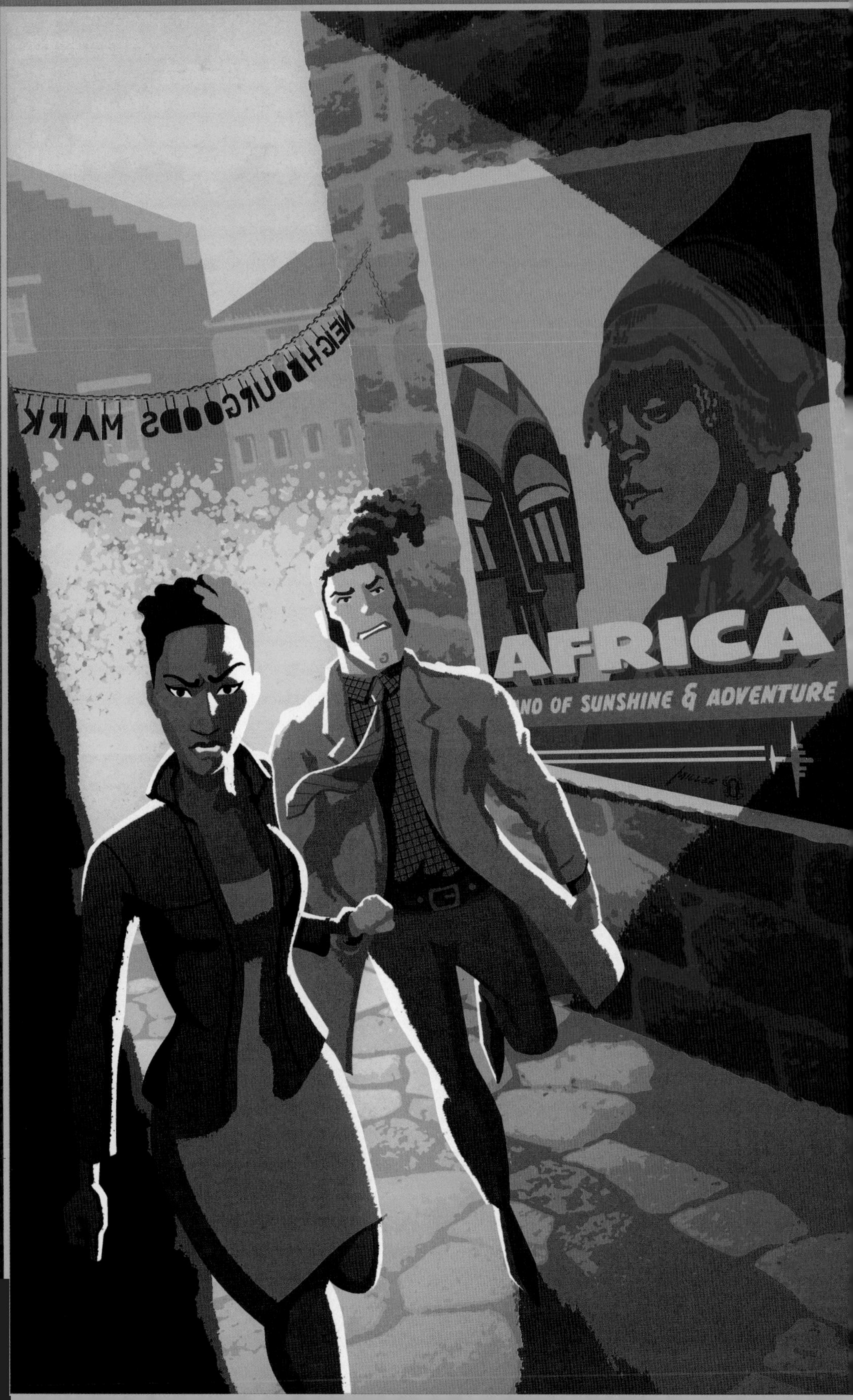
AFRICA
OF SUNSHINE & ADVENTURE

Cover Art by **BRIAN MILLER**

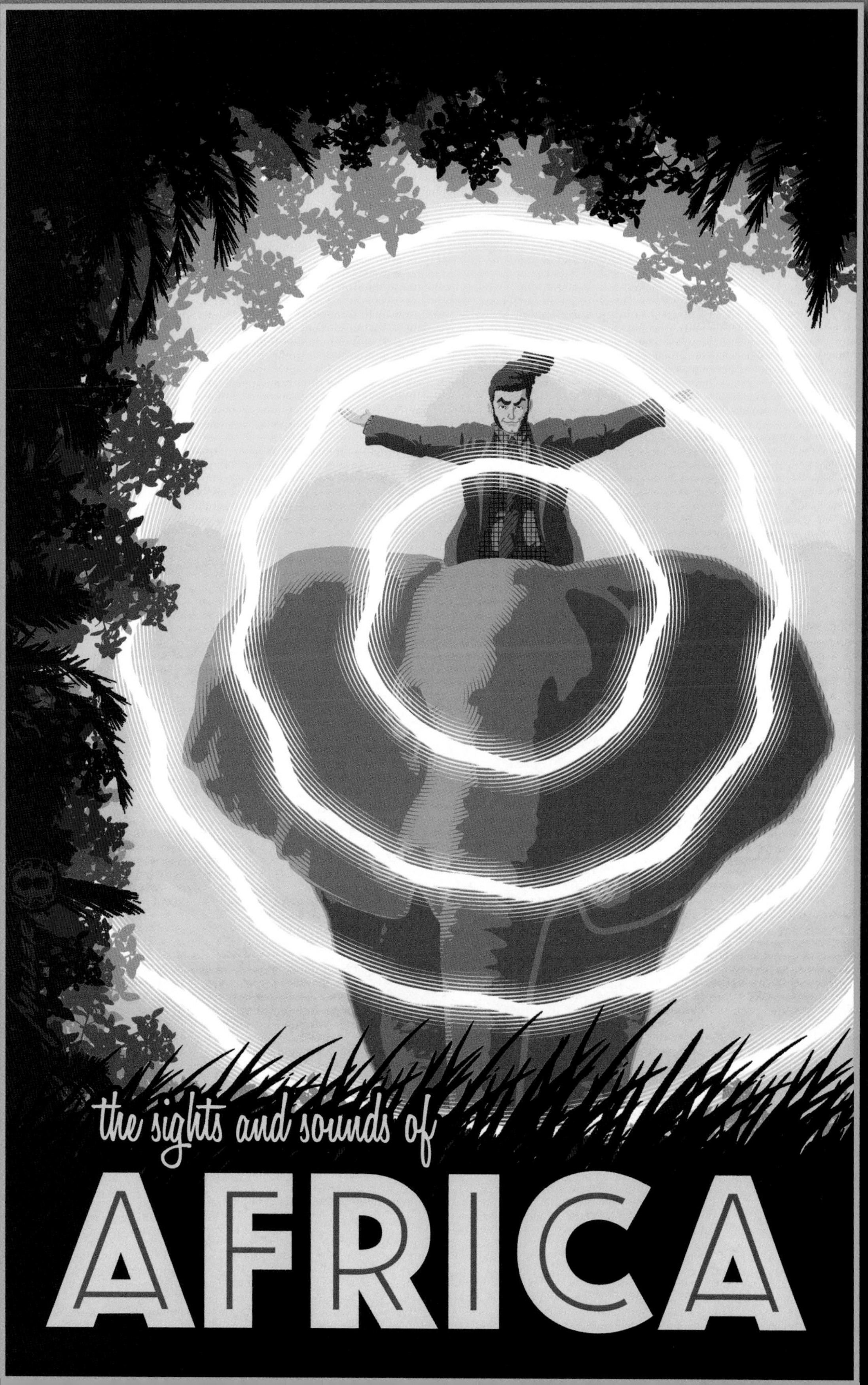
the sights and sounds of
AFRICA

Cover Art by **ROBERT HACK**

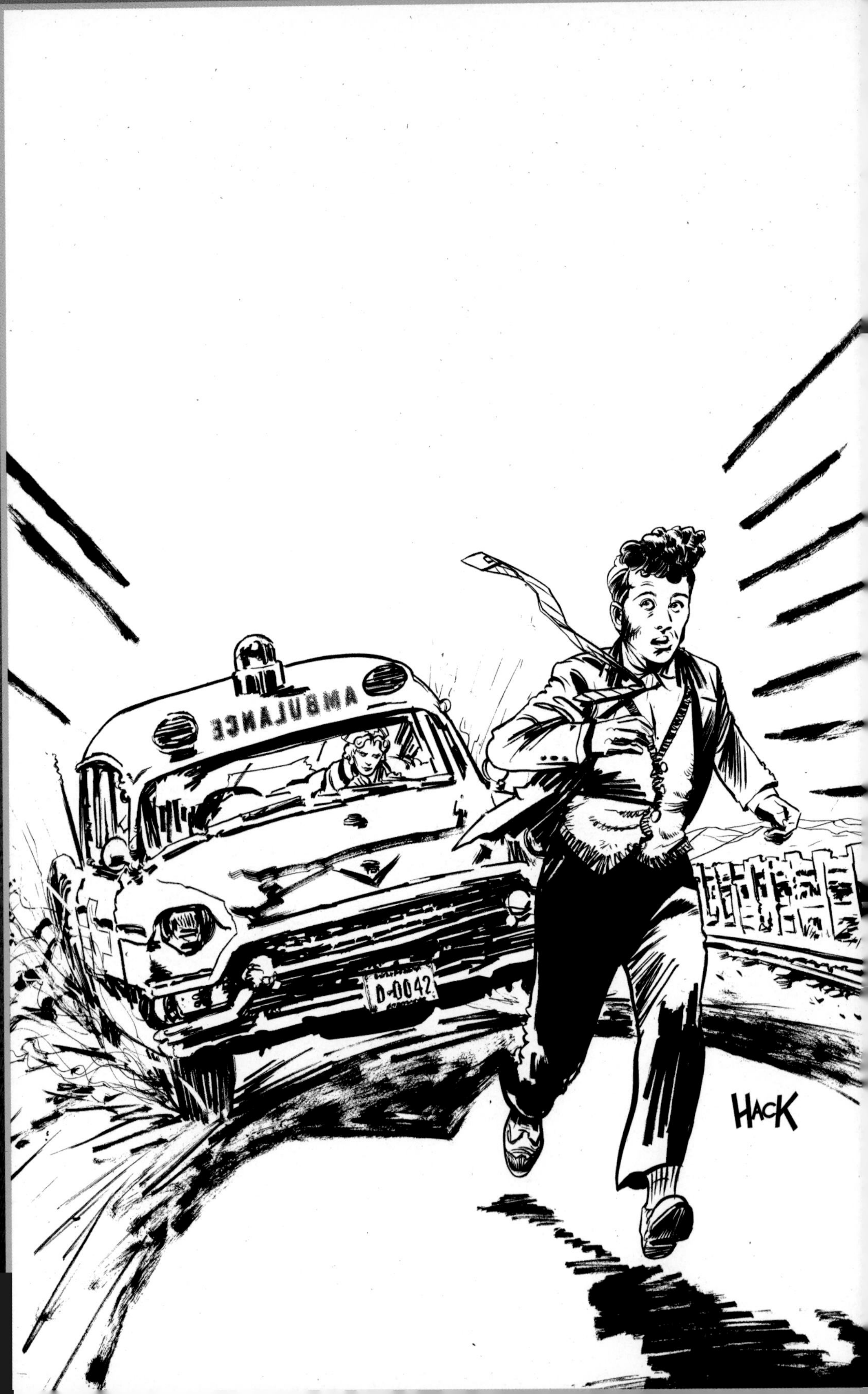

AMBULANCE
D-0042
HACK

Cover Art by **ROBERT HACK**

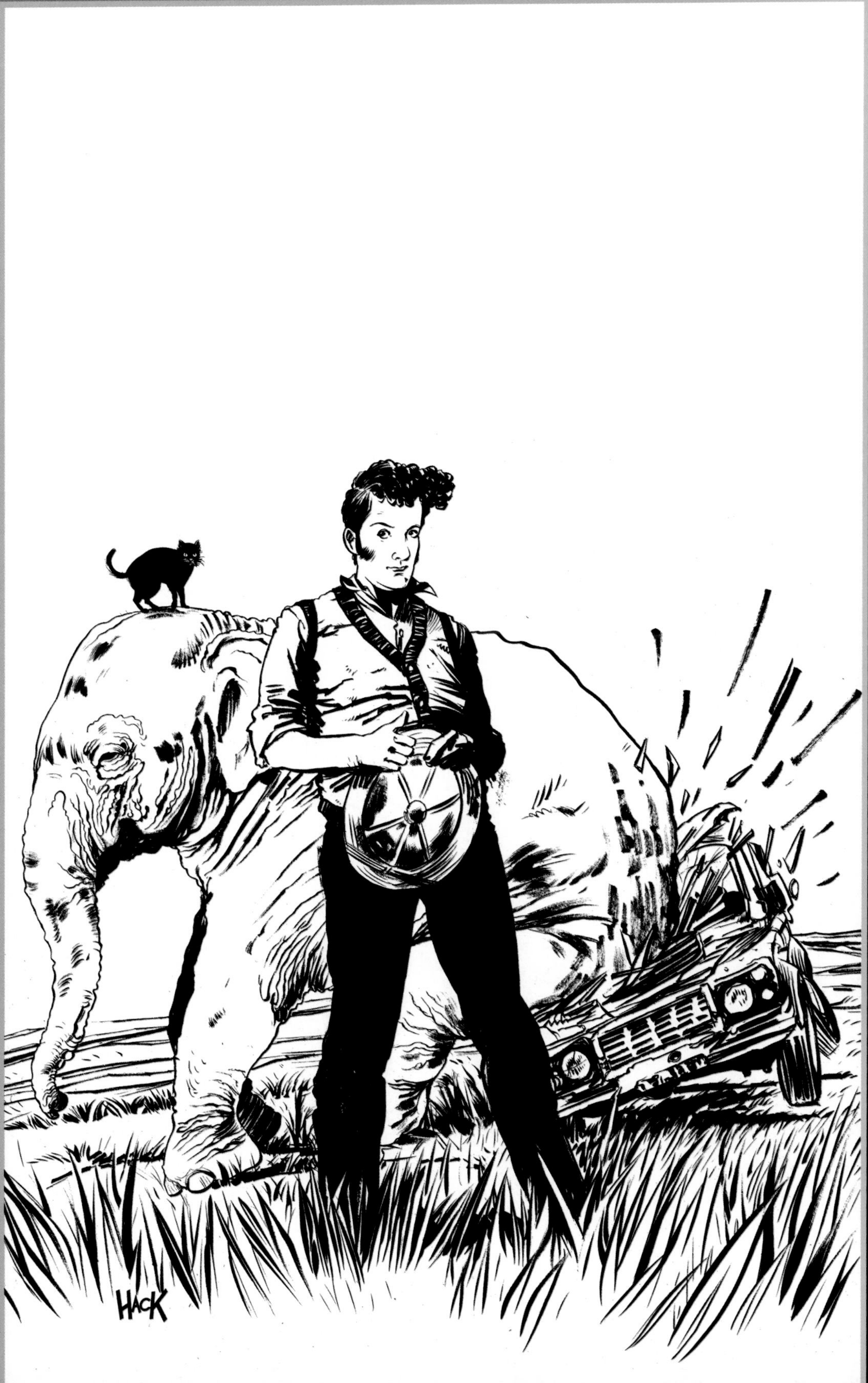
HACK

Cover Art by **ROBERT HACK**

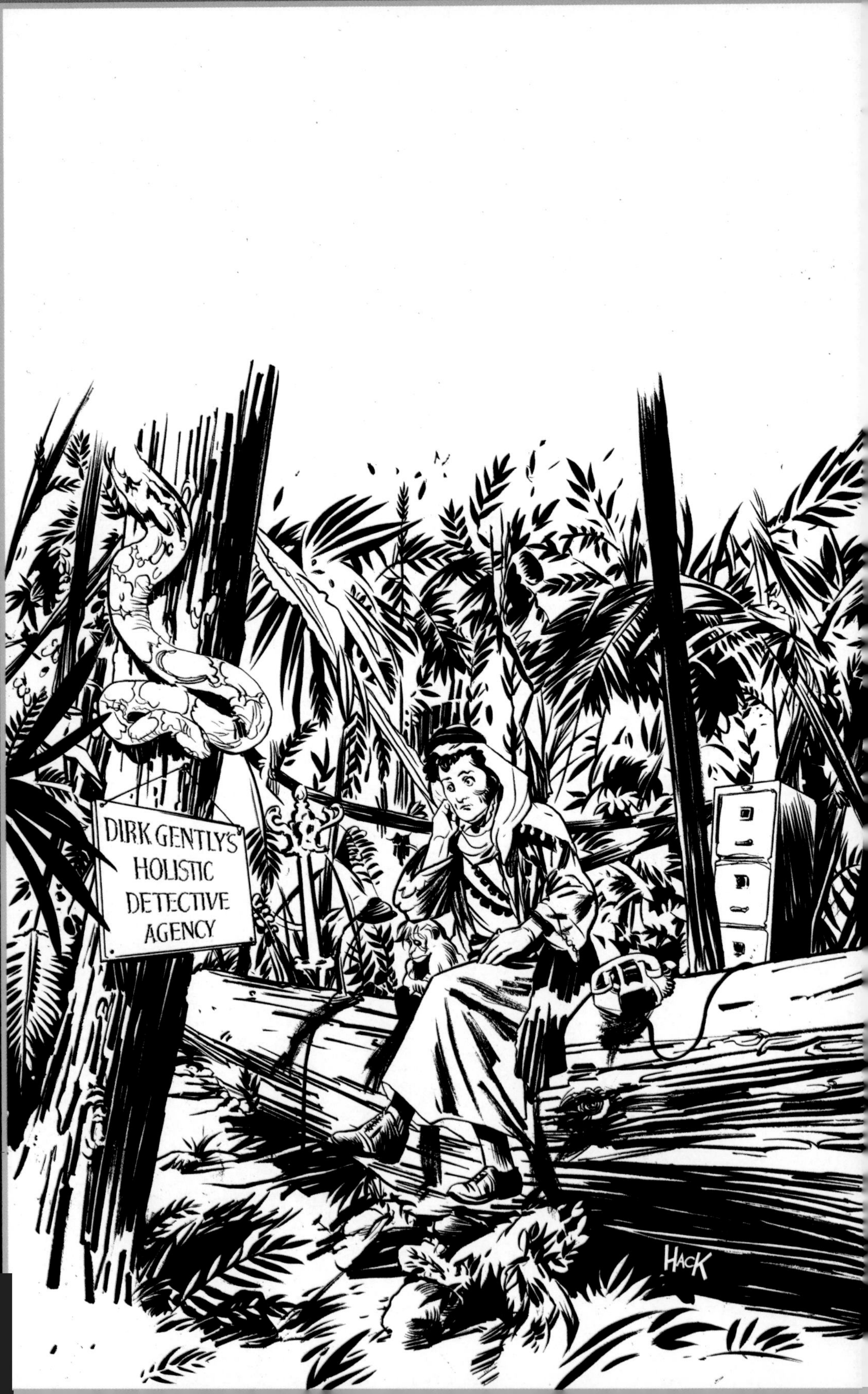
DIRK GENTLY'S
HOLISTIC
DETECTIVE
AGENCY
HACK

Cover Art by **ROBERT HACK**

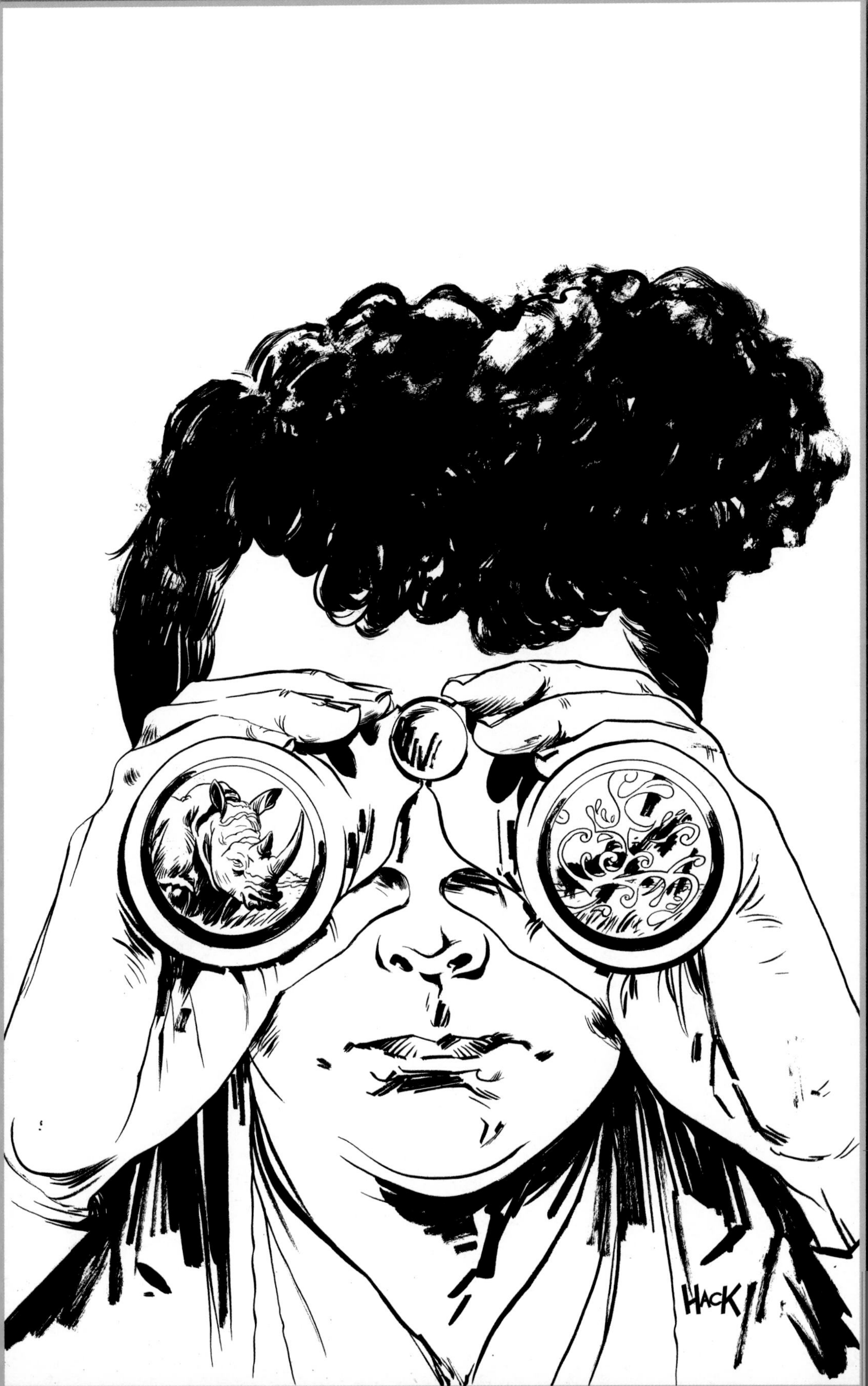
HACK

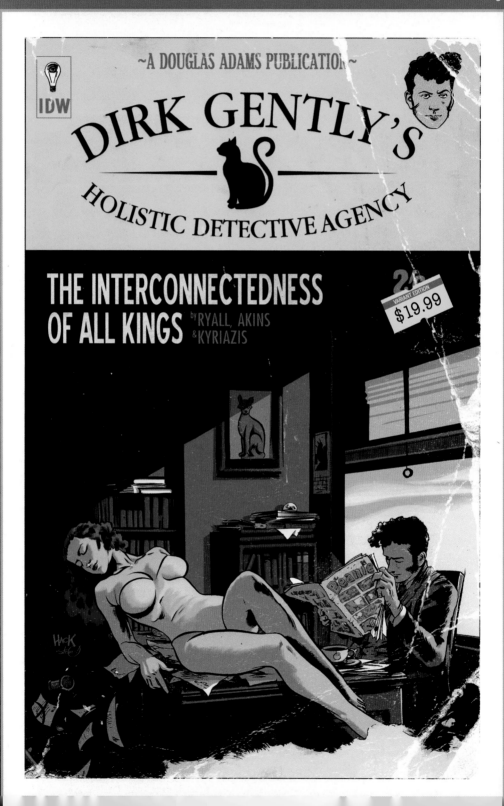